Institute for Early Christianity
in the Graeco-Roman World,
Cambridge

FIRST-CENTURY CHRISTIANS
IN THE GRAECO-ROMAN WORLD

Andrew D. Clarke
Series Editor

Seek the Welfare of the City:
Christians as Benefactors and Citizens
Bruce W. Winter

Secure the Well-Being of the Family:
Christians as Householders and Servants
Bradley B. Blue

Serve the Community of the Church:
Christians as Leaders and Ministers
Andrew D. Clarke

Solicit the Progress of the Gospel:
Christians as Partners and Stewards
G. Walter Hansen

Strengthen the Fellowship of Believers:
Christians as Élites and Havenots
David W.J. Gill

Strive for the Faith of the Gospel:
Christians as Public Speakers and Apologists
Conrad Gempf

FIRST CENTURY CHRISTIANS
IN THE GRAECO-ROMAN WORLD

Seek the Welfare of the City

Christians as Benefactors and Citizens

by

Bruce W. Winter

WILLIAM B. EERDMANS PUBLISHING COMPANY
GRAND RAPIDS, MICHIGAN

THE PATERNOSTER PRESS
CARLISLE

© 1994 Wm. B. Eerdmans Publishing Company
255 Jefferson Ave. S.E., Grand Rapids, Michigan 49503

First published 1994 jointly
in the United States by
Wm. B. Eerdmans Publishing Company
and in the U.K. by
The Paternoster Press,
P.O. Box 300, Carlisle, Cumbria CA3 0QS

Printed in the United States of America

00 99 98 97 96 95 94   7 6 5 4 3 2 1

Eerdmans ISBN 0-8028-4091-4

British Library Cataloguing in Publication Data

Winter, Bruce W.
Seek the Welfare of the City: Christians as Benefactors and Citizens. —
(First Century Christians in the Graeco-Roman World Series)
I. Title II. Series
261.1

ISBN 0-85364-633-3

Dedicated to
Sir Kirby Laing
A modern-day Christian Benefactor and Citizen

Table of Contents

INTRODUCTION

The title of this book, *Seek the Welfare of the City* is borrowed from Jeremiah 29:7. There the prophet instructed the exiled people of God to 'seek the welfare of the city' in which they lived. A second-century A.D. proconsul of Asia also used the phrase when he rebuked the bakers who went on strike in Ephesus accusing them of being indifferent to 'the welfare of the city' (τὸ τῇ πόλει συμφέρον). In the same inscription he speaks of the city's leaders as 'those in charge of the community's welfare' (τοῖς ὑπὲρ τοῦ κοινῇ συμφέροντος ἐπιταττομένοις).[1] During the reign of Claudius an imperial official, Pallas, is commended for having thought less of his own status than the welfare of the state *i.e.* the public good (*usui publico*) and remained in the service of the imperial household.[2] There is, then, in the concept of 'the welfare of the city' a convergence of OT and Graeco-Roman ideas. Christians had grown up in societies which had long-established conventions by which the welfare of the city's inhabitants was secured with the help of leading citizens. This book shows that Christians in the first-century Graeco–Roman world were taught to embrace this tradition in order to help sustain and enhance the life of the cities in which they lived. It will be suggested that Jeremiah's injunction provided a paradigm which enabled Christians as citizens to adopt and adapt the rôle of benefactor as they sought the city's welfare.

---

[1] *I Eph* 215 *ll.* 3, 8.
[2] Tacitus, *Ann.* 12.53.

1

The subtitle of this book *Christians as benefactors and citizens* was chosen to summarise 'public life', *politeia*, in the first century. When the Greek term πολιτεία is transliterated, it is immediately divested of much of its first-century meaning if it is assumed that *politeia* = 'politics'. It has a much wider application than the term 'politics' does today. The term referred to the whole of life in the public domain of a city, in contrast to private existence in a household.[3] In an attempt to maintain this first-century understanding, it was thought best to use the term throughout this book in its transliterated form and only translate it where thought appropriate. It is largely because of the view that πολιτεία = 'politics' that the discussion of Christians in 'public life' has proceeded along the Western world's concerns of the narrow, well–worn track of 'church and state' derived largely from Romans 13:1–7 and 1 Peter 2:13–17. Because of this limited focus on what *politeia* is perceived to have meant, much material which is relevant for the Christians' participation in *politeia* has been overlooked. The different spheres of activity covered by the ancient meaning of the term *politeia* will be discussed in this book in a series of soundings which maps out the public place of early Christians.

To aid this enquiry, the book is divided into two parts. The first will deal with benefactions and the second will explore the rôle of Christians as citizens. In the New Testament, the responses of Christians to the existing social institutions of the Graeco–Roman world will be seen to have varied. Ordinary Christians at times imitated the welfare syndrome of their own secular culture as this study will show. They could even use Christian ethics as a pretext for avoiding legal and filial *providentia*. There was a dichotomy in some instances between apostolic teaching and the Christian community's behaviour in *politeia* which was, of course, also true in the other spheres of life. In the face of such aberrations it was underscored that they were 'to seek the welfare of the city' and, in effect, 'not to seek great things' for themselves (Jer. 29:7, 45:5). In Part I it emerges that Christian teaching endorsed the rôle of benefactors but expanded the definition of who they were in a remarkable way which gave the Christian community a distinctive public face. Part II seeks to explore what a Christian's civic obligations and privileges were—what was now prescribed and what was proscribed for them as the people of God.

---

[3]C. Meier, *The Greek Discovery of Politics* (ET Harvard: University Press, 1990) 13ff. For a similar study of this long established understanding see J. Bordes, *Politeia dans la pensée grecque jusqu 'à Aristote* (Paris: 'Les Belles Lettres', 1982) 116ff.

Naturally, the way in which cities were governed determined in part how Christians operated in that society. Roman imperial policy permitted cities to be largely self-governing. They used the ancient tradition of honorary, annually-elected holders of public office who were drawn from the élite class. These honorary officials were civic benefactors. They ruled with the support of 'the Council and the People' and operated from a personal power base drawn largely from their clients.[4] Discussions on 'the rôle of the Christian in the world' have failed to consider this or the institutions of Graeco–Roman society which were part of the world of *politeia*. For example, a short monograph by J. Schneider, *Gemeinde und Welt im Neuen Testament*, makes no reference to precisely what happened 'in the world' in terms of what he calls 'the secular orders of life'.[5] More recently, Wayne Meeks sets out to help us discover 'the ethos and ethics' of early Christian communities by examining 'their involvement in the culture of their time' and 'the patterns they made of old forms in order to hear the new songs they composed from old melodies'.[6] He concluded that 'There is a self-conscious communal dimension of the sect's ethic which is far removed from the civic mindedness of Greek ethics.'[7] This book argues a rather different position *viz.* that the early church taught a civic consciousness among its members. It endorsed the concept of 'seeking the welfare of the city'. Their new-found faith did develop new perspectives on social ethics and thereby brought 'new songs' from 'old melodies' in the sphere of *politeia*, to use Meeks' helpful analogy.

It will be seen that little or no reference is made to Christians who sought the welfare of the city in the province of Judaea. The two exceptions have been in the chapters dealing with the care of the widows and the use of arbitrators. The only reason for mentioning the former is the difficulty which appears to have been created by the straight transfer of the Jewish system of welfare into the Gentile situation reflected in 1

---

[4]P.A. Brunt, 'The Romanization of the Local Ruling Classes in the Roman Empire', in D.M. Pippidi (ed.), *Assimilation et résistance à la culture gréco-romaine dans le monde ancien: Travaux du VI e Congrès International d'Etudes Classiques* (Bucharest and Paris: 'Les Belles Lettres', 1976) 161-73.

[5](Wuppertal: Onchen Verlag, 1955) E.T. *Church and World in the New Testament* (Macon: Mercer University Press, 1983).

[6]W. Meeks, *The Moral World of the First Christian* (London: SPCK, 1987) 97.

[7]Meeks, *The Moral World of the First Christian*, 130. More recently he suggests 'The Christian group's engagment with the city is thus in a sense buffered by their distance from the decurial class' *The Origins of Christian Morality; The First Two Centuries* (New Haven: Yale University Press, 1994) 46. On the social register of some Christians see secondary sources cited p. 38 n. 44 and discussion p. 203 ff.

Timothy 5:3–16 (pp. 66-7). There is a passing reference to the use of private arbitrators in litigation in Jewish situations as well as in the Graeco–Roman world in another discussion (p. 116). Why is there no systematic examination of the Jewish material?

The chapter on the widows drew attention to the fact that the way Christians related to public life in Jewish society and the Gentile world was determined in part by the distinctive ethos already existing in their different worlds of *politeia*. Goodman saw a fundamental difference between them when he wrote 'euergetism in the form common to both Greek and Roman society was never practised by the Judaean ruling class. . .they did not pick up the epigraphic habit and did not subscribe to public buildings.'[8] It became clear that a comparable book needs to be written for the Jewish world. It would be able to draw on those sections of the New Testament corpus not encompassed by this study because of their Jewish rather than Gentile backgrounds.[9] This book belongs in the series on early Christians in the Graeco–Roman world, so it must be left to others to proceed along parallel lines to this volume. It is clear that a comparable work from the Jewish Christian side would be invaluable, for *politeia* was determined by very different cultural roots.[10]

Another obvious gap will be perceived and here an *apologia* is also needed. It was not felt necessary to write a chapter or chapters on the whole of what has been seen to be *the* passage on 'church and state', Romans 13:1–7 although one chapter is devoted to 13:3–4. E. Bammel at the end of his essay 'Romans 13' called for a reconsideration of this passage by giving it 'its proper focus'.[11] There is a concentration in chapter two on Romans 13:3–4 where an important aspect has been lost

---

[8]M. Goodman, *The Ruling Class of Judaea: The Origins of the Jewish Revolt against Rome A.D. 66–70* (Cambridge: CUP, 1987) 126–7. For some recent modifications of this views see T. Rajak and D. Noy, '*Archisynogogoi*: Office, Title and Status in the Graeco–Roman World', *JRS* 83 (1993) 75–93 where they show something of the Graeco–Roman influence on certain synagogue traditions.

[9]For a very brief discussion of the Jewish and Greek charity system in Judaea see G. Hamel, *Poverty and Charity in Roman Palestine: First Three Centuries C.E.*, Near Eastern Studies 23 (Berkeley and Oxford: University of California Press, 1990) 216–19 and 219–20 respectively. Hamel, unwilling to draw on gospel sources because he felt the 'thorny choices in source and tradition criticism' would mean 'a very arduous task with few assured results', *ibid.* 2, was thus deflected from what would have been a fruitful undertaking.

[10]The two works together might well help the polarized discussion of kingdom *v.* creation ethics.

[11]'Roman 13', in E. Bammel and C.F.D. Moule (edd.), *Jesus and the Politics of His Day* (Cambridge: CUP, 1984) 365–83, citation 383.

from sight by many who discuss 'Romans 13'. The aim has been to refocus the discussion on the subject matter of the first part of this book *i.e.* the benefaction tradition. This was one of the two spheres perceived by ancient secular writers to be 'the rôle of government'—the other being the administration of justice.[12] The method of dealing with Romans 13 in this book has been to take 'the flesh off the fish without disturbing the bones' to quote the Malay saying. The bones of the fish have already been well and truly examined and they have generated a large body of important secondary literature. This book therefore does not deal with the concept of 'the powers that be' (13:1) which has been much used and misused in contemporary debate on 'church and the state'. Rather the aim has been to analyse that part of the body, to continue the metaphor, which relates to one of the two aspects of this book *i.e.* the rôle of civic benefactions. Romans 13:3–4 is one of the prime concerns of the first half of the book because it is one of the most significant texts discussing *politeia* that was immediately relevant to some early Christians.

The interpretations of some of the New Testament passages contained in these chapters are perhaps new. They have arisen out of an attempt to draw evidence from the Graeco–Roman world of *politeia* perceived to be relevant to our study of the New Testament. If a justification is needed for the meaning attributed to certain key words and their influence on our interpretation of some passages, then it is done ever so briefly on pages 83-4. A fuller work is to be undertaken on the influence of semantic fields on word meanings.[13]

Four of the chapters of this book have already been published as journal articles,[14] and some of the primary material discussed elsewhere has been drawn into two other chapters.[15] I was originally exploring what seemed to be four disparate areas in keeping with my general interests in the intersection of the New Testament with the Graeco–Roman world. Through the kindness of Dr Koh Eng Soo and his wife, Christian benefactors and friends from a decade of work in

---

[12]There was possibly only one Christian who exercised 'the sword' with the emperor's *imperium*, *viz.* Sergius Paulus, the proconsul of Cyprus (Acts 13:7–12)—the more recent evidence of the 'Tiber' inscription may well have solved at least his identification. See the discussion of an ancient historian, A. Nobbs, 'Cyprus' in edd. D.W.J. Gill and C. Gempf *The Book of Acts in its Graeco–Roman Setting*, The Book of Acts in its First Century Setting (Grand Rapids and Carlisle: Eerdmans and Paternoster, 1994) ch. 8 and esp. 284–7 on her positive identification.

[13]My work on the social context of certain New Testament semantic fields as a way of determining more precisely word meanings awaits completion for the series of 'Studies in Biblical Greek' to be published by Peter Lang.

Singapore, an opportunity was provided to take stock of future research during a break in the Swiss Alps.

It became clear in reviewing what I had already written, that the place of the early Christian in public life warranted an extended treatment. In the first essay, 'The Public Honouring of Christian Benefactors' which was researched through the generous benefactions of the Jubliee and Witness Foundations, I had reached conclusions on the rôle of Christians in their society based on the texts of Romans 13:3–4 and 1 Peter 2:14–15. They were examined in the light of epigraphic evidence of rulers praising those who did good.[16] These conclusions ran counter to a commonly held view, originally shared by me, that the early Christians were a small group operating in a low profile way in a hostile world. Was not their outlook eschatological and their endeavours primarily evangelistic? It seemed a logical development to trace the place of early Christians in *politeia* more fully, given the profitable explorations already undertaken. After research on other chapters had been completed, the conclusions of that first essay were revisited, and were felt to be substantially correct. Four of the chapters already published in journals were reworked in order to integrate them into the overall theme of this book. Some material was excised and further supporting material, especially primary sources, added. Six new chapters were written to complete the book.

Early this year the kind invitation of an old friend and former colleague, Dr. Choong Chee Pang, to return to Trinity Theological College, Singapore, to lecture his graduate students firmed up certain aspects of the book. It provided a helpful reminder that in some areas of *politeia*, the Asian scene has more in common with the Graeco–Roman world than the present Western world. That happy experience was followed by a visiting fellowship kindly awarded by the Society

---

[14]'The Public Honouring of Christian Benefactors: Romans 13:3 and I Peter 2:14–15', *JSNT* 34 (1988) 87-103 reproduced by permission of the Sheffield Academic Press, '*Providentia* for the Widows of 1 Timothy 5:3-16', *Tyn.B.* 39 (1988) 83-99, '"If a man does not wish to work. . ." 2 Thessalonians 3.6–16: A Social and Historical Context', *Tyn.B.* 40 (1989) 303–315 reproduced by permission of Tyndale House, Cambridge and 'Civil Litigation in Corinth: The Forensic Background to 1 Cor. 6.1–8', *NTS* 37 (1991) 559–572 reproduced by permission of the Cambridge University Press.

[15]'Seek the Welfare of the City: Social Ethics According to 1 Peter', *Themelios* 13 (1988) 91-94 and 'The Problem with "church" for the Early Church', in D. Peterson and J. Pryor (edd.), *In the Fullness of Time: Biblical Studies in Honour of Archbishop Robinson* (Sydney: Lancer 1992) ch. 13.

[16]'The Public Honouring of Christian Benefactors', 95-7.

for the Study of Early Christianity and my appointment as a visiting fellow in ancient history in the School of History, Philosophy, and Politics, Macquarie University, Sydney. Dr. Alanna Nobbs, the Associate Professor of Ancient History, and Dr. Ray Nobbs, Senior Lecturer in Modern History, went out of their way to make sure that this was a very productive time. The staff at Macquarie's Ancient History Graduate Seminar chaired by Dr. Ted Nixon provided very helpful comments on the chapter on Christians and social mobility. Mr Darryl Palmer, Senior Lecturer in Classics at Newcastle University also thoughtfully arranged a seminar involving their ancient historians during my stay. I also benefitted much from their discussion of Part I of this book. Five of the six chapters of Part II were completed in Australia in the idyllic setting of its autumn of 1994 during a short sabbatical break.

It is appropriate that I should acknowledge my long-term indebtedness to the 'school' (σχολή) of Emeritus Professor E.A. Judge of Macquarie University. He, together with Professor A.J. Malherbe of Yale Divinity School, have spawned much of the current interest and fruitful work being undertaken on early Christianity in the context of the Graeco–Roman world. My thanks are due to the editor of the series *First-Century Christians in the Graeco-Roman World*, Dr. Andrew Clarke, for his careful reading of the text and many helpful suggestions for its improvement. I am also indebted to my dear wife who worked around me on the sabbatical leave and also read and commented on the manuscript, as did my daughter, Elizabeth and son–in–law, Orlando Saer. As is the case of the series *The Book of Acts in its First Century Setting*, due acknowledgement must be given to Mr. Bill Eerdmans Jr., the President of Wm.B. Eerdmans Publishers for his unflagging interest in new ideas and projects, and his Christian approach to publishing.

September, 1994.

PART ONE

EARLY CHRISTIANS AS BENEFACTORS

CHAPTER ONE

SEEKING THE WELFARE
OF THE CITY

1 Peter 1–2:11ff.

Although the early church looked for a city whose architect and maker was God, (Heb. 11:10) it also encouraged its members to develop another focus by taking 'part in everything as citizens'. This included the provision of civic benefactions for earthly cities as chapter 2 will argue in detail.

> They reside in their respective countries, but only as aliens (πάροικοι) they take part in everything as citizens (πολῖται) and put up with everything as foreigners (ξένοι). Every foreign land is their home and every home a foreign land. They find themselves in the flesh, but do not live according to the flesh.[1]

These comments by a second-century Christian in the epistle to Diognetus explain the nature of the dual citizenship of Christians and indicate that there was an appropriate place for Christians in *politeia*. The writer provides a second-century reflection on the place of Christians in *politeia* and does so in language which is similar to that used in 1 Peter 1:1 and 2:11. There Christians are spoken of as 'sojourners of the Dispersion' and again as 'resident aliens' and sojourners' (πάροικοι, παρεπίδημοι). Was this understanding of the duality of the Christian's citizenship and their participation 'in everything as citizens' (μετέχουσι πάντων ὡς πολῖται) also a correct summary of the rôle of first-century Christians in the public place?

Of all the letters in the New Testament, it is 1 Peter which considers the theme of the welfare of the city in detail. 1 Peter 2:11–3:17 is a sustained discussion of ethical conduct which is undergirded by a theological prolegomena in 1:1ff. The situation was one in which the public place of Christians needed urgent discussion, given the antagonism experienced in the provinces mentioned in 1:1.

In this opening chapter it is proposed (I) to evaluate briefly the approaches to the issue of Christians in *politeia* in the first-century Roman East and to suggest that the discussion in 1 Peter 2:11ff. concerns the welfare of the city, (II) to show how the theological paradigm from the Old Testament indicates the way the dispersed people of God should relate to the cities in which they live, (III) to demonstrate the contrast between their position of spiritual security and their insecure position in the cities, (IV) to set this in the context of a threefold call to the people of God to bless and not retaliate, and (V) to explore how 1 Peter argues that Christians in public life should express this in their rôle of benefactors.

---

[1]*Epistle to Diognetus* V.5, 8.

I. Recent Social History and Sociological Studies

The explanation that Christians in early centuries 'take part in every-thing as citizens' as part of their spiritual and temporal self–definition does not reflect the twentieth-century perception of the *politeia* of early Christians. Recent discussions have taken rather different approaches.

The solution of a social historian has been to suggest that Christians had an 'acute sensitivity to public opinion' and aimed 'to avoid upsetting the government'. 'Plainly their security as groups was felt to depend to a large extent on their activities escaping public attention'.[2] But were Christians encouraged to maintain a low profile? Good works in general are the subject of the overarching preliminary comment in 2:11–12 and to pursue them was the alternative to a lifestyle of self-indulgence. They were meant to be seen in the public arena and are referred to as 'your good works which they behold' (2:13). The writer of the letter is sensitive to the way in which the Christian life-style is perceived in public life. In the light of this, it is hard to see how those who performed good works could have a low profile, or why they should not have let 'their lights so shine before men that they would see their good works and glorify their Father in heaven' (Mt. 5:16). Social ethics is defined in 1 Peter as 'the doing of good works' in all spheres of life and was every Christian's calling and a central theme (2:11ff.). Another consideration was that Christians were to be seen to do good which would counter those who brought allegations against them as evildoers who warranted prosecution (2:11-15).

It has also been said that Christians were required 'to stand aloof from public life'. This attitude came from Epicurean teaching on withdrawing from society. While this comment has not been applied specifically to a discussion of 1 Peter, those conclusions can readily colour our overall perception of the early Christian's participation in, or withdrawal from, public life. In Macedonia they were said to have been taught to 'live quietly'. This is seen as a reference to political quietism—the Christian was 'to attend to one's own affairs', and not 'to attend to public affairs' (1 Thess. 4:11–12).[3] It will be argued in chapter 3 that this passage, along with 2 Thessalonians 3:6ff., relates specifically to the former clients of patrons withdrawing from a

---

[2]E.A. Judge, *The Social Pattern of Early Christian Groups in the First Century* (London: Tyndale, 1960) 73.
[3]R.F. Hock, *The Social Context of Paul's Ministry: Tentmaking and Apostleship* (Philadelphia: Fortress, 1980) 46, following A.J. Malherbe, *Social Aspects of Early Christianity* (Baton Rouge: Louisiana State University Press, 1977) 26.

disruptive involvement in *politeia*. It was not a command for a blanket withdrawal by all Christians from public life. The evidence for involvement in *politeia* in 1 Peter will be discussed later in this chapter, but by way of initial comment 2:12ff. seems to suggest that political quietism was not a Christian social ethic for the early communities.

Others have felt that the place of Christians in society can be better accounted for by using sociological models rather than social historical approaches. For instance, it has been argued that 'social marginality' and 'social separation' were actively encouraged in 1 Peter. This conclusion has been reached with the use of the sociological model of the 'conversionist sect', which is said to have encouraged 'the maintenance of social distance' in order to preserve coherence and distinctiveness as a means of attracting potential converts. In the same way sociologists believe that rigorous religious distinctiveness accounts for the growth of sectarian groups in the twentieth century.[4] New Testament scholarship has rightly questioned the linguistic basis of this treatment of 1 Peter 1:1 which is crucial to this sociological model.[5] The foundations of this approach have been questioned more recently by other sociologists. Furthermore, neither does this socio-logical model fit the evidence of the setting up of another religious group with its own pagan shrine and the obligations required of members. In this case it was not a social limitation but moral para-meters that were required of its adherents.

> Let those who enter this shrine, men and women, free and slaves, swear by all the gods that they are aware of no deceit exercised against man or woman, nor know nor carry out any evil spell or wicked enchantment against persons, nor love–potents nor abortificient nor contraceptive, nor any other means of infanticide, that they neither made these themselves nor advised nor assisted another so to do, that they have cheated no one'.[6]

The reason for maintaining purity was not to generate distinctiveness but to avoid the judgement of the gods.[7] The sociological model does not fit that ancient data any more than it does first-century Christianity reflected in 1 Peter. In the latter it is suggested that the means by which

---

[4]J.H. Elliott, *A Home for the Homeless: A Sociological Exegesis of 1 Peter, Its Situation and Strategy* (Philadelphia: Fortress, 1981) 74-77 cites substantially from B.R. Wilson, 'An Analysis of Sect Development', *American Sociological Review* 24 (1959) 3-15.
[5]See for example M. Chin, 'A Heavenly Home for the Homeless: Aliens and Strangers in 1 Peter', *Tyn.B.* 42 (1991) 96–112.
[6]See *SIG* [3] 985.

God's virtues are declared are not social separation but the social involvement of Christians in the everyday life of the city through good works (2:9ff.). This is not to deny that 1 Peter may have been written in part to overcome any possible social separatist tendencies developing among Christians as a defence mechanism against hostile pressure. The teaching of 1 Peter does not encourage separation from society but rather from sin (*cf.* 1:17, 2:11).

There is an alternative sociological model which seeks to show that the opposite activity is occurring in 1 Peter *i.e.* the integration of this movement into society. This 'acculturation' model was developed from social patterns of South Pacific peoples and the Indians and Amish people of North America, and has been used to argue that 1 Peter reflects 'the social function of contradictory actions' with an 'enthusiastic reception' of social patterns and at the same time a firm rejection of other behaviour.[8] Again this does not appear to explain the motivation for ethical conduct in 1 Peter, nor does the evidence from that letter itself support the view that Christians were aiming for acculturation. The difficulty there addressed is the problem created by society's response to Christians.

This brief analysis shows that recent discussions of social history and sociology appears to offer no explanation consistent with the extant data on the relationship of early Christianity in Asia Minor to the public life of its adherents, which is a major concern in 1 Peter.

II. The People of God in *politeia* in 'the Dispersion'

A paradigm for the rôle of the Christian in society in 1 Peter can be found in Jeremiah 29:7. This appears to have been foremost in the thinking of the writer of this letter, for the self–definition of Christians is expressed in terms of the 'Diaspora' (1 Peter 1:1). In Jeremiah's day the Jews in Exile were exhorted to settle in Babylon, marry, 'seek the welfare of the city' to which the Lord had carried them, and pray for its

---

[7]The text suggests that the concern was to insist on certain behaviour for superstitious purposes. See discussion by S. Barton and G.H.R. Horsley, 'A Hellenistic Cult Group and the New Testament Churches' *JbAC* 24 (1981) 7–41.

[8]D.L. Balch, 'Hellenization Acculturation in 1 Peter', *Perspectives on First Peter, NABPR Special Studies Series* 9 (1986) 83 who is critical of Elliott's use of the early ideas of Wilson's sociological model, which was later refined, and argues that Elliot has not applied the correct model for the data. Hence his use of the acculturation explanation.

peace. The suggested alternative was that the community should perceive its present existence as temporary. Some of their prophets saw return from exile as an event which would occur almost immediately (Jer. 29:8). The people of God in that Diaspora, however, were to continue to seek the welfare of their city for seventy years, and then their return to the promised inheritance of their forefathers would be realised (Jer. 29:4-14). It has been shown that the treatment of the Jews in exile was no different from that experienced by other dispossessed minority groups in Babylon.[9] What was unique was the attitude Israel was called upon to adopt—not to plot the destruction of their conquerors, but to seek their blessing. 'The people are to intercede with the Lord on behalf of the well-being of their new home',[10] and Bright notes 'the command is a remarkable one for the Jews to pray for the hated heathen power, and to seek the peace *i.e.* the prosperity of their city'.[11]

Likewise in 1 Peter 1:1 the Christians are aptly called 'elect sojourners of the Dispersion'. This is a theological and not a social description of the letter's recipients.[12] It was an appropriate phrase for the elect pilgrim people of God in their present temporal situation.[13] Far removed from their promised inheritance or homeland, they are assured that they will reach their promised destination preserved by the power of God. They will not be disappointed with the nature of their inheritance as were the exiles when they returned from their Bab-

---

[9] For a discussion of Jeremiah and Jews and other ethnic groups see E. Eph'al, 'The Western Minorities in Babylon in the 6th-5th Centuries B.C.: Maintenance and Cohesion', *Orientalia* 47 (1978) 74-90.

[10] R.P. Carroll, *Jeremiah* (London: SCM, 1986) 556.

[11] As J. Bright, *Jeremiah* (New York: Doubleday, 1965) 211 notes, the command is a remarkable one for the Jews to pray for the hated heathen power, and to seek the peace *i.e.* the prosperity of their city. See also S. Wagner, *TWOT* III, 296. *Cf.* Est. 10:3 'seek the wealth (or good) of his people' and Deut. 23:6 'do not seek their peace or prosperity'.

[12] V.P. Furnish, 'Elect Sojourners in Christ: An Approach to the Theology of 1 Peter', *Perkins School of Theology Journal* 28 (1975) 1-11 and D.E. Hiebert, 'Designation of the Readers of 1 Peter 1:1-2', *Bibliotheca Sacra* (1980) 65-67.

[13] Elliott, *A Home for the Homeless*, 24-49, esp. 47 suggests the terms describe their legal status as two types of non-citizens in the cities of the Jewish Dispersion in Asia Minor. If however παρεπιδήμοι = visiting strangers and πάροικοι = resident aliens, why is only the former greeted in the opening of the letter and the latter group ignored until both words occur together in 2:11? The terms appear together in the LXX in Gen. 23:3 where Abraham sought a burying place for Sarah because he was technically a stranger and a sojourner in the land, but in Ps. 39:12 the writer acknowledged that before God he was a spiritual stranger and sojourner on earth as were his fathers. See J.W. Pryor, 'First Peter and the New Covenant', *Reformed Theological Review* 45 (1986) 45ff. for his arguments against Elliott's position.

ylonian captivity (1:4-9). They are not to retaliate, but are to bless (3:9). The twin concepts 'to do good' (ποιεῖν ἀγαθόν) and 'to seek peace' (ζητεῖν εἰρήνην) are picked up later in the letter (3:11) in a citation from Psalm 34:12-16, but the language is also reminiscent of the theme of Jeremiah to seek the welfare of the city and to pray for its peace (29:7). The parallels between Jeremiah 29 and 1 Peter 1 are compelling.[14]

How then should the Christians in 1 Peter spend their days on earth? It is clear that as spiritual 'sojourners' and 'alien residents' they must withdraw from the self–indulgent lifestyle of their contemporaries (2:11) and seek the welfare of the society in which they live. They were instructed to spend their days in this earthly city seeking the blessing of its inhabitants (2:11ff.).

In 1 Peter the theological paradigm which demanded that Christians seek the welfare of the city was derived from the Old Testament. The era of salvation history chosen was not the promised land but the exile, in keeping with the careful selection by the writer of an apposite Old Testament citation or era.[15]

III. Eschatology and the Welfare of the City

1 Peter's focus on life in the city is intriguing in the light of the emphasis of its opening section. 'The true grace of God' in which the Christian is to stand (5:12) is the stated theme of the letter. 'Every home (is) a foreign land', to cite again the letter to Diognetus, because of the unseen, yet certain inheritance reserved in heaven for God's people (1:4-5). No inheritances would remain unclaimed because the power of God would be keeping the Christians so that they could ultimately enjoy them. This is the work of the Triune God, Father, Son and Holy Spirit, who has secured such a salvation for the Christians (1:2–12). This future hope and confidence was intended to occupy the horizons of Christians who were commanded to fix their gaze on the future

---

[14]*Contra* W.A. Meeks, *The Origins of Christian Morality*, 47–8 who simply sees here an implicit analogy of the convert as the Jewish immigrant which has been 'commandeered by the new offshoot cult'.

[15]For a careful treatment of the theme where it is argued that a technique akin to midrashic exegesis is used with great sensitivity to the stated OT context of the passages cited in 1 Peter see G.L. Green, 'The use of the Old Testament for Christian Ethics in 1 Peter', *TynB.* 41 (1990) 276–89. However he makes no comment on the theological foundation of the OT *Sitz im Leben* in 1 Pet. 1:1.

grace which was to come to them at the revelation of Jesus Christ (1:13ff.).

If this is the case, the ethical injunctions which taught Christians how to relate positively to their city and its inhabitants (2:12ff.) are somewhat unexpected. This is particularly the case in the insecure situation which these elect sojourners faced. We know of discrimination against Christians 'with sporadic outbursts of local suspicion, resentment, and hostility'.[16] Rumour-mongering could result in public disorder (στάσις), or litigation against Christians initiated by an accuser, leading to private prosecution before magistrates or governors with accompanying testings and trials (1:6, 4:12). There were public allegations against them (2:15). There are examples of similar troubles in the cities mentioned in Acts (19:16ff., 16:19, 17:6, 18:12 and 24:1). Why then should those whose future inheritance was so secure seek to promote the welfare of a city whose inhabitants created such tension and uncertainty for them? This question may have been the primary motivating force behind the writing of the circular letter to Christians in the provinces named in 1 Peter 1:1, especially when cities could be so hostile towards them.

During the Jewish exile,there was an almost total preoccupation with the future and the expectation of its immediate realisation. Jeremiah curbed this by assuring them of the promised return although some seventy years hence, and coupled this with a demand that they focus on the present. The people of God were to seek the welfare of the present cities in which they resided.

If the Christians were to gird up their minds and fix their hope perfectly on the coming grace to be revealed at the final revelation of Jesus Christ (1 Pet. 1:13), could the welfare of their present secular city possibly matter to them? The sense of eschatological confidence in 1 Peter did not provide the Anatolian Christians with the excuse to abstract themselves from society. On the contrary they were encouraged to develop double *foci*. Social ethics are clearly assumed to be the

---

[16]J.H. Elliott, 'Peter, Its situation and strategy: A Discussion with David Balch', in C. H. Talbert (ed.), *Perspectives on 1 Peter*, (NABPR Special Studies Series 9; Macon: Mercer University Press, 1986) 62. The word 'discrimination' has been used advisedly and not 'persecution' because there is no clear evidence in 1 Peter that the imperial persecutions of the force of Nero's localized one in Rome or Domitian's were being suffered in 1 Peter. See also E.G. Selwyn, 'The Persecutions in 1 Peter', *BNTS* 1 (1950) 44 for the same view and his comments in *The First Epistle of St Peter* (London: Macmillan, 1947) 55 that the trials were spasmodic, 'a matter of incidents rather than policy, at once ubiquitous and incalculable.'

norm for Christians in 1 Peter 2:11ff. In 1 Peter the reality of the *parousia* was a motivating reason and not an escape for seeking the welfare of the city because of the eschatological judgement. The assessment of their life by the impartial judgement of their works at the Assize would provide a salutary motive (1:17). The good works of Christians were obviously orientated towards the needs of others in the temporal cities in which they lived.

Surprisingly, no mention is made of the church *per se*. This general epistle deals with the difficulty of fulfilling their responsibility as benefactors in the unsettled circumstances in which Christians found themselves. The crucial framework of their future hope provided a vital perspective.

The teaching, then, about social ethics by the pilgrim people of God in 1 Peter holds together two crucial, but related biblical doctrines, eschatology and social ethics.[17] To stand in 'the true grace of God' demanded a deep commitment to the welfare of the city within the framework of a living eschatological hope. That enabled the Christian to place personal concerns second to the needs of others in the city. This firm, eschatological hope of a secure inheritance meant that their present or impending suffering would be no ultimate catastrophe for them (4:12). The setting of one's hope on the grace to be revealed at the revelation of Jesus Christ (1:13) provided the perspective for fulfilling the Christian mandate to seek the welfare of the earthly city and not personal aggrandisement.

IV. The Calling to do Good

The good works performed by God's people were an expression of holiness. This attribute was based on the character of the God who called them (1:14) and was an essential ingredient of the Christian lifestyle, 'all manner of living' (ἀναστροφή, 1:15). That expressed itself in good deeds which would be subject to scrutiny by an impartial Father at the great assize (1:13-17). He would judge everyone on the basis of their deeds.

There are three reasons given why the transient Christian should be concerned for the welfare of the hostile and ungrateful city. They

---

[17]For a general discussion of the place of ethics between the two aeons see H. Thielicke, *Evangelical Ethics: Foundations* (E.T.; Philadelphia: Fortress Press, 1966) I, ch. 4

are to be found in the concept of the calling of God's people—a theme introduced in three places with the verb 'to call'. They were called upon 'to declare', 'to follow' and 'to bless', all of which, it will be argued, are related to social ethics.

Firstly, the fundamental purpose of the elect race, the royal priesthood, the holy nation, the formerly stateless group who were now the people of God, was to declare the virtues or characteristics of the One who called them out of darkness into his marvellous light (2:9-10). The following verses indicate how this was to be done in terms of a compelling Christian lifestyle seen from their good works (2:11ff.). J.H. Elliott notes that 'this was manifested through a positive witness to all men'.[18] That witness occurred through their good works which outsiders beheld.

Secondly, in the face of unjust treatment the Christian household servant was also called to follow the example of the patiently suffering Messiah. 'For to this you were called, because Christ also suffered on your behalf, leaving you an example, that you should follow in His steps' (2:21). In the face of mistreatment they were to follow their calling to perform good deeds as their *imitatio Christi*.

Thirdly, discrimination might well reach flash-point in the wider society. The whole church was exhorted not to repay evil with evil, or abuse with abuse, but the exact opposite. They were to impart the blessing of doing good 'because you were called for this very purpose that you should inherit a blessing' (3:9). God's calling demanded that Christians relate to others in the way He had related to them with His great blessings in Christ. The apt quotation from Psalm 34:12-16 in the verses following (3:9) lays out what the blessed and blessing life was. It was 'doing good', not 'evil', it was 'seeking peace', not 'speaking evil'.

This was a calling similar to that given to God's exiled people in Jeremiah 29:7 who were to seek the welfare of the city in which they lived, to pray for its peace and to bless it by means of good deeds.[19]

---

[18]J.H. Elliott, *The Elect and the Holy. An Exegetical Examination of 1 Peter 2.4-10 and the Phrase basileion hierateuma*, Nov.T. Sup.12 (Leiden: E.J. Brill, 1966) 184-5 on the outward orientation to the world of the Christian as the meaning of 2:5, 9. *Contra* D.L. Balch, *Let Wives Be Submissive; The Domestic Code of 1 Peter*, SBL: Monograph 26 (Chico: Scholars Press, 1981) 133-6 for an attempt to refute Elliott's argument.
[19]See C.W. Mitchell, *The Meaning of BRK "To Bless" in the Old Testament*, SBL Dissertation Series 95 (Atlanta: Scholars Press, 1987) ch. 4.

V. *Politeia* and Benefactors

The Christians' good works were intended to be 'observed' (ἐποπτεύω, 2:11-12).[20] As sojourners and temporary residents they were commanded to abstain from fleshly conduct in order to present an attractive lifestyle (ἀναστροφὴ καλή, 2:11). The observation of their high-profile good works would not only be an eloquent defence of ill-founded allegations against Christians accused of being evil-doers, it would also be the means by which critics became converts who glorified God 'in the day of visitation' *i.e.* the day referring to personal salvation.[21]

There were three areas of life where they were called upon to engage in these high-profile good works. One was clearly in *politeia* (2:13-17), another in 'private', *i.e.* servants in the household and wives and husbands in marriage (2:18-3:7), and the last was not restricted to either public or private relationships (3:8ff.).

The Christian citizen's duties were discharged in part by obedience to civic ordinances. One of the dual functions of rulers was to punish the law-breakers. The other was to praise those who did good in the public arena (2:14).[22] The latter, it will be argued in the following chapter, referred to the important duty of the official recognition of a public benefactor.[23] The cities of Anatolia and other regions of the East had long been supported by public benefactors.[24] This method of providing for the needs of the city was well-established in Greek times and was certainly continued during the early centuries of the Roman empire.[25] In 2:14-15 Christians of substance were called upon to con-

---

[20]*Contra* 'Plainly their security as groups was felt to depend to a large extent on their activities escaping public attention', Judge, *The Social Pattern of Early Christian Groups*, 73.

[21]*Cf.* Lk. 1:68 where God visits and redeems his people and 19:44 where Jerusalem did not know the day of its visitation *i.e.* salvation. J. Ramsay Michaels, 'Eschatology in 1 Peter II.17', *NTS* 13 (1967) 397 says it refers to the 'salvation of the heathen', *contra* W.C. van Unnik, 'The Teaching of Good Works in 1 Peter', *NTS* 1 (1954) 104-5 where he argues from 1 Enoch that it refers to the day of doom and desolation.

[22]For the literary evidence of this dual function of government see W.C. van Unnik, 'Lob und Strafe durch die Obrigkeit Hellenistisches zu Röm.13.3-4', in E. Earle Ellis and Erich Grässer (edd.), *Jesus und Paulus: Festschrift für Werner Georg Kümmel zum 70 Geburtstag* (Göttingen: Vandenhoeck & Ruprecht, 1975) 336-40.

[23]For a discussion of this and the epigraphic evidence to support it see chapter 2.

[24]See chapter 2.

[25]C.P. Jones, 'Benefactions', *The Roman World of Dio Chrysostom*, Loeb Monograph Series (Cambridge, Mass. and London: Harvard University Press, 1978) ch. 12.

tinue to be benefactors. This was declared to be 'the will of God' and public recognition by rulers was the means of silencing the rumours of ill-informed men.

There was an established procedure by which the particular gift of a benefactor was recognised. This was done by the erection of an inscription commemorating the event, the public praising with words of commendation, the crowning with a crown of gold, and being allocated a permanent seat of honour in the theatre.[26] The term 'benefactor' conferred status in society.[27] The public declaration of a Christian man as 'good and noble' acknowledged his benefaction.[28] As the following chapter will show, civic benefactions were also honoured in public with customary civic conventions including places of honour.[29] The writer of 1 Peter was not simply endorsing public benefactions *per se* but emphasizing their importance as God's way to refute charges that Christians were not good citizens.

The need for this exhortation could well have arisen because of the natural tendency for Christians to withdraw from being benefactors in the face of open discrimination or possible persecution. It is not unlikely that the wisdom of such actions by public benefactors who became Christians and continued to spend their resources on public works or emergency relief was now being questioned in the church. The New Testament stance is clear—their light was to shine that men would see their good works and glorify their Father in heaven. Furthermore the rich, be they Christian or non–Christian, would have been expected, either by custom or by law, to undertake public office as part of their liturgy.[30]

Finally, there was a message to the Christian community threatened by the cities in which they lived (3:8-16). They were reminded that they must give to others what has been given to them *viz.* a blessing (v. 9ff.). That blessing was not only the absence of malicious speech and evil actions, but also 'the doing of good' and 'the pursuit of peace' (v. 11). Again the use of this citation from Psalm 34:14 reflects the same

---

[26]See pp. 30-3.

[27]A.R. Hands, *Charities and Social Aid in Greece and Rome*, (London: Thames and Hudson, 1968) 36, 'the very title. . .did not simply state a fact but conferred a status'.

[28]For evidence of this public declaration see p. 32.

[29]Judge, *The Social Pattern of Early Christian Groups*, 73.

[30]See P. Garnsey, *'Taxatio and pollicitatio in Roman Africa,'* JRS 61 (1971) 116, P. Garnsey and R. Saller, *The Roman Empire: Economy, Society and Culture*, (London: Duckworth, 1987) 33.

theological and ethical framework of Jeremiah 29:7 where the exiles were to seek the welfare of the city and to pray for its peace. The call is to be zealous for the good (deed) (τὸ ἀγαθον), to be able to give a ready answer for the Christian hope when asked by fellow inhabitants, and to accompany this with the witness of a good lifestyle in Christ (ἀγαθὴν ἀναστροφήν, vv. 13-16). To suffer for doing good is better than to suffer for having done evil (v. 17).

Underlying the important place given to social ethics within eschatology is the biblical perspective of the goodness of God who showers His providential care regardless of the world's response. God does good, because good needs to be done. His pilgrim people must do the same. This theme of doing good and not evil is central in 1 Peter even in the far from eirenic atmosphere that prevailed. The fact that the committing of one's soul to a faithful Creator is accomplished by 'doing good' reflects the strong encouragement given to Christians to make positive contributions to everyday life even in the face of an unappreciative or hostile city (4:19. Despite the complex and far from ideal social situations of the Christians addressed in 1 Peter, there were no extenuating circumstances which exempted them from seeking the blessing of the city.

It is right to see this New Testament text as 'an incitement for Christians to live up to this standard of first-class citizens', the theme of Romans 13:1-7 developed in 1 Peter 2:13-17 to meet the new reality of slanderous rumours against Christian communities.[31] Official endorsement of Christian benefactors by public honouring and permanent epigraphic record would have shown to all the city that 'they take part in everything as citizens', to cite the second century observation in the Epistle to Diognetus.[32]

This view of Christians in *politeia* was seen as both something that was obligatory and also distinctive.

> While they dwell in both Greek and Barbarian cities, each as his lot was cast, and follow the customs of the land in dress and food and other matters of living, they show forth the remarkable and admittedly strange order of their *politeia* (θαυμαστὴν καὶ ὁμολογουμένως παράδοξον ἐνδείκνυνται τὴν κατάστασιν τῆς ἑαυτῶν πολιτείας).[33]

---

[31]W.C. van Unnik, 'The Teaching of Good Works', 99.
[32]*The Epistle to Diognetus*, IV.5.
[33]*The Epistle to Diognetus*, V.4.

CHAPTER TWO

CIVIC HONOURS FOR CHRISTIAN BENEFACTORS

Romans 13:3–4 and 1 Peter 2:14–15

The welfare of the city in the Graeco-Roman world depended on the ongoing contributions of civic-minded benefactors. They paid for public works from their private resources in order to enhance the environs of their cities and, in times of famine, to ensure the supply of grain at a cost affordable to every citizen. This was a means of maintaining social order. The epigraphic and literary evidence to be cited will demonstrate that there were established conventions for the acknowledgement of benefactors. Rulers praised and honoured those who undertook good works which benefited the city. At the same time they made the conventional promise to honour publicly those who in the future would undertake similar benefactions.

The purpose of this chapter is to show that the praising by rulers referred to in Romans 13:3 and 1 Peter 2:14 was related to a specific area of *politeia viz.* public benefactions. Christians of substance were taught to seek the welfare of the city in the public domain by undertaking benefactions as part of their responsibilities in accordance with the will of God (*cf.* Rom. 12:1ff., 1 Pet. 2:15). In order to establish that this is the case, it is proposed to discuss (I) the form of the benefaction inscription, (II) the future promise implied in benefaction inscriptions, (III) the importance of gratitude and incentive in the empire, (IV) conventions surrounding the public praising of civic benefactors, and (V) New Testament teaching on Christians as civic benefactors.

I. The Form of the Benefaction Inscription

Greek benefaction inscriptions from the fifth century B.C. through to the second century A.D. generally followed a standard literary form.[1] They began with an announcement that 'the Council and the People resolved' (Ἔδοξεν τῇ βουλῇ καὶ τῇ δήμῳ) to honour a benefactor who is named. Then followed the actual resolution which began with the customary 'whereas' (ἐπειδή) and recounted the benefactions bestowed on the city. This clause prefaced the resolution proper, which was almost universally introduced by the statement, 'it has been resolved' (δεδόχθαι).[2] It announced the honours which the city was awarding to the benefactor. At the conclusion of the honours, there was a final clause introduced by the connective 'in order that. . .' (either ὅπως or

---

[1]See A.S. Henry, *Honours and Privileges in Athenian Decrees: The Principal Formulae of Athenian Honorary Decrees* (Hildesheim and New York: G. Olms, 1983) for a general discussion.

ἵνα). The purpose of that clause was to draw to the attention of all those who read the inscription that the city fathers knew how to bestow honours appropriate to benefactions.

The following is a typical inscription. Its purpose was to grant citizenship in Ephesus to a benefactor from Rhodes.[3]

Resolved by the Council and the People

> Dion, son of Diopeithes, moved that 'whereas' (ἐπειδή) Agathocles, son of Hegemon of Rhodes, having imported a quantity of wheat, and finding that the corn in the market was being sold at more than (?) drachmae, persuaded by the superintendent of the market and wishing to please the People, sold all his corn cheaper than that which was being sold in the market: it is hereby 'resolved' (δεδόχθαι) by the Council and the People to grant citizenship to Agathocles of Rhodes, upon equal and similar terms, to himself and to his descendants; further, that the Essenes allot to him a place in a tribe and a thousand, and that the Temple-wardens inscribe these (grants) in his honour— in the Temple of Artemis where they inscribe the rest of the grants of citizenship; to the end that all may know (ὅπως ἅπαντες εἰδῶσιν)[4] that the People understand how to repay with its favours those who are benefactors to it (ὅτι ὁ δῆμος ἐπιστάται χάριτας ἀποδιδόναι τοῖς εὐεργε-τοῦσιν αὐτόν).

The Greek epigraphic benefactor *genre* conveyed the following information: Whereas A did X and Y for our city, it is therefore resolved to honour A as follows. . .in order that all may see that the People appropriately honour benefactors commensurate with their benefactions.[5]

---

[2]For an exception, see the resolution of citizenship decrees in Athens from the fifth to the third centuries B.C. with the use of εἶναι αὐτόν, although δεδόχθαι was implied and later used. See Henry, *Honours and Privileges in Athenian Decrees*, 64ff. and M.J. Osborne, *Naturalization in Athens: The Law and Practice of Naturalization in Athens from the Origins to the Roman Period* (Brussels: AWL^SK, 1983) IV.155. Other Athenian grants during this period used δεδόχθαι *e.g. IG* I. 223 (343 B.C.).

[3]*Ancient Greek Inscriptions in the British Museum—Ephesus* cited in *BMI* 455 (150 B.C.).

[4]The final clause cited above uses one of two verbs. The other is φαινεῖν as in ὅπως οὖν καὶ ἡ βουλὴ καὶ ὁ δῆμος φαίνωνται τιμῶντες, *IG* II² 992.

[5]For the extent of the form of the final clause see over seventy examples of extant inscriptions published to 1914. W. Larfeld, *Griechische Epigraphik* (ed 3; München: C.H. Beck, 1914) 226. For similar inscriptions from Ephesus see *Die Inschriften von Ephesos* cited as *IEph* 1390, 1405, 1408, 1411, 1412, 1440, 1442, 1443.

II. The Future Promise to Civic Benefactors

There was a promise of rewards for future benefactors in the ὅπως/ἵνα clause of the resolution. Its aim was to indicate to those who read the inscription that the city authorities knew how to reward benefactors. An inscription from the island of Cos affirms what is implicit in *BMI* 455 (cited on page 27). It reads that the People might continue to be seen to give fitting rewards to those who choose to be their benefactors.[6]

The bestowing of honours on future benefactors is more explicitly stated in two inscriptions:

> so that we ourselves may be seen by those who propose to bestow benefactions on us (ὅπως οὖν καὶ ἡμεῖς φαινώμεθα τοῖς προαιρουμένοις εὐεργετεῖν) to give appropriate rewards. . .to praise (ἐπαινέσαι) . . .and to crown (στεφανῶσαι) them.[7]

> in order that our people may continue to be seen to bestow gifts on benefactors, and that those who come in future to serve as judges [independent arbitrators] in our city might seek to render verdicts worthy of praise (ἔπαινος) and honour, knowing that the People both praise and honour (ἐπαινεῖ τε καὶ τιμᾷ) the fine and noble men (καλοὺς καὶ ἀγαθούς).[8]

In other examples, the word 'always' (ἀεί) is added. 'The city of Eritrea always takes great thought for its friends'.[9] There is also an Ephesian inscription which promises rewards to 'each and all of the benefactors'.[10]

This sample of inscriptions provides sufficient evidence of a widespread convention of promising public recognition to intending benefactors.[11] It demonstrates that the assurance of Romans 13:3, 'do

---

[6] *c.* 200 B.C. For the text see J. Benedum, 'Griechische Arztinschriften aus Kos', *ZPE* 25 (1977) 271.

[7] J. Benedum, 'Griechische Arztinschriften aus Kos', 266.

[8] *BMI* 420 (150 B.C.).

[9] C. Michel, *Recueil d'inscriptions grecques*, 345 (3rd century B.C.).

[10] *IEph* 1412.

[11] One may cite examples of benefaction inscriptions with the 'promise' clause from specific locations related to the NT, *i.e.* Rome: *IG Urbis Romae²*; Corinth: B.D. Meritt, *Corinth: Results of Excavations conducted by the American School of Classical Studies at Athens 1896-1927* (Cambridge, Mass.: Harvard University Press, 1931) 8.1 No. 4 and a first-century A.D. inscription, *SIG* 800 (Claudius). For the widespread use of provenances, see Larfeld, *Griechische Epigraphik*, 377-81, 422-3.

the good and the authority will praise you', was not 'daringly promised' as Käsemann suggests,[12] for NT writers endorsed a long-established social custom of appropriate recognition of public bene-factors. The very existence of these inscriptions century after century in city after city shows that the promise was fulfilled. This convention was not only confined to the Greek and Hellenistic periods. It remained as vital for the welfare of Greek cities in the Roman empire, and thus '. . .it would not be an exaggeration to say that the prosperity of the cities rested in large part on the generosity of their leading citizens'.[13]

III. Gratitude and Incentives

If the final statement in Greek inscriptions aimed to promise future benefactors that public works would be met with appropriate rewards, the resolution wished to show that, in the case of the particular benefactor, the city had met its obligation of gratitude for the present public work bestowed on it. The use of ὅπως or ἵνα makes a clear connection between the first part of the resolution and the final clause. The city had indeed fulfilled its obligation by bestowing appropriate honours on the person concerned 'so that all might know the People understood how to reward with honours. . .' Those who read the inscription would be able to see that this was the case. It was not simply that honours were given, but that honours were seen by all to have been given by the rulers of the city. These were regarded as being commensurate with the value of the benefaction. Many of the inscriptions declared this by calling the honours 'worthy' (ἄξιαι) or 'highly worthy' (κατάξιαι).

Literary sources strongly support the epigraphic evidence. They show that great importance was attached to meeting the obligation with gratitude. Some saw this obligation not simply as a cultural con-vention but as 'a law'. Benefactions could be called 'loans' which were to be repaid with gratitude or, if not properly acknowledged, reclaimed with monetary compensation. Such was the expectation of the benefactor that due recognition would be given in the appropriate

---

[12]E. Käsemann, *Commentary on Romans* (E.T. London: SCM, 1980) 358.

[13] Jones, *The Roman World of Dio Chrysostom*, 104-14 and his discussion of Dio's benefactions to his native Prusa c. A.D. 101; P. Garnsey, '*Taxatio* and *Pollicitatio* in Roman Africa', 116.

way. Others saw failure to acknowledge public works adequately as a
sin.[14] There was a sense of 'indignation' (βαρύτης) whenever a benefactor received little or no gratitude for his benefaction.[15]

The purpose of this public recognition, according to Demosthenes, was to provide an incentive for others: 'the whole vast
audience is stimulated to do service to the commonwealth and
applauds the exhibition of gratitude rather than praising the one who
is crowned and that is why the state has enacted this statute'.[16]

The explicit affirmation in the final clause of the inscription
shows that the persuading of other benefactors to emulate the one
being honoured was of great importance for the future welfare and
enhancement of the city.

IV. The Praising of Civic Benefactors

An important Hellenistic Ephesian inscription promises incentives to
future benefactors by detailing the public honours.

> . . .whereas Skythes, son of Archidamus, has been good to the citizens
> with whom he has been involved, eagerly coming forward and with-
> out hesitation. . .as it is right and proper for a man who loves his city
> and is concerned for honour and good standing among the citizens,
> that the People, being grateful to such and having seen the fine and
> noble character of the man, have resolved to praise (ἐπαινέσαι) Sky-
> thes because of the diligence and the forethought he has in both sacred
> and secular affairs and, in addition, resolved by popular decision, and
> to crown (στεφανῶσαι) him with a gold crown during the games at
> the Festival of Dionysus. . .that announcement taking place in the

---

[14]See J.W. Hewitt, 'The Development of Political Gratitude', *TAPA* 55 (1924) 35-51
and more recently S.C. Mott, 'The Power of Giving and Receiving: Reciprocity in
Hellenistic Benevolence', *Current Issues in Biblical and Patristic Interpretation—Studies in Honor of Merrill C. Tenney* (ed. G.F. Hawthorne; Grand Rapids: Eerdmans,
1975) 60-72 and especially evidence cited from Greek and Latin authors in the section 'The Obligation of Gratitude', 61-3; Cicero, *De officiis* 1.47 on the great
importance of returning gratitude; Philo, *De decalogo* 165-7, for whom this obligation of honouring one's benefactor comes within the purview of the Old
Testament's commandment on honouring parents; and Seneca, *De beneficiis* 1.1.3,
4-8, 13 on benefactors expecting 'repayments' and the sin of ingratitude committed
if ignored because 'he who does not return a benefit sins.'
[15]Hermogenes, *On Types of Style* (trans. C.W. Wooten; Chapel Hill and London:
University of North Carolina Press, 1987) 364.
[16]*De corona* 120.

assembly of citizens, 'The People crown Skythes of Archidamus a fine and noble man who is well-disposed to the city', so that all may know the people are eager to honour its best men. . .[that] they might become zealous. . .and might eagerly give themselves. . .[17]

How were benefactors publicly recognised for their good deed? The procedure was that an individual 'moved' (εἶπεν) in the Council that a benefactor be granted certain honours. His formal motion, duly endorsed by the assembly, constituted the wording of the inscription.[18] Some of the resolutions explain what was involved, with the use of the terms 'praise' (ἔπαινος) and 'crown' (στέφανος).[19] The first term means a 'formal commendation',[20] and the second means literally 'a crown'.[21]

Dio Chrysostom, writing at the end of the first century A.D., provides valuable information on the rewards for a benefaction which has been 'established' (πεποίηκε) viz. 'a crown and a proclamation and a seat of honour' (στέφανος καὶ κήρυγμα καὶ προεδρία). He adds that the public proclamation contained 'three words' and notes that with them 'each good man is publicly acclaimed'. Dio does not say what they were, on the assumption that his audience knew them.[22] It has been suggested that the words might be 'he is a good man' (ἀνὴρ ἀγαθός ἐστι).[23] The Ephesian inscription noted above records the actual citation to be announced at the ceremony, 'The People crown Skythes, son of Archidamus, a good and noble man who is also well-disposed to the city'.[24] The official who honoured the benefactor in the theatre with the gold crown in this inscription declared that he was 'good and

---

[17]*IEph* 1390 (Hellenistic period).

[18]Motions were almost universally moved by an individual whose name was often recorded in the inscription.

[19]*E.g. BMI* 452, 457. See A.S. Henry, *Honours and Privileges in Athenian Decrees*, 7-9.

[20]See A. Strobel, 'Zum Verständnis von Rom. 13', *ZNW* 47 (1956) 82-4.

[21]C.B. Welles, *Royal Correspondence in the Hellenistic Period* (New Haven: Yale University Press, 1934) 363. This was originally a crown made of a sacred plant and valued for the significance of honour attached to it. Later a sum of money was given with a wreath, and still later, the crown was made of gold. It could be shaped like an olive branch (θαλλός) or a headband of gold (ταινία), Jones, *The Roman World of Dio Chrysostom* , 110, citing G.E. Bean, 'Notes and Inscriptions from Caunus', *JHS* 74 (1954) No. 22 and more recently Henry, 'Crowns', *Honours and Privileges in Athenian Decrees*, ch. II. See also *BMI* 29A 466.

[22]*Or.* 75.7-8 οὗτος ὁ τὰ τρία ῥήματα and seen by Dio as 'a law' *i.e.* an established custom. On proclaiming see P. Gauthier, *Les cités grecques et leurs bienfaiteurs*, Bulletin de correspondence hellénique Suppléments XII (1985) 33.

[23]H. Lamar Crosby, *Dio Chrysostom LCL* V 247 n. 2.; *IEph* 1412.

noble' (καλὸς καὶ ἀγαθός). In the political arena the terms stood for the truly noble person who put the interest of the state above his own.[25] Other inscriptions which record what is to be said at the crowning ceremony use 'virtue and benevolence' (ἀρετὴ καὶ εὔνοια) or 'virtue and righteousness and benevolence' (ἀρετὴ καὶ δικαιοσύνη καὶ εὔνοια) to describe the character of the benefactor.[26] Dio adds that 'the three words' were for some 'more precious than life itself'.[27] He mentions the third reward of the granting of a permanent seat of honour in the front row of the theatre.[28]

All the evidence presented to this point from diverse epigraphic sources is reflected in Demosthenes, *De corona*. It records his defence in 330 B.C. against legal proceedings by Aeschines, an orator who objected to the provisional decree (προβούλευμα) of the Athenian Council to award Demosthenes with the customary crown for his public benefaction. This literary source records the actual wording of four benefaction resolutions and cites the legal requirement that the crowning in Athens would occur in the theatre. It also notes that the crowning occurred at a notable event; in his case it was to have been at the 'performance of the new tragedies'.

In arguing his defence, Demosthenes observes that public accounts require audit and auditors, but the benefaction—in this case his gift to the theatre—deserves gratitude and [formal] thanks' (χάρις καὶ ἔπαινος). He puts the matter bluntly 'I made donations. For those

---

[24]*IEph* 1390 mentions 'praising. . .crowning. . .announcing'. See also *BMI* 452, 'to crown with a gold crown and proclaim. . .in the theatre. . .'; *cf.* Dio Chrysostom, *Or.* 66.2.

[25]*E.g. OGIS* 215, 339; *BMI* 420; *SIG* 312, 762; *IEph* 1395, 1412; *Michel* 307, 468, 487. Some have καλὸς κἀγαθός, *e.g. SIG* 307, and *IEph* 1390 prefaces the announcement with the term καλοκαγαθία. On the importance of καλὸς καὶ αγαθός see A.W. Gomme, 'The Interpretation of ΚΑΛΟΙ ΚΑΓΑΘΟΙ in Thucydides 4.40.2', *CQ* (1953) 658; G.E.M. De` Ste. Croix, 'Additional Note on KALOS KAGATHOS, KALOKAGATHIA', *The Origins of the Peloponnesian War* (London: Duckworth, 1972) Appendix xxix; and W. Den Boer, *Private Morality in Greece and Rome* (Leiden: Brill, 1979) 161-2.

[26]*OGIS* 339, *SEG* XXII 266, and XXIV 1099 use the first phrase and *SIG* 193 uses the second, having already noted that the benefactor was ἀνὴρ ἀγαθός. For Athenian terminology see Henry, *Honours and Privileges in Athenian Decrees*, 42-44.

[27]*Or.* 75.8, 66.2.

[28]προεδρία meant the seat of dignity and the privilege of the front seat at the theatre. Dio, *Or.* 75.7 is not alone in referring to the seat of honour as a reward: *BMI* 448 suggests it was one of the honours given 'to the rest of the benefactors'. For examples of inscriptions including this honour see *BMI* 448, 452, 453 and for discussion see Henry, 'Seats in Theatre and Stadium, Statues and Painted Portraits', *Honours and Privileges in Athenian Decrees*, ch. X.

donations I am thanked', (ἐπαινοῦμαι διὰ ταῦτα). It was not the first time he had undergone this public ceremony. He thus expresses his sense of injury at the possible deprivation of this honour recommended some six years prior to the trial but deferred for final resolution pending the decision of the court on the legal objections of an opposition group.[29] *De corona* shows how firmly established the literary form and the supporting legal conventions were in Athens in 330 B.C. It confirms both the epigraphic evidence and the witness in the first century of Dio Chrysostom already discussed.

There was, then, not only a formal recognition by way of a resolution by the Council to the Assembly and the erecting of an inscription, but also a public ceremony at which the benefactor was proclaimed. The term 'praise' referred to this public recognition.

V. Christians as Civic Benefactors

Did well-to-do Christians in Greek cities in the East undertake these public benefactions as did their secular counterparts, and more importantly were they exhorted to do so as part of Christian social ethics? If and when they did, the customary public recognition of their contribution by ruling authorities would be considered appropriate. In fact, they would have been expected to do so like any other well-to-do citizen. Their conversion to Christianity would not have exempted them from fulfilling their customary rôle as public benefactors. There is evidence in the first century of the Christian seeking the welfare of the city in this way and being taught to do so as part of his obligations in the sphere of social ethics. It throws further light on the Christians' involvement in society in the first century A.D. whereby they contributed to the well-being of the community at large.

When Paul wrote to the Romans, 'Do the good [deed] and you shall have praise (ἔπαινος) from the [civil] authority' (13:3), he was giving 'absolute assurance' that this would happen to the Christian.[30] Käsemann has noted, 'Furthermore the ἔπαινος is daringly promised (without even a "perhaps")'. The latter has suggested that the reference is to '. . .the honouring which the public authorities mentioned

---

[29]See *De corona* 84, 114-6, 118, 120, 113 respectively for the four resolutions, the legal stipulation of crowning, the reason for public crowning, the firm expectation of ἔπαινος, and the resolution commending him for ἀρετή. . .καὶ καλοκαγαθία.

[30]C.E.B. Cranfield, *A Critical and Exegetical Commentary on the Epistle to the Romans* (Edinburgh: T. & T. Clark, 1979) II. 655, n. 1.

customarily grant'.[31] While primary literary sources show that the ruler's functions were epitomised as honouring the good citizens and punishing the lawless ones,[32] it has been noted that none of them appears to match the absolute certainty of Paul in Romans 13:3-4, where the apostle writes that public benefactions would *ipso facto* be praised by rulers.[33] The discussion to this point, however, has demonstrated that literary sources from the time of Xenophon and Demosthenes through to the second century A.D. have reflected that one function of the ruler was to honour publicly those who were benefactors. Epigraphic evidence has shown that this function was fulfilled. Paul, or indeed any traveller of the ancient world, would naturally have known of this convention, for cities recorded for posterity in public places the work of benefactors on inscriptions which were officially erected by 'the Council and the People'. Paul's certainty that this would be the case, and a similar conviction in 1 Peter 2:14, were fully justified if these references are to public benefactions.

Do these biblical texts refer to public benefactions? It is one thing to show a convention existed in the Graeco-Roman world, but quite another to demonstrate that particular texts in the NT refer to it. The phrase 'the good [work]' (τὸ ἀγαθόν) in Romans 13:3-4 was also used in inscriptions to refer to a public benefaction. The injunction 'to do good' (τὸ ἀγαθὸν ποιεῖν) in Romans 13:3 was used in epigraphy to refer to the performing of a public benefaction. For example, concerning a benefactor of the city the People of Athens resolved '. . .to praise him because he is a good man (ἀνὴρ ἀγαθός) and he does whatever good he can (καὶ ποιεῖ ὅτι δύναται ἀγαθὸν) for the people of Athens. . .it is

---

[31]Käsemann, *Commentary on Romans*, 358. He does not cite any evidence of these customary grants.

[32]W.C. van Unnik, 'Lob und Strafe durch die Obrigkeit Hellenistisches zu Röm. 13,3-4' in E. Earle Ellis and E. Grässer (edd) *Jesus und Paulus, Festschrift für Georg Kümmel sum 70 Geburtstag* (Göttingen: Vandenhoeck and Ruprecht, 1975) 336-40 for the literary evidence of the ruler punishing the evil and praising the good. Although he cites Dio Chrysostom's *Or.* 39.2, he did not note the reference to honouring benefactors as a binding 'law', *i.e.* convention, in *Or.* 75.7-8.

[33]See Cranfield, *Epistle to the Romans*, II. 655, n. 1 and M. Borg, 'A New Context for Romans XIII', *NTS* 19 (1973) 205-18, who also adopts the same position. This interpretation has, however, been rejected for lack of proof, and some have argued that 'the good' in v. 4 refers to a morality related to salvation and not to public benefactions. Käsemann, *Romans*, 358 rejects Cranfield's position in the latter's earlier work, *A Commentary on Romans 12-13*, SJT Occasional Papers 12 (Edinburgh and London: 1965) 74-5, but incorrectly argues that 'the good' refers simply to 'earthly well-being, in fact scarcely more than security against attacks'. It is being argued that general public benefactions are being referred to here in these NT passages.

resolved that Menelaus be considered a benefactor. . .' Another is described as 'a benefactor of the city, a good man. . .and he does whatever good he is able to', and yet another has sought to do 'whatever good he is able to do for the city'. The linking of doing good to being a benefactor is clearly made—'to do whatever good he is able to perform for the citizens (ποιεῖν ἀγαθὸν ὅτι ἂν δύνηται τοὺς ἐντυγχάντας αὐτεῖ τῶν πολιτῶν). . .and to be a benefactor for all in the city (καὶ κατὰ κοινὸν εὐεργετεῖν τὴν πόλιν)'.[34]

But would the congregations have understood the term ἀγαθόν to refer to a public benefaction? Apart from the *politeia* context of both NT passages which would have readily suggested the meaning of benefaction because of the praising by rulers, Paul refers to 'the good man' in Romans 5:7. His argument is that for a righteous man one would hardly be prepared to lay down one's life, 'although perhaps for a good man one will possibly (τάχα) dare to die'. The order is, first, 'the righteous' (δίκαιος) and then 'the good' (ἀγαθός). Paul believes that the latter is a greater possibility because of obligations established through the receiving of a benefaction, and the latter term has been rightly taken to refer to one's private benefactor.[35] It was a binding obligation in the first century that one would honour one's benefactor—the argument is whether a person felt himself to be under such an obligation that he might consider laying down his life.

How would the term ἔπαινος in Romans 13:3 and 1 Peter 2:14 have been understood by its readers? Epigraphic evidence includes the following words of praise, doing good and being a benefactor: ἐπαινέσαι. . .ὅτι εὖ ποιεῖ ἐπειδὴ εὖ ποιεῖ. . .ἀναγραψάτω. . .καὶ εὐεργέτην ποιεῖν ὅτι δύναται ἀγαθὸν καὶ εὖ ποιεῖ. . .ἐπαινέσαι τὸ αὐτῷ καὶ

---

[34]*SIG* 174; *GDI* 5464, 5698, 5366; see also *SIG* 127, ἀνδρὸς πολλὰ καὶ ἀγαθὰ ποιη-῾σαντος τὴμ πόλιν. . .καὶ λόγῳ καὶ ἔργῳ. . .καὶ οὓς εὐεργέτας τῆς πόλεως; *SIG* 167, ἐπειδὴ ἀνήρ ἐστι ἀγαθός. . .περὶ τὴν πόλιν. . .ποιεῖν ὅτι δύναται ἀγαθόν, καὶ εὖ ποῖει. . .εὐεργέτην Ἀθηναίων; *SIG* 114, τὸ ἔργον καλὸν καὶ ἄξιὸν ἐποίησαν *SIG* 1105. Compare Cranfield, *The Epistle to the Romans*, II. 664, n. 5, who states that the terms 'are naturally understood as denoting that which is morally good. . .*pace* Käsemann', whereas the epigraphic evidence links them clearly to public benefactions and service.

[35]C.E.B. Cranfield, *The Epistle to Romans*, (Edinburgh: T. & T. Clark, 1975) I. 264-5, feels this gives the best sense. For a full discussion based on primary sources which establishes the view of the last century that ἀγαθός refers to a benefactor, see A.D. Clarke, 'The Good and the Just in Romans 5:7', *Tyn.B.* 41 (1990) 129-142. Elsewhere in the same epistle Paul uses the language of a patron who distributes to the needs of others (ὁ προιστάμενος, 12:8) and, following Cranfield, *ibid.*, I. 626 notes that the cognate προστάτης was used of a patron of resident aliens in Athens and was translated as *patronus*.

ἀναγράψαι αὐτὸν. . .εὐεργέτην Ἀθηναίων.[36] Because this term appears in the discussion of the rôle of leaders in the city, it would have been connected immediately with the conventions surrounding public recognition of benefactors.

This epigraphic evidence throws considerable light on Romans 13:3 and 1 Peter 2:14.[37] It demonstrates that the semantic field from which these words come was that of public benefactions and shows that both NT writers were on very secure ground promising Christian benefactors public recognition.[38]

Those who reject the interpretation offered on Romans 13:3-4 and 1 Peter 2:14 are driven to the vague position that Cranfield was forced to adopt in concluding that 'Paul means that consciously or unconsciously, willingly or unwillingly, in one way or another, the power will praise the good work and punish the evil'.[39] In writing to the Christians in the vast city of Rome, how could Paul expect the emperor or those in authority to observe their good works, if the refer-

---

[36]*IG* I² 82, 93, 118.

[37]A substantial study has recently been undertaken on the benefaction theme in relation to New Testament word usage. F.W. Danker, *Benefactor: Epigraphic Study of a Graeco-Roman and New Testament Semantic Field* (St Louis Missouri: Clayton Publishing House, 1982). It includes over fifty inscriptions and documents in translation and aims to identify key words from them in order to illuminate their meaning in the NT *corpus*. What is missing from this study is any reference to Rom. 13:3, even though there is ample evidence of the final clause promising recognition of benefactors cited in his inscriptions. What he says of Rom. 13:1-7 is 'And benefactors deserve honour'. Hence the concluding words in v. 7, 'Render honour to whom honour is due' (*ibid.*, 401). The 'honouring' Paul has in mind is that due to rulers; it was the ruler who gave praise to benefactors. In his section, 'Response to Benefactors', reference is made to the theme of 'honour' but none to 'praise' by authorities, although adequate reference to this is to be found in Danker's collection of inscriptions. The parallel passage in 1 Pet. 2:14 is not discussed in relation to the theme of Christians as public benefactors. Danker (*ibid.*, 452) regards 1 Pet. 2:13-5:11 as a 'benefit' response theme with no specific comment on public acknowledgement of good works in 2:14.

[38]The twenty literary sources noted by van Unnik, 'Lob und Strafe durch die Obrigkeit Hellenistisches zu Röm. 13,3-4', 336-40 in support of the rôles of rulers as reflected in Rom. 13:3 and 1 Pet. 2:14 are explicated from the inscriptions. The value of the epigraphic evidence is that it has shown that the ruler's role discussed in literary sources was certainly carried out with respect to the honouring of public benefactors.

[39]C.E.B. Cranfield, 'Some Observations on Romans XIII.1-7', *NTS* 6 (1959-60) 245. In his most recent work, *Romans: a Shorter Commentary* (Edinburgh: T. & T. Clark, 1985) 322-23 he has reiterated this comment and regards this explanation 'though admittedly difficult, seems preferable. . .' to 'the true and natural duty of the magistrate' which he notes was Calvin's explanation.

ence is simply to unspecified good moral conduct? How could the authorities know of the good morals of its Christian citizens in the cities mentioned in the provinces of Asia Minor referred to in 1 Peter, *viz.* Pontus, Galatia, Cappadocia, Asia and Bithynia? The authorities would certainly be aware of those who did evil, *i.e.* transgressed the law. The petitioning of the authorities by an accuser for the commencement of litigation to bring the accused to justice would do this. There is no difficulty in identifying the exercising of this role in Romans 13:4b and 1 Peter 2:14, as scholars have universally done. The other role for leaders of the long-established tradition which guaranteed that city benefactors would be publicly praised should also be seen in these NT passages. The objection to van Unnik's conclusions which Cranfield raised in his extended commentary on Romans 13 is overcome by the epigraphic and literary evidence discussed in this chapter.[40] Käsemann's conclusion, that the reference is to the public honours customarily granted, is justified, although different from the scope he envisaged.[41]

The use of singular 'you' (σοί) in Romans 13:4 shows that it is addressed to the individual rather than the whole church. The cost of a benefaction was very considerable and beyond the ability of some, if not most, members of the church. Benefactions included supplying grain in times of necessity by diverting the grain-carrying ships to the city, forcing down the price by selling it in the market below the asking rate, erecting public buildings or adorning old buildings with marble revetments such as in Corinth, refurbishing the theatre, widening roads, helping in the construction of public utilities, going on embassies to gain privileges for the city, and helping the city in times of civil upheaval.[42] There must have been Christians of very considerable means to warrant Paul's injunction in verse 3 and that of 1 Peter 2:15.[43] This further evidence supports the view that there were members of significant social status and wealth in a number of congregations in the early church.[44]

---

[40]Cranfield, *The Epistle to the Romans*, II. 666.

[41]'The good in v. 4 is simply earthly well-being, in fact scarcely more than security against attacks', Käsemann, *Romans*, 358.

[42]This reflects some of the activities of benefactors in the Ephesian epigraphic material, *BMI* 449, 450, 452, 455. On Corinthian buildings see Kent, *Corinth:* 8.3. 20-21 (for discussion), No. 123-37 (for inscriptions). For a discussion by Dio of Prusa of the bestowal of benefactions on a city see Jones, *The Roman World of Dio Chrysostom*, ch. 12.

[43]Judge, *The Social Pattern of the Christian Groups* 49ff. and 'The Early Christians as a Scholastic Community', *Journal of Religious History* 1 (1960-61) 130.

Paul sees the ruler as God's 'servant' (διάκονος) with respect to the benefaction (εἰς τὸ ἀγαθόν, v. 4). The use of γάρ explains why he 'praises' the benefactor—ἕξεις ἔπαινον ἐξ αὐτῆς θεοῦ γὰρ διάκονος κ.τ.λ. The best translation of εἰς is 'with respect to' the benefaction (v. 4a). The sentence would read 'For he is God's minister to you because of the benefaction'. In v. 4b the other traditional function of the ruler is referred to: 'For God's minister is the prosecutor or avenger (ἔκδικος) with respect to wrath (εἰς ὀργήν) to the one who does the evil deed'. In this verse the dual functions of the ruler are referred to, as they are in 1 Peter 2:14—a phenomenon not peculiar to NT literature. Demosthenes argues that the strength of the state depended on zeal for those laws which assigned rewards to those who 'do good' (ἀγαθὸν ποιεῖν) and the punishment of those who do evil. 'Wrongdoing' (κακὸν ποιεῖν) is described as a breach of the law and good deeds as 'benefactions' (εὐεργεσία) for which there are public rewards for those who are ambitious for honour.[45] Paul declares that the ruler is acting as God's vicegerent when he officially recognises the benefactor with the accolade that he is a good man, for in Romans 2:10 God gives 'glory and honour and peace to every man who works the good (τὸ ἀγαθόν)'. The public recognition of a Christian benefactor in the theatre before the multitude was appropriate in the NT with the ruler acting as God's 'servant' for this purpose. Christians were not taught to undertake civic benefactions for pragmatic reasons but rather for theological ones.

In the clearly civic context of 1 Peter 2:14-16 public benefactions are commended to Christians as God's will, because they will also silence the unfounded rumours against Christians by ill-informed men. 'Rulers praise those who do good. Because this is the will of God

---

[44]To hold public office citizens had to be 'persons of relatively great means', S.V. Tracey, 'IG II² 336: Contributions of First Fruits for Pythaïs', *Beiträge zur klassischen Philologie* 139 (1982) 171ff. For Christians of means, see E.A. Judge, 'The Social Identity of the First Christians: A Question of Method in Religious History', *Journal of Religious History* 11 (1980) 201-7; G. Theissen, 'Social Stratification in the Corinthian Community: A Contribution to the Sociology of Early Hellenistic Christianity', *The Social Setting of Pauline Christianity: Essays on Corinth* (Edinburgh: T. & T. Clark, 1982) 69-119; W.A. Meeks, 'The Social Level of Pauline Christians', *The First Urban Christians: The Social World of the Apostle Paul* (New Haven and London: Yale University Press, 1983) ch. 2, and D.W.J. Gill, 'Acts and the Urban Élites' *The Book of Acts in its Graeco-Roman Setting*, The Book of Acts in its First Century Setting (Grand Rapids and Carlisle: Eerdmans and Paternoster, 1994) ch. 5.
[45]Demosthenes, *Against Leptines* 504. See van Unnik, 'Lob und Strafe durch die Obrigkeit Hellenistisches zu Röm. 13,3-4', 336-40 for literary evidence.

that by doing good, you put to silence the ignorance of uninformed men' (vv. 14b-15).[46] The public acknowledgement of a generous Christian benefactor by crowning him as a noble person and the permanent reminder of the benefaction on an inscription would be the means of refuting unfounded rumours against a Christian as being a man of ill-will or a threat to the peace and welfare of a city.[47] The title 'benefactor' bestowed enormous status.[48] The doing of public good in verses 14-15 is but one example of the theme from 2:12–3:6, where 'doing good' in the context of less than easy circumstances is seen as the means of establishing Christian credibility in social relationships and the sphere of *politeia*.[49]

The chapter has shown how public benefactors of a city were duly recognised by its rulers. This also applied to the Christian who acted as a public benefactor (Rom. 13:3-4 and 1 Pet. 2:14-15).[50] These verses confirm the Christian's involvement in civic life in the first century A.D. and the warrant for it.

The picture emerges of a positive rôle being taken by rich Christians for the well-being of the community at large and the appropriateness and importance of due recognition by ruling authorities for their contribution. The Christians in Greek cities in the East were exhorted to undertake the same benefactions as did their secular counterparts. In fact this would have been expected of them by their fellow citizens if they were 'well-to-do'. Conversion to Christianity did not mean that civic benefactors ceased to seek the welfare of their earthly cities in keeping with their Old Testament counterparts in the Exile (Jer. 29:7). It was an ethical imperative which

---

[46]W.C. van Unnik, 'The Teaching of Good Works in 1 Peter', *NTS* 1 (1954) 99, rightly argues that the good works in 2:14 are something more than 'doing one's duty' they are doing something deserving 'special distinction', since 'public honours' will be bestowed on them. '. . .it is well known that εὐέργεται of Greek communities were often honoured by tablets in the market place extolling the great services they rendered to the State'. He makes this observation without epigraphic evidence, citing the general comment of E.G. Selwyn, *The First Epistle of St Peter* (London: Macmillan, 1946) 173.

[47]Elliott, *A Home for the Homeless*, 87, argues that 1 Peter does not reflect the view of the state as a 'servant of God' in Rom. 13:1-7 but simply a human institution, worthy of respect and deputed to administer justice. F. Schröger, *Gemeinde im 1 Petrusbrief* (Passau: Passavia Universitätsverlag, 1981) 148, argues that both passages are loyal and friendly to the state. Certainly both passages have the same expectation of public recognition for Christian benefactors.

[48]Hands, *Charities and Social Aid in Greece and Rome*, 36.

[49]See p.19ff.

Christians were commanded to fulfil within this aspect of *politeia*, and as a result would have made them very visible in the public place.

---

[50]This is not to be confused with rulers who were 'called benefactors' and whose description as such is mentioned in Lk. 22:25. On this role see E. Skard, 'Zwei religios—politische Begriffe: Euergetes Concordia', *Norske Videskaps Akademi i Oslo, Avhandlinger* 13 (1932) 1-66. His study incorporates epigraphic evidence. The literary evidence deals especially with Isocrates' view of the monarch as benefactor, but he does not discuss the role of the citizen as benefactor. As F.W. Danker, *Benefactor*, 324, notes, the ruler was called a benefactor because he was seen as the provider of benefits such as security and welfare for the people. I.H. Marshall, *The Gospel of Luke: A Commentary on the Greek Text* (Exeter: Paternoster Press, 1978) 812, cites some of the evidence of rulers from Ptolemy III to Trajan. The prohibition (ὑμεῖς δὲ οὐχ οὕτως) is not against Christians operating as benefactors. See D.J. Lull, 'The Servant-Benefactor as a Model of Greatness (Luke 22:24-30)', *Nov.T.* 28 (1986) 296, where he notes that the phrase 'those in authority are called benefactors' is a descriptive term. The point of Lk. 22:25 is that Christians were not to operate in an overbearing and dictatorial fashion as Gentile kings and those in authority who were commonly called 'benefactors'. For the most recent discussion of Rome as benefactor of the early empire see A. Erskine, 'The Romans as Common Benefactors' *Historia* 43 (1994) 70–87.

CHAPTER THREE

FROM SECULAR CLIENTS TO CHRISTIAN BENEFACTORS

1 Thessalonians 4:11–12 and
2 Thessalonians 3:6–13

The rôle of the Christian benefactor would no longer be the sole responsibility of the rich. The call for those in the church 'to do good', (a term used for undertaking benefactions),[1] would have come as a shock to those who were clients of patrons on converting to Christianity. Rich citizens were expected to be civic benefactors. Paul would not endorse a Christian continuing as the recipient of private benefactions by way of the parasitic client relationship with a patron (προιστάμενος, *patronus*) even though it was widely accepted in the secular world as an important element in the social fabric of public life.[2] This relationship would have been the one reason why some citizens apart from the rich in the city of Thessalonica, or in any other city in the empire, did not have to work. The purpose of this chapter is to show that from the early days of his ministry in Thessalonica, Paul set out to change the established convention of the *providentia* relationship between a patron and his client. In doing this he was initiating in Gentile regions a radical social ethic which he regarded as binding on Christians. The secular client must now become a private Christian benefactor.   When this social change was introduced into new Christian communities, it must have been the most distinctive public feature of this newly-emerging religion in the Roman East.

That Paul had to use such sharp language in 2 Thessalonians 3:6–13 to re–enforce this teaching demonstrates the great strength of the patron/client relationship. It also shows there was a reluctance on the part of some to renounce it permanently for the Christian alternative, *i.e.* that every Christian be a benefactor in his or her society. He reminded them yet again, in greater detail, of what he had taught them concerning work when he was initially with them.

> . . .with toil and labour we worked day and night, that we might not burden any of you. It is not because we have not that right, but to give you in our conduct an example to imitate. For even when we were with you, we gave you the command, 'If any one does not wish to work, let him not eat'. For we hear that some of you are living in idleness, mere busybodies, not doing any work. Now we command and exhort such persons in the Lord Jesus Christ to do their work with quietness and earn their own living. Brothers, in the doing of good you must not grow weary (2 Thess. 3:8-11).

---

[1]See p. 35.
[2]See R.P. Saller, *Personal Patronage under the Early Empire* (Cambridge: CUP, 1982).

Paul had already taught the church in Thessalonica in an earlier letter, instructing them to do their work, to earn their own living, *'as we charged you,* so that you may command the respect of outsiders, and be dependent on nobody' (1 Thess. 4:10–12).[3]

In a recent discussion about why certain Christians in Thessalonica refused to work, R. Russell has made the important observation that 'whatever encouraged their behaviour preceded these eschatological problems because disorderly behaviour existed from the beginning'.[4] He rightly justifies this conclusion from 2 Thessalonians 3:7–9, 'for you yourselves know how you ought to imitate us. . .with toil and labour we worked day and night. . .to give you in our conduct an example to imitate. For even when we were with you, we gave you the command'. The initial problem in Thessalonica, in Russell's estimate, was a social rather than an eschatological one.

To what might this problem be attributed? A number of suggestions have been made. Russell himself argues that 'the opportunities for employment were limited, and with scarcity of work idleness was more widespread and wages even lower'. Thus, as a result of unemployment, some had become poor and had received support from rich members of the congregation.[5] If this is correct, then Paul's solution was an unsympathetic and impractical one, for if any were unem-

---

[3]The reasons for the traditional ordering of the two letters may be fortified by the argument of this chapter. At the very least 2 Thess. 3:6–13 should be seen as a record of Paul's initial visit and the social situation he set about to rectify, even by those who reject the Pauline authorship of 2 Thess. It would hardly have been invented for a congregation, some of whose members would have been aware of the radical demands that Paul made when he first came. Pauline authorship of 2 Thess. has been the subject of considerable debate: in favour of its authenticity see for example the arguments of I.H. Marshall, *1 and 2 Thessalonians* (London: Marshall Morgan and Scott, 1983) 28–45, against those put by the most influential antagonist, W. Trilling, 'Untersuchungen zum 2. Thessalonicherbrief', *Erfurter theologische Studien* 27 (Leipzig: St. Benno–Verlag, 1972).

[4]R. Russell, 'The Idle in 2 Thess 3.6–12: an Eschatological or a Social Problem?', *NTS* 34 (1988) 108. For the most recent attempt to make a connection between the two issues, see J.J. Menken, 'Paradise Regained or Lost? Eschatology and Disorderly Behaviour in 2 Thessalonians', *NTS* 38 (1992) 271–89, with his critique of Russell (pp. 272–3). He acknowledges that the nexus is impossible to prove (p. 288).

[5]Russell, 'The Idle', 112, 108. As Menken, 'Paradise Regained', 274, points out with respect to Russell's argument that while the people were without work, he has not satisfactorily explained why they will not work.

ployed through lack of job opportunities, then *ipso facto* they could not eat at the expense of other Christians (2 Thess. 3:10b).

A. Malherbe speculates that the fact that 'converts abandoned their trades and took to the streets (as Cynic preachers did) helps to explain Paul's preoccupation with his own and his converts' employment'.[6] Dio Chrysostom, in his Alexandrian oration dated *c.* A.D. 70, provides evidence of the Cynic teachers offering their instruction free of charge in contrast to others who accepted fees. They begged for support on street corners from all and sundry.[7] However, the esteeming of Christian teachers on the one hand (1 Thess. 5:12–13) and the exhortation to 'admonish the idlers' on the other, which follows immediately after, seem singularly out of place if it is true that the unemployed had left their work to preach, as the Cynic teachers did.

Was the reluctance to work related to attitudes to manual labour, *i.e.* working with their hands? The view has been canvassed that the first-century disdain for manual work was at the heart of the Thessalonian problem.[8] Certainly artisans were not esteemed even if their work was admired. Plutarch, for example, states that 'while we delight in the work [of craftsmen and artisans], we despise the workman. . .it does not necessarily follow that, if the work delights you with its graces, the one who wrought it is worthy of your esteem'.[9] This is but one comment reflecting the upper class' attitude to manual workers. It does not, however, explain why some in Thessalonica assumed responsibility to provide for their fellow-citizens. 2 Thessalonians 3:6–8 implies that there was a convention of *providentia* which existed prior to Paul's initial coming to Thessalonica, and one which he set about resolving while still there. He refers to 'the tradition you received from us.[10] For you yourselves know how you ought to imitate us. . .we

---

[6]A. Malherbe, *Paul and the Thessalonians* (Philadelphia: Fortress Press, 1987) 101.
[7]Dio Chrysostom, *Or.* 32.9.
[8]*E.g.* I.H. Marshall, *1 and 2 Thessalonians*, 223.
[9]*Pericles*, 1.4–2.2. In denigrating their opponents, the sophists, who were from the social élite, boasted they 'knew nothing of labour' (πόνον οὐκ εἰδότες) and they spoke of those who had to work as 'easy to despise' (εὐκαταφρόνητοι), Philo, *Det.* 33–4.
[10]παρελάβοσαν, an aorist tense, v. 6. See G.S. Holland, *The Tradition that You Received from Us: 2 Thessalonians in the Pauline Tradition* (Tübingen: J.C.B. Mohr [Paul Siebeck], 1988). The implication of Paul's statement is that, both by word and example, Paul drove home this message in Thessalonica, undertaking what he himself did not need to do because of his gospel right of local support while preaching the gospel, *cf.* 1 Cor. 9:6, 12b, 14 where he cites the dominical *fiat*.

worked day and night. . .to give you in your conduct an example to imitate' (2 Thess. 3:6-9).

In order to discover why Paul felt it was necessary to have given this 'tradition', both by precept and example, while he was in Thessalonica, and subsequently found it so difficult but important to re–enforce this teaching, it is proposed to discuss (I) The patron/client relationship, (II) the requirement of 'political' quietism by former clients, (III) Paul's call not to be dependent on a patron, (IV) *providentia* for clients after Paul's departure, and (V) Paul's re-enforcement of radical Christian teaching on the rôle of all Christians as benefactors.

I. The Patron/Client Relationship

Russell suggests without further analysis that because the poor 'developed a relationship (friendship) with a benefactor or patron whereby they would receive support, money or food in exchange for the obligation to reciprocate with an expression of gratitude', so too some of the Christian 'urban poor. . .may have formed a client relationship and obligation to the benefactor'.[11] Patrons did not establish client relationships with 'the urban poor'. They were great inferiors. They did so with those who possessed the same status as they did, but not their wealth, or with those who were their former slaves but were now their freedmen. If they were clients, then it gives an indication of their moderately high social register in contrast to that normally understood for the Thessalonian Christians.

What did such a relationship involve? What is said of the Republic applied equally to the early empire.

> The aristocratic social milieu of the Republic continued into the Principate, and with it the basic notion that a man's social status was reflected in the size of his following—a large clientele symbolising his power to give inferiors what they needed. If a man's *clientela* was indicative of his current status, his potential for mobility depended on the effectiveness of his patrons whose wealth and political connections could be indispensable. Perhaps partly because of the unchanging social structure and values, financial institutions developed little, and so Romans appear to have continued to rely largely on patrons, clients and friends for loans or gifts in time of need, and assistance in financial activities.[12]

---

[11]Russell, 'The Idle', 112–3.

At the heart of patronage was the social convention which was called 'giving and receiving'.[13] This meant more than simply an expression of gratitude at the time of receiving a gift. Once financial support had been given and received, a relationship was created which could be further exploited by the receiver. The very return of profuse thanks for a gift was the means of asking for more. The act of benefiting set up a chain of obligations. The beneficiary had an obligation to respond to the gift with gratitude; profuse expressions of gratitude then placed the benefactor under obligation to do something further for his client.[14]

One of the requirements of a client was that he should attend the morning 'greeting' (salutatio) in the reception room of his patron and receive a gift of food or money.[15] The houses were designed architecturally to accommodate the greeting of clients and friends every morning—'the opening of the doors [of the house] at dawn to the crowd of callers, the accessibility of the dominus to the public, his clients and his friends'.[16]

There were certainly some in the church who were wealthy and therefore potential private and even public benefactors. Aristarchus from Thessalonica, who is mentioned in Acts 19:29 and 20:4, is possibly one such person. If he is the same person as Aristarchus, son of Aristarchus who heads a list of politarchs in that city, then he would have been a person of means.[17] Jason, who appears to have been Paul's host in Thessalonica and who sends his greeting to the church in Rome, may well have been a wealthy man.[18] There were 'not a few of the leading women' who became converts, according to Acts 17:4. As such, they were not precluded from giving public and private benefactions, as illustrated by the inscription to Junia Theodora of Corinth c. AD 43.[19]

---

[12]R.P. Saller, *Personal Patronage under the Early Empire*, 205. See also P. Marshall, *Enmity in Corinth: Social Conventions in Paul's Relations with the Corinthians* (Tübingen: J.C.B. Mohr [Paul Siebeck], 1987) 143.

[13]Marshall, *Enmity in Corinth*, 157–164.

[14]S.C. Mott, 'The Power of Giving and Receiving: Reciprocity in Hellenistic Benevolence', 60–72, esp. 63: 'the expression of gratitude placed a valid claim for further benefits upon the benefactor'. '"Gratitude for one favour is the best method of securing another"', he states, citing C.B. Welles, *Royal Correspondence in the Hellenistic Period: A Study of Greek Epigraphy* (New Haven: Yale University Press, 1934) 108.

[15]See Juvenal, *Satires* III *ll.* 129–130 on paying morning respects to a patron.

[16]P.R.C. Weaver, *Familia Caesaris: A Social Study of the Emperor's Freedmen and Slaves* (Cambridge: CUP, 1972) 63–4.

[17]See C.J. Hemer, *The Book of Acts in the Setting of Hellenistic History* (Tübingen: J.C.B. Mohr, 1989) 236.

Even if the Acts account contained no references to people of status in the church in Thessalonica, the existence of a few wealthy members would need to be presupposed. As Jewett comments, 'the archaeological evidence in the Greek cities renders it essential to assume the presence of a few patrons whose houses were large enough to serve as centres for house churches'.[20]

If some patrons were now Christians, what would have happened to their clients? A Christian patron would still have been under an obligation to support non-Christian clients. Changing his religion would not automatically have abrogated his patronal responsibilities. There is good reason to suppose that converted patrons would have made every attempt to share their new-found faith with the former, for they would have constituted an immediate sphere of influence. Becoming a Christian would not thereby have relieved a patron of his obligation to continue to give help to Christian clients if they asked for support. In fact, refusal to do so would have created a relationship of enmity which could not but affect relationships in the church, especially if it met for worship in a Christian household or households.[21] This may well explain why Paul set himself the task of working, although clearly he need not have done so—'Not because we did not have the right' (2 Thess. 3:9).[22] He wished to break the strong social convention which was part of the fabric of the life in *politeia, i.e.* the

---

[18]Acts 17:5–7 and Rom. 16:21: see R. Jewett, *The Thessalonian Correspondence: Pauline Rhetoric and Millenarian Piety* (Philadelphia: Fortress Press, 1986) 120, *contra* G. Theissen, 'Social Stratification in the Corinthian Community: A Contribution to the Sociology of Early Hellenistic Christianity', *The Social Setting of Pauline Christianity* (Philadelphia: Fortress, 1982) 95, who believes that the social status of Jason remains an open question.

[19]See D.I. Pallas, 'Inscriptions Lyciennes trouvées à Solomos près de Corinthe', *BCH* 58 (1959) 498–500 (for the texts) and L. Robert, 'Recherches épigraphiques', *REA* 62 (1960) 324ff. no. 7 (for the dating of the decree *c.* AD 43). For a discussion of the rôle of Roman women, see A.J. Marshall, 'Roman Women and the Provinces', *Ancient Society* 6 (1975) 108–27 and R. MacMullen, 'Women in Public in the Roman Empire', *Historia* 29 (1980) 208–20.

[20]Some have doubted the integrity of the account of the social composition of the new church in Acts 17:4 because of the exhortations for the idle to work in the Thessalonian *corpus,* See R. Jewett, *Thessalonian Correspondence*, 120, commenting on J. Murphy-O'Connor, 'Archaeology', in *St. Paul's Corinth Texts and Archaeology* (Wilmington: M. Glazier, 1983) Part 3.

[21]Marshall, *Enmity in Corinth*, 20.

[22]For an explanation of this right and Paul's rejection of it see 1 Cor. 9 and my discussion in *Philo and Paul among the Sophists: a First-Century, Jewish and a Christian Response,* (Macquarie University Ph.D., 1988) 172–4 *forthcoming SNTSMS.*

patron/client relationship, because it contradicted the Christian's new
obligation to 'do good'.

II. 'Political' Quietism for Former Clients

In 1 Thessalonians 4:11 Paul is encouraging former clients to 'stand
aloof from public life'.[23] This was not similar to the Stoic stance of
withdrawing from public life. Paul is here proscribing the boisterous,
political rabble–rousing behaviour by clients on behalf of their patrons
in *politeia*. He calls on them to be 'eager to live quietly' (φιλοτιμεῖσθαι
ἡσυχάζειν), to undertake their own activities (πράσσειν τὰ ἴδια),[24] and
'to work with their hands'. Are these commands the alternative to the
public activities of a client on behalf of his patron? R.F. Hock has suggested that this command to 'live quietly' refers to political 'quietism',
which he contrasts to public life.[25] Certainly the verb φιλοτιμοῦμαι followed by an infinitive means 'to strive earnestly to. . .' The former was
used in the semantic field of *politeia* to refer to those who act in a public-
spirited way as benefactors. Dio Chrysostom, for example, speaks of
those who 'strive earnestly [to be] good and noble' (καλὸς καὶ ἀγαθός)
i.e. public benefactors,[26] who are 'zealous to serve the city' and are
'ambitious to exalt it'.[27] It was also used to describe those who 'strive
earnestly to have more than their neighbour' in Dio Chrysostom's oration on covetousness (17.20). Clients were ambitious for themselves,
living as they did in the hope of securing substantial gifts for their
political loyalty through the generosity of their patron, on whose
behalf they were politically active in the secular ἐκκλησία. Juvenal tells

---

[23]The interpretation runs counter to that of Meeks, *The Origins of Christian Morality*,
49 who sees this text as the response of 'any migrating group' and not a prohibition
against client participation in *politeia*.
[24]Herodotus 5.63 δημοσιῷ, ἴδια πράσσω ἢ στρατοῦ ταχθείς, *cf.* Thucydides 1.82.6;
2.61.4, where it is used as an antonym to 'public' *i.e.* πόλις and κοινός respectively.
[25]Hock, *The Social Context of Paul's Ministry* 46, following Malherbe, *Social Aspects
of Early Christianity* 26. Hock supports his view from the political nature of Paul's
language citing E. von Dobschutz, *Thessalonicker–Briefe* (Göttingen, 1909) 179-81.
That view was rejected at the time by J.E. Frame, *The Epistles of St. Paul to the Thessalonians* (Edinburgh: T. & T. Clark, 1912) 161, and more recently by I.H. Marshall,
1 and 2 Thessalonians, 116-7 who argue from the context and the further reference
to idleness (4:13-5:11; 5:14). This idleness, however, could refer to that of the clients
who definitely did not work with their own hands.
[26]See p. 32 on the use of this phrase to refer to benefactors.
[27]*Or.* 13.28, 31.105, 43.4*cf.* Plato, *Alcibiades* 146a where it is used of political jostling.

us that a client might live in the unrealistic hope that his patron would bestow on him a gift of 400,000 sesterces, the sum required for the client to become a knight.[28]

The term 'to live quietly' (ἡσυχάζειν) was also used to describe a person who had given up his honorary public duties in order 'to be at rest' (ἡσυχάσαι), although others sought to put pressure on that person to remain in his duties' (ἐπιμεῖναι ἐν τοῖς πράγμασιν, P.Oxy. 128). The alternative in 2 Thessalonians 3:6 to disorderly conduct and being 'busybodies' was to work with their own hands. Just as the command to the brethren is given 'in the name of our Lord Jesus' not to feed those who refused to work, so too is a most solemn command and exhortation registered in the same name, requiring that they 'work with quietness' (μετὰ ἡσυχίας), and eat your own bread' (2 Thess. 3:12). ἡσυχία is the cognate noun of the verb used in 1 Thessalonians 4:12 to describe the way in which their daily activity is to be undertaken. There would have been a stark contrast in lifestyle between the activity of a client in the public place and working quietly, eating the fruits of that labour.

Paul's call to 'undertake your own activities' (πράσσειν τὰ ἴδια) is followed by the exhortation 'to work with your own hands, as we charged you' (v. 11b). The former injunction is made as the antithesis to attending to the affairs of another.[29] Plato uses the same term in *The Republic* 433a–b, where he speaks of 'this principle of doing one's own business' and commands that the person be 'not a versatile busybody'. Plato refers to this principle being enshrined in a popular adage—'"to do one's own business (τὸ τὰ αὐτοῦ πράττειν) and not to be a busybody is just" is a saying that we have heard from many and have very often repeated ourselves'. In *Gorgias* 526c he mentions Callicles, who is described as a 'private man' who 'minded his own business' and had not been 'a busybody in his lifetime'.[30] It therefore makes sense to see this comment concerning 'minding one's own affairs' in 1 Thessalonians 4:12 as taken from a popular description of public and private life. It was clearly the opposite to being concerned about the public activities of one's patron. The patron's very purpose in establishing a financial relationship with a client was that the latter

---

[28] *Satire V. l.* 132.

[29] Paul here is not juxtaposing this comment with civic euergetism, 'the doing of good' as in Rom. 13:3–4. For discussion see ch. 2.

[30] For a discussion of this in Athens see V.J. Hunter, 'The Politics of Reputation: Gossip as a Social Restraint', *Policing Athens: Social Control in the Attic Lawsuits, 420–320 B.C.* (Princeton: Princeton University Press, 1994) ch. 4.

would not need to attend primarily to his own affairs. He was being supported by his patron in order to give attention to the latter's concerns in the public domain. The statement πράσσειν τὰ ἴδια would be better translated 'to do one's own business' in contrast to the 'full time' activity of doing the bidding of a patron. Paul intends the καί which separates the two statements to be epexegetical, *i.e.* attending to one's own business means working with one's own hands in order to provide for one's own needs.

The extra–biblical examples cited in the previous paragraph record the juxtaposition of 'minding one's own business' with 'being a busybody'. These concepts clearly referred to *politeia*. Paul makes the same nexus in his subsequent discussion in 2 Thessalonians 3:11. Those not working are specifically described as busybodies—'those not working but being busybodies' (μηδὲν ἐργαζομένους ἀλλὰ περιεργαζομένους). The statement there is preceded by a reference to their disorderly conduct, περιπατοῦντας ἐν ὑμῖν ἀτάκτως. Russell has taken this to refer to their activity in the actual Christian meeting, ἐκκλησία.[31] The context, however, suggests that it is much more likely to be a description of the activity of a client supporting his patron's cause in *politeia*.[32] Epictetus commends the person in public life who is neither a 'busybody' (περίεργος) nor a 'meddler' (πολυπράγμων) for, it is explained, 'he is not meddling in other people's affairs when he is overseeing the actions of men when this is his proper [official] concern (τὰ ἴδια)' (III.22.97). So the term τὰ ἴδια, both here and in 2 Thessalonians 3:11, refers to one's proper tasks: the Christian's being 'a busybody' as a client is not one, but his working certainly is.

In discussing Paul's use of the two terms, ἐργάζω and περιεργάζω, attention has been drawn to their occurrence together in Demosthenes where it is said that there is a play on words.[33] Whether this was the case or not is uncertain. What is important is the illumination of the latter's discussion for our understanding of Paul's comments. Demosthenes refers to 'to the person who meddles'

---

[31]Russell, 'The Idle', 107–8.

[32]*Cf.* Aristotle, *Politics* 1319B 15. ποιεῖν τὴν πολιτείαν ἀτακτοτέραν. See A. Lintott, *Violence, Civil Strife and Revolution in the Classical City* (London & Canberra: Croom Helm, 1982) and B. Rawson, *The Politics of Friendship, Pompey and Cicero* (Sydney: Sydney University Press, 1978). This suggestion is far more convincing than the argument of Jewett, *Thessalonian Correspondence*, 125, who explores the possibility that the members of the congregation understood Paul's proclamation in political terms and that they possibly comprised 'disenfranchised labourers who were known to be restive under Roman rule'.

[33]Demosthenes, *The First Philippic Oration* 7 and the comment in *BAGD*.

(περιεργάζω) in public affairs, and sees the utmost danger from the activity he describes as 'bustling' (ἐργάζω) and 'meddling' (περιεργάζω). The latter term is, for both Demosthenes and Paul, used in a pejorative sense.

Paul is concerned with the public association of Christians with a lifestyle that should commend itself to the outsiders: 'command the respect of outsiders' (ἵνα περιπατῆτε εὐσχημόνως πρὸς τοὺς ἔξω, 1 Thess. 4:12). It could not be said that those who were clients were admired by all, nor that their pleas for substantial benefactions were always warmly entertained by their well-to-do patrons.[34] It is possible that the outsiders to whom Paul refers had been patrons of some of the Christians. The client now had a financial source to call upon for his daily food. If he made no further claims as was his right, would he not earn the respect of others?

Ought we then to see Paul's discussion in 1 Thessalonians 4:11ff. and 2 Thessalonians 3:6–13 as a demand for political quietism on the part of all the church, or is it specifically directed towards those who were or would be clients of patrons? 1 Thessalonians 4:11 refers to 'some', i.e. those who do not work, while verse 12 begins with the reference to 'such' who are to work with quietness and eat their own bread. What should not be concluded is that Paul is deflecting wealthy Christians from bestowing benefactions in politeia, nor, as we have seen in chapter 2, from their public obligations. He is forbidding the life of a client for members of the Christian community. Paul here requires political quietism for clients.

III. 'Dependent on Nobody'

Paul was as concerned for the public image of Christians as he was that they should not be dependent upon others. The solution to both these issues lay in clients making it their ambition to be quiet, to pursue their own affairs and to work with their own hands (1 Thess. 4:11–12). What was meant by his phrase 'dependent on nobody' (μηδενὸς χρείαν ἔχητε)?[35]

---

[34]Juvenal, Satire V ll. 1–5. See also Satire III ll. 124–5, 'Nowhere is it so easy as at Rome to throw an old client overboard', viz. because of the vastness of the city.
[35]μηδενός is either masculine or neuter and can be translated as either 'nobody' or 'nothing'. See examples in BAGD under χρεία.

In his satire on 'How Clients are Entertained', Juvenal belittles the 'plan of life' whereby some are happily dependent on their patron and 'still deem it to be the highest bliss to live at another man's board' (*ut bona summa putes aliena vivere quadra*). He describes the demeaning behaviour of a patron who may have his client served inferior food at the same dinner at which the former is given the very best.[36] An aggrieved client speaks to his patron at the dinner in the hope of overcoming this humiliation:

> No one asks of you such lordly gifts as Seneca or the good Piso or Cotta used to send to their humble friends: for in the days of old, the glory of giving was deemed grander than titles or *fasces*. All we ask of you is that you should dine with us as a fellow-citizen: do this and remain like so many others nowadays, rich for yourself and poor to your friends.[37]

His patron may be mean, for if the client's wife produced three boys, at the birth of each he would 'order little green jackets to be given to them, and little nuts, and pennies too *if they be asked for*, when the little parasites present themselves at his table'.[38]

As well as attending on their patrons throughout the day as the latter went about their public business, clients were expected to greet their patron with a salutation when he appeared every morning as a sign of honouring him.[39] The fawning nature of a client to his benefactor is well illustrated by Lucian when a client slips up in the greeting of his patron.[40] He begins:

> When I came to you to give you the morning greeting, I ought to have used the usual expression 'Joy to you' but, like a golden ass, I blundered and said 'Health to you', a pleasant enough greeting, but not suitable—it is not for the morning. As soon as I had said it I was all at sixes and sevens. I began to sweat and went pink.

The remainder of the discussion was an attempt to mend his relationship with his patron because this insecure client saw the slip as a serious breach of etiquette.

Such an existence was not appropriate for Christians, who were to be 'dependent on nobody', for they were to work with their own

---

[36]*Satire* V. *ll*. 2, 80ff.

[37]*Satire* V. *ll*. 110–13.

[38]*Satire* V. *ll*. 142–5.

[39]See Saller, *Personal Patronage under the Early Empire*, 128.

[40]'A Slip of the Tongue in Greeting' 1. See also *CPR* 19 (first or second century)

hands 'as we charged you'. This teaching was given *in situ* (1 Thess. 4:11–12 and 5:14). Paul himself would not be dependent upon the Thessalonian church while he was there, although he was within his rights to do so. Working 'night and day', he felt that he had provided an example for them to imitate (2 Thess. 3:8–9).[41] Paul's purpose was to wean such persons away from the welfare syndrome, be their source a wealthy Christian or non-Christian patron.

IV. *Providentia* after Paul's Departure

How can it be explained that some in the congregation had abandoned his teaching on work? What were the circumstances which resulted in others supporting those who were unwilling to work? It has been suggested that only the second letter reveals an internal problem for the church, caused by the idleness of the Thessalonian Christians.[42] It is true that in his first letter Paul is simply reminding the church to work and that, in contrast to the second letter, he invokes 'the name of the Lord Jesus' as he issues his command (2 Thess. 3:6), using strong imperatives in dealing with the matter. It is for this reason that the problem of idleness in the church is felt to sound like 'a new topic' in 2 Thessalonians 3:11, whereas in retrospect it sounds 'old' in 1 Thessalonians 4:11. Moreover it is thought strange that Paul refers back to his own example in 2 Thessalonians rather than to his previous letter.[43]

A famine subsequent to the writing of 1 Thessalonians would account for the fact it was 'a new topic' because the church had now to cope with such a situation with all its endemic social disruption and its aftermath for the Christian community. There was a famine in Greece in the forties and fifties and one can be dated to A.D. 51.[44] Tacitus declared that A.D. 51 was an 'ominous' year. 'There were earthquakes and subsequent panic in which the weak were trampled underfoot.' He also notes that there was a shortage of corn again, as a consequence of the famine, and that this was construed by some as 'a supernatural warning'.[45] Famine and earthquakes were seen as divine portents not only by pagans but also by Christians who attached significance to these disasters as but the beginning of the tribulation.[46] This may well

---

[41]Hock, *The Social Context of Paul's Ministry* 48, suggests that 'we may assume a paradigmatic function for his paraenesis on work'.
[42]Marshall, *Enmity in Corinth*, 172.
[43]I.H. Marshall, *1 and 2 Thessalonians*, 25–6.

account for the heightened eschatological concerns of the Thessalonians.[47] It does not, however, necessarily follow that the expectation of the *parousia* resulted in the Thessalonian Christians refusing to work.[48] That is clearly an assumption.

How did the 'Council and the People' in Greek cities handle the enormous problems associated with famine which threatened its peace and the welfare of their citizens? 'The grain supply provides the mainsprings of hatred and popularity. Hunger alone sets cities free, and reverence is purchased when rulers feed the lazy mob.'[49] Officially, the authorities would appoint a *curator annonae*, curator of the grain supply, whose task was to ensure that grain was available at a lower price in the market place. This was done either by purchasing grain at a substantially reduced price and dumping it on the market thus forcing down the price, or by initiating a corn fund with donations from wealthy benefactors to subsidise likewise the price of grain.[50]

How did the various groups in cities in the East cope with the actual shortages during famines? The monthly corn dole in Rome was sufficient, whether in plenty or in dearth. For more than a century in the imperial capital, the corn dole was the right of a vast number of inhabitants for whom this concession was based, not on need, but on citizenship.[51] Did Roman citizens in Thessalonica receive the corn dole

---

[44]Another possibly occurred a little later if Corinth suffered the same grain shortage as did the citizens of Thessalonica. For evidence of a further famine after A.D. 51 see my, 'Secular and Christian Responses to Corinthian Famines', *Tyn.B.* 40 (1989) 99 for the date of 53 or 54 and 'Acts and Food Shortages' *The Book of Acts in its Graeco–Roman Setting*, The Book of Acts in its First Century Setting (Grand Rapids and Carlisle: Eerdmans and Paternoster. 1994) ch. 3 esp. 61–9. 2 Cor. 8:1 notes the extreme poverty of the churches of Macedonia which may well be related to a severe grain shortage and made Paul's Jerusalem collection even more difficult; *cf.* Phil. 4:14. See also Garnsey, *Famine and Food*, 261, on famines in Greece in the 40s and 50s.

[45]Tacitus, *Ann.* XII.43.

[46]Mk. 13:8; Mt. 24:7–8.

[47]1 Thess. 5:13 and 2 Thess. 1:5–2:12. For a similar explanation of the situation in Corinth, see my 'Secular and Christian Responses', 92-3.

[48]For the most recent treatment in a long line making the connection between the *parousia* and work in Thessalonica see Jewett, 'The Millenarian Model', *The Thessalonian Correspondence*, ch. 9. He bases this on sociological investigations into millenarian movements including the twentieth-century cargo cult, and presupposes a dispossessed or oppressed class in Thessalonica, an idea derived from Meeks, *The First Urban Christians*, 73, that the 'typical' Christian in the Pauline churches was 'a free artisan or small trader'.

[49]Lucan, *Pharsalia* III.55-8.

[50]See Jones, *The Roman World of Dio Chrysostom*, 19.

as their counterparts did in Rome, or were these citizens actually from Rome and claimed the dole when absent from the capital? It is known that in a later period Roman citizens in Oxyrhynchus were entitled to the monthly corn dole,[52] and they came from three groupings. Some had established their eligibility on the grounds that their parents were Alexandrian or Roman citizens. Others were people of means who had undertaken liturgies and thus qualified, while others had one 'metropolite' parent.[53] Whether this applied in Thessalonica is not known, but if it did, then Rome and Oxyrhynchus are a guide to who would have been eligible, *viz.* mostly well-to-do citizens. According to the Acts account of the social status of the church, there may have been some in the Thessalonian congregation who would have qualified if the dole was given to Roman citizens in that city.

Wealthy householders could afford to buy grain at either inflated or subsidised prices. They stored sufficient grain for everyone, including their slaves, in expectation of food shortages. There were legal obligations for a master who had conditionally manumitted his slave and, in effect, had become the patron of the former slave who was now his client. He was bound to feed him as his freedman if he was unable to do so himself.[54] So the freedman and the slave were cared for.

To whom could the lower social group who 'worked with the hands', *i.e.* the non-slave labourers and artisans, turn in order to cope in a time of famine? 'Mutual support between ordinary citizens linked by kinship, proximity of residence or friendship, and exemplified in the interest-free loan, was a defence against poverty, hardship and the personal patronage of the wealthy'.[55] While the last was something which the Athenians wished to avoid for ideological reasons,[56] there

---

[51]See Juvenal, *Satire I ll.* 117–26 on the senior official calculating how much the corn dole will bring in, 'how much it adds to their income' and some of the abuses of the system.

[52]See R.J. Rowland, 'The "Very Poor" and the Grain Dole at Rome and Oxyrhynchus', *ZPE* 21 (1976) 69–72.

[53]See J. Bingen, 'Declarations pour l'epichrisi', *Chronique d'Egypte* 16 (1956) 116; C.A. Nelson, 'Epikrisis: The Identity and Function of the Officials', in E. Kiessling and H.A. Rupprecht (edd.), *Akten XIII Internationalen Papyrologenkongresses* (München, 1974) 309–14. For discussion of the status and numbers in Oxyrhynchus see Garnsey, *Famine and Food*, 265–6.

[54]A.M. Duff, *Freedmen in the Early Roman Empire* (Cambridge: W. Heffer, 1958) 98 and K. Hopkins, *Conquerors and Slaves*, Sociological Studies in Roman History I (Cambridge: CUP, 1978) 148.

[55]Garnsey, *Famine and Food*, 80.

were always those who were glad to have a patron support them in time of want, or even permanently.

Members of this recently founded church would have been faced with a 'new situation'. It was 'new' in that it was now an internal one for the church because for the first time the Christian ἐκκλησία, as distinct from the city's ἐκκλησία or kinship groupings, was faced with the problem of how to react to members who needed help to purchase grain. It would have been available for purchase in the market but, as has been noted, at a price which could be crippling for artisans and non-slave labourers. The civic solution was to provide it inexpensively or as a gift, depending on money provided by benefactors. Christian compassion would have demanded some action by the community on behalf of its members who were affected by the dearth of grain.

However, the Thessalonian epistles do not suggest that the church as a whole was feeding those who refused to work.[57] There is no evidence that the congregation had set up a soup-kitchen to cope with the crisis, as happened in a Jewish synagogue in the third century A.D.[58] Needy members of the congregation appear this time to have sought the 'patronage' of individual Christians, instead of that of secular private benefactors, for the purpose of obtaining money to buy grain or of providing a handout of free grain. Others with Christian patrons would have looked to them as their former benefactors. That relationship would not have been severed simply because clients had not asked for money or food in the intervening period but had worked instead. If they were freedmen, their patron still had a legal obligation to feed them in times of necessity.[59]

Once the grain shortage had passed, did those who had been assisted now presume on their former client/patron relationship and, by means of their ongoing profuse thanks, continue the cycle of giving and receiving? It is being proposed that subsequent to the writing of 1 Thessalonians, Paul learnt that there were some who did not now wish

---

[56]For discussion see pp. 59-60. P. Millett, 'Patronage and its avoidance in Classical Athens,' in A. Wallace-Hadrill (ed.), *Patronage in Ancient Society* (London and New York: Routledge, 1989) 15-47.

[57]*Contra* Marshall, *1 and 2 Thessalonians*, 226 who argues that Paul is not telling the church to cut off their supply of food to the idle, but rather admonishing the idle to change their ways.

[58]J. Reynolds and R. Tannenbaum, *Jews and Godfearers at Aphrodisias*, Proceedings of the Cambridge Philological Society Association Supp 12 (Cambridge: Philological Society, 1987) 27.

[59]See p. 68 n. 32.

to work. This would suggest that they had reverted to a client/patron relationship as the permanent means of support.

This reconstruction is a more complex explanation, but it does take into account the external evidence of famines and earthquakes and explains the heightened eschatological expectation which would have been attributed to such signs in 2 Thessalonians. An alternative explanation is the more simple one. Either those who were converted after Paul left refused to surrender their relationship with their patron, or those former clients, who had begun to work while Paul was there, resumed their dependent relationship with their patron after he left the city. Furthermore, the loss of a following of clients would certainly have been felt by a patron, as his prestige and power in the public place depended upon the number who accompanied him in *politeia*.

Which explanation is to be preferred? The latter fits more easily if the epistles are seen as having been written in very close succession and if social circumstances were largely unchanged. The former possibility accounts for the much stronger apocalyptic element in the second letter and could refer to the 'present dislocation' in 1 Corinthians 7:26 which, it has been suggested, is also a reference to social dislocation which normally accompanied famines.[60]

V. Christians as Benefactors not Clients

Whatever the explanation for the Thessalonian Christians reverting back to 'old' ways, it is important to remember that Paul's *paradosis* in word and deed was being flouted. He intended to re-enforce his teaching on this issue, such was the importance he attached to Christians working and also fulfilling their obligations in this area of social ethics.

Paul's prohibition on feeding any 'who did not wish to work' (εἴ τις οὐ θέλει ἐργάζεσθαι μηδὲ ἐσθιέτω) was directed towards 'brethren' who were to keep away from any brother who was living in idleness (2 Thess. 3:6). This serious apostolic injunction was commanded 'in the name of the Lord Jesus', as was the command to those who did not wish to work. It was as much a binding admonition on the rich and the generous not to give, as it was on others not to ask (2 Thess. 3:6, 14).[61]

---

[60]For evidence see my 'Secular and Christian Responses to Corinthian Famines', 86–106.

[61]The term 'brethren' as an inclusive term for Christians would not rule out this injunction's applying to patronesses or to their οἰκονόμοι who had the responsibility of distributing food and money in a household.

Paul's intervention with the command to 'keep away from a brother who is idle' would have been the only way of relieving the Christian patron of his obligation. The latter's refusal to provide food would certainly be seen as an act of unfriendliness or enmity.[62]

After Paul has reminded those who did not wish to work that they were to engage in paid activity to support themselves, he then gives the general injunction that they were to do good (οἱ καλο-ποιοῦντες, 2 Thess. 3:13).[63] It was not simply a matter of keeping out of trouble, nor indeed of becoming self-supporting, as important as both of those reasons were. There was a far more over-arching consideration which stood at the centre of Christian reflection and activity, *viz.* the doing of good which benefited the lives of others.

Paul's exhortations, then, do not have as their primary focus a concern about offending civic order.[64] His concerns are far wider because of the ongoing commitment of Christians to provide benefactions. Given his commitment to social ethics which aimed to bestow help and blessing on the everyday life of other citizens, his deep worry about some Thessalonians' welfare syndrome is explicable.[65] Christians were not only to command the respect of outsiders by being self-sufficient, but they were to seek the welfare of their city by having the wherewithal to do good to others. Paul perceived that this involved sharing self-generated financial resources.

The section ends with the exhortation to all the brethren that in the midst of doing good, they were not to grow weary (v. 13).[66] There may have been those benefactors who were somewhat disillusioned with other Christians because the latter had continued to exploit them to their own advantage, in spite of Paul's specific example and teaching, both in and away from Thessalonica. Others may have called into question whether Christian benefactors of means should continue to seek the welfare of other citizens, given the hostility of the city.[67] Paul appears to anticipate this with the injunction, 'You yourselves, brethren, must not tire in doing good' (ὑμεῖς δὲ ἀδελφοί, μη ἐγκακήσητε

---

[62]It has been assumed that those from whom the idle were receiving assistance in Thessalonica were all Christians. See Russell, 'The Idle', 113.

[63]This is a benefaction term and a synonym for ἀγαθοποιέω. See pp. 34-5.

[64]Russell, 'The Idle', 109, believes that 'this exhortation (2 Thess. 3:10) is given so that the Thessalonian believers will not offend the pagans' conception of civic order, περιπατῆτε εὐσχημένως in 1 Thess. 4:12'.

[65]See p. 78.

[66]Cf. Gal. 6:9, τὸ καλὸν ποιοῦντες μὴ ἐγκακῶμεν.

[67]See ch. 1.

καλοποιοῦντες, 2 Thess. 3:13). It is clear that he is not forbidding either private or public benefactions. The direction to all was that they must not cease to be benefactors.

VI. Abolition of Personal Patronage

Paul treated this issue with the utmost seriousness. While 2 Thessalonians 3:14 indicates that disobedience to his word in this letter is not necessarily confined to 2 Thessalonians 3:6ff., there are no grounds for arguing that the matter is excluded from this overall injunction. The idle are precluded from continuing to place individual Christians under an obligation to support them. The latter are to have no fellowship with the idle, but are not to treat them as enemies; rather they should see them as brothers to be admonished and encouraged to engage in work (2 Thess. 3:14–15).

It was not possible for some of the Thessalonians to opt out of work simply because others would support them. While in secular society 'it was less disgraceful to depend idly on the state or on a patron for subsistence than to earn it by sordid labour',[68] it was not to be so in the Christian community—those who did not wish to work were not permitted to be supported by their fellow-Christians acting as patrons.[69]

This examination of the Thessalonian *corpus* has also made it clear that the Christian community was not obliged or indeed permitted, to shower money or goods in kind indiscriminately on those who asked. In the Christian community there were the undeserving *i.e.* those who could, but would not work. Christians were to be benefactors to those with real needs.

This deliberate avoidance of patronage has a striking parallel in classical Athens and therefore the Thessalonian situation provides interesting evidence for the ancient historian. Millett points out, 'democratic ideology, with its emphasis on political equality, was hostile to the idea of personal patronage, which depended on the exploitation of inequalities in wealth and status'.[70] He draws on

---

[68]Duff, *Freedmen in the Early Roman Empire*, 106.
[69]In the light of the discussion in this chapter it is perhaps somewhat misleading to speak of Christians who played the part of patrons to the Christian groups and suggest that the pattern of client/patron 'trickled down. . .to those who provided the household bases of the Christians', Meeks, *The Origins of Christian Morality*, 46.
[70]Millett, 'Patronage and its avoidance in Classical Athens', 17.

evidence outside Athens where patronage systems had developed, citing Sparta. Hesiod's *Works and Days* which stressed the need for self-sufficiency, and other evidence illustrates that which Athens wished to avoid in its public life. The Athenian solution recognised 'that patron-client relationships, inasmuch as they are generated by inequality and are a constraint on an individual's freedom, are inappropriate to democracy'.[71] What was known as 'public pay' or 'crisis insurance' and reciprocal obligations with relatives, friends, and neighbours made it possible to borrow, in times of emergency, interest-free loans. A loan, as it was called, provided an alternative to the patronage system and was recoverable at law.[72] Roman Athens did not escape the patronage system.

In his day Paul determined to see the abolition of the patronage system in the Christian community but not for the democratic reasons of the Athenians. One of the tasks of Christians was to go beyond their own needs to the needs of others. It constituted the most visible signal to the society of its day of a new community in which a function of all able-bodied members of this new community was to do good. This created a whole new class of benefactors. They did good because good needed to be done, and did so without expectations of reciprocity or repayment. This conclusion leads into the following chapter, which deals with the benefactions of Christian widows and the discriminating provision for them related to their legal entitlement in the public place and their record of having themselves been bene-factors to others.

---

[71]Millett, 'Patronage and its avoidance in Classical Athens', 25.
[72]Millett, 'Patronage and its avoidance in Classical Athens', 37.

CHAPTER FOUR

WIDOWS AND LEGAL AND CHRISTIAN BENEFACTIONS

1 Timothy 5:3-16

In the previous chapter it was shown that Christian social ethics in
Gentile contexts did not indulge the wishes of those who sought to replicate in the Christian community the secular, parasitic client/patron
benefaction relationship for those who did not wish to work. Christians were to work and thereby be able to be benefactors to those who
were in genuine need in their society.

There was another community in the Gentile Christian world
where the provision of benefactions needed to be re-evaluated with the
passage of time. All its widows were being supported by that community. It was not only in the Jerusalem Christian community of Acts
6:1-5 that the problem of adequately providing for its widows had
arisen. Some of them felt discriminated against in the daily distribution on ethnic grounds. In 1 Timothy 5:3-16 the church's benefactions
for widows were being misdirected and, as a result, its resources were
so stretched that those who were 'true' widows were being deprived
of adequate support. As in the case of Thessalonica, the perception of
Christian social ethics relating to an area of benefactions for another
group in the church needed to be corrected. That discussion provides
additional evidence of the benefaction rôle for all Christians, including
widows.[1]

However, in more recent discussions this has not been the
significance attached to 1 Timothy 5:3-16. The passage has been cited
as an example of the suppression of Christian women by the church.
One writer has suggested that these widows were seen as 'a disruptive
force',[2] and the intention in proscribing distributions to some Christian
widows was to subvert their charismatic claim to office in the church.[3]
A sociological perspective of 'equality and freedom' has been invoked
in order to argue that this passage sees the commencement of the
erosion of egalitarianism for women in the early stages of Christianity
and the adoption of secular society's hierarchical and patriarchal
structure.[4] It has also been concluded that 'predictably, the new

---

[1]For a brief survey of views, see B.B. Thurston, *The Widows: A Women's Ministry in
the Early Church* (Minneapolis: Fortress Press, 1989) 40–44. The passage has proved
to be an exegetical minefield for commentators, *e.g.* D.C. Verner, *The Household of
God: The Social World of the Pastoral Epistles*, SBL Dissertation Series 71 (Chico:
Scholars Press, 1983) 161-66 and J.M. Bassler, 'The Widows' Tale: A Fresh Look at
1 Tim. 5:3-16', *JBL* 103 (1984) 23-41.
[2]This observation on 1 Tim. 5:3-16 by S.C. Humphreys, *The Family, Women and
Death: Comparative Studies* (London: Routledge and Kegan Paul, 1983) 47.
[3]H.W. Bartsch, *Die Anfänge: Evangelischer Rechtsbildungen: Studien zu den Pastoralbriefen* (Hamburg: Herbert Reich, 1965) 34.
[4]Verner, *The Household of God*, 39-40.

Christian norms (including 1 Tim. 5:3-16) are much like the old defensive rules of Judaism' and constitute a post-Pauline regression of 'charismatic customs developed previously'.[5] The passage has been said to be connected with 'the widow's order' in the church.[6] On the last suggestion it has been conceded that 'None of these textual elements by itself proves the establishment of an order of widows in 1 Timothy 5:3–16. Taken together, however, they make a good case'.[7]

In 1 Timothy 5:3–16, 'the writer is not initiating a new benevolence. . .but is seeking to limit an existing one'.[8] What was being reformed? The text itself suggests that all widows, young and old, were being supported by that Christian community. As a result, its resources were clearly stretched far too much to meet adequately the needs of the widows who really deserved to be supported. 'Let the church be not burdened, so that it may assist those who are indeed widows' (v. 16). The reorganisation of an existing system defined 'real' widows and proscribed support for those who could and should rightly draw their support from elsewhere. The discussion also throws important light on the spheres of benefactions by the widows.

As in the case of benefactions in Thessalonica where the client/ patron relationship was the key for understanding the situation and its implications for social ethics, so too the abuse of benefactions in 1 Timothy 5:3–16 needs to be understood within the context of social conventions. These were backed up by the legal stipulations for widows, young and old, and their support in the Graeco-Roman world.[9] The following discussion argues that the passage is better understood if it is seen to be dealing primarily with the abuse of the well–attested legal benefactions guaranteed by the dowry and the rejection of legal stipulations to remarry by some widows, rather than the uncertainties of an early ecclesiastical order of widows. The importance of 1 Timothy 5:3–16 for our understanding of benefactions by and for Christian widows will then be discussed.

---

[5]B.J. Malina, *The New Testament World: Insights from Cultural Anthropology* (Atlanta: John Knox Press, 1981) 116.

[6]See Thurston, 'The Origins of the Widow's Order', ch. 3.

[7]Thurston, 'The Origins of the Widow's Order', 46.

[8]Bassler, 'The Widows' Tale', 34.

[9]Of the commentaries consulted, E.K. Simpson, *The Pastoral Epistles* (London: Tyndale Press, 1954) 73, refers to the Greek legal requirement that children support their parents in Athens, but none mention the dowry, for which legal stipulations existed concerning widows.

It is proposed to deal with (I) legal benefactions for widows, (II) wholesale adoption of the Jerusalem church's benefaction mechanism, (III) the avoidance of benefactions by children and grandchildren, (IV) benefactions from believing women (V) benefactions for the 'real' widows, (VI) disqualifying young widows from Christian benefactions, (VII) 1 Timothy 5:3–16 in its context, and (VIII) 1 Timothy 5:3–16 and benefactions in order to demonstrate further the radical Christian innovation that all who were able to work were required to be benefactors.

I. Legal Benefactions for Widows

The dowry, which was provided by the bride's father always accompanied a woman to her marriage. It constituted an important legal aspect of marriage. Greek marriage contracts specified the nature and value of it and this continued to be done in the Roman period. The dowry's 'basic object was to provide for the maintenance of the woman'.[10] 'The only legal obligation that the groom acquired toward the wife upon receipt of the dowry was her maintenance'.[11] W.K. Lacey notes that 'the law was explicit; the person who had charge of her dowry had the obligation to maintain her'.[12] This then was a legal requirement.[13]

In the event of a husband's death, the laws governing that dowry were clearly defined.[14] A widow was cared for by the person in charge of that dowry. Two options were open to her. If she had children, she might remain in her deceased husband's home. There she would be maintained by the new 'lord' (κύριος) of the household, possibly her son. She could also return to her parents, taking her dowry back to her family.[15] The choice appears to have been hers. The minutes of legal proceedings before Flavius Titianus, Prefect of Egypt, record 'if the marriage had not been annulled (or the husband deceased) the father had no power either over the dowry or over the daughter he had given away'.[16] The returning of the dowry to the widow's father meant the legal severance of her relationship with her late husband's house-

---

[10]A.R.W. Harrison, *The Law of Athens: Family and Property* I (Oxford: Clarendon Press, 1968) 57.

[11]D.M. Schaps, *Economic Rights of Women in Ancient Greece* (Edinburgh: Edinburgh University Press, 1979) 75.

[12]W.K. Lacey, *The Family in Classical Greece* (London: Thames and Hudson, 1968) 117.

[13]Schaps, *Economic Rights of Women*, Appendix IV.

hold.[17] Rules governing the repayment of the dowry were enforced by a provision known as δίκη προικός and those dealing with the interest rate to be charged on the value of the dowry from the time of the husband's death until its return by δίκη σίτου.[18]

In Athens there was a legal, as well as a moral obligation placed upon children to care for not only the widow but also both parents. Failure to do so rendered one liable to prosecution in which 'the prosecutor ran no risk of punishment'.[19] Roman women had similar security and had what S. Dixon describes as 'a dowager's life interest in her husband's holdings' based on the understanding that she would, at death, pass it to children from that issue.[20] The Hellenistic Jewish period allowed the wife a share in her own property during marriage, and when made a widow, to retain part of her dowry.[21]

The Graeco-Roman world sought to make sure that the widow had security with her dowry, either by sheltering in the (οἶκος) of the sons of her late husband or in that of her parents. As Schaps comments 'Legally, then, a woman was never as thoroughly protected as she was in her old age'.[22]

---

[14]Schaps, 'The Dowry', *Economic Rights of Women*, ch. 6 and appendices gives an excellent discussion of the dowry and issues of its inheritance on the husband's death; and A.R.W. Harrison, *The Law of Athens*, I. 145-60. See also R. Taubenschlag, *The Law of Greco-Roman Egypt in the Light of the Papyri 332 B.C. - 640 A.D.* (Warsaw: Panstwowe Wydawnictwo Naukowe, 1955) 120-7 for evidence of the continuation of this through the Hellenistic and Roman periods. For examples of extant marriage contracts, all of which refer specifically to the contents or value of the dowry and its importance, see *P. Ryl.* 154 (AD 66), 'received from him as a dowry on his daughter', *P. Eleph.* 1 (311 BC), *P. Tebt.* 104 (92 BC), and *BGU* 1052 (13 BC), cited in A.S. Hunt and C.C. Edgar, *Select Papyri* I (London and Cambridge Mass.: Heinemann, 1970). On the Roman side see J.P.V.D. Balsdon, *Roman Women: Their History and Habits* (ed 2; London: Bodley Head, 1974) 186-9, where the recovery of a dowry, in part or whole, was for its future use, *i.e.* remarriage.

[15]Harrison, *The Law of Athens*, I. 38, 57.

[16]*P.Oxy.* 237, col. vii, *ll.* 28-9 (AD 133).

[17]Just as the dowry set up the marriage, A.R.W. Harrison, *The Law of Athens*, I. 45, points out that its return saw the termination of the relationship. See S.C. Humphreys, *The Family, Women and Death*, 46 citing *BGU* 1104 (first century BC).

[18]A.R.W. Harrison, *The Law of Athens: Procedures* II (Oxford: Clarendon Press, 1971) 22.

[19]Furthermore all who aspired to public office were asked 'Do you treat your parents well?', Lacey, *The Family in Classical Greece*, 116-18.

[20]S. Dixon, *The Roman Mother* (London and Sydney: Croom Helm, 1988) 47 and A. Watson, *The Law of Persons in the Later Roman Republic* (Oxford: Clarendon Press, 1967) 67ff.

[21]Z.W. Falk, *Introduction to Jewish Laws of the Second Commonwealth* (Leiden: E.J. Brill, 1978) 290.

However worthy these legal intentions were, there were always those who slipped through the net, especially those at the lower end of the economic scale.[23] The church had to be responsible for Christian widows who were from this group and unable to support themselves financially (1 Tim. 5:16). In order for the church to fulfil this rôle adequately, there was the need to define 'real' widows and to demand individual members of the congregation to assume or resume legal and filial responsibility for any relatives bereft of husbands.

II. Adopting the Jerusalem Church's Benefaction Mechanism

The adoption by the Jerusalem Church of the procedures of the synagogues in the charitable distributions to the poor appears to have occurred almost from the beginning of Christianity.[24] The Jewish synagogues had an established programme for the needy, with the weekly distribution from the money chest on Fridays to the sojourners and the resident poor, including the widows.[25] The Jerusalem church followed suit, but with a daily distribution. The reason for this adjustment is not explained, but it may be related to its daily corporate activity described in Acts 2:46, rather than to the weekly gatherings in the synagogues. The synagogues' tried and tested method of collection and distribution proved to be an appropriate model to use to fulfil the injunction of Jesus to meet the needs of the poor whom the church found to be always with them.

The apostles who initially assumed the rôle of the receivers and distributors of alms in the synagogue drew sharp criticism from the Hellenists because of allegations of the neglect of their widows in the distribution. Arrangements that suited a smaller ἐκκλησία apparently

---

[22]Schaps, *Economic Rights of Women*, 84.

[23]Hands, *Charities and Social Aid in Greece and Rome*, 71-3. Athens had made provision for girls who were from poor families or whose fathers had proved great compatriots, to have their dowry provided by the state, S.B. Pomeroy, 'Charities for Greek Women', *Mnemosyne* 35 (1982) 115-135.

[24]E. Schürer, *The History of the Jewish People in the Age of Jesus Christ* (ed 2; Edinburgh: T. & T. Clark, 1979) II 437 n. 45, who notes that the 'officers charged by the primitive church with the care of the poor (διακονεῖν τραπέζαις)' in Acts 6:1-5 are fulfilling an identical role.

[25]K.F. Nickle, *The Collection: A Study in Paul's Strategy*, SBT 48 (London: SCM, 1966) 93-4.

proved to be unsatisfactory with an increasing number of disciples coming into the Christian community, including widows (Acts 6:1a). The NT gives no further indication that the mechanism for distribution to the poor in Jerusalem needed subsequent adjustments. It does, however, reveal that the problem continued to be a lack of resources from within the Jerusalem church. Only collections from the Diaspora Jewish and Gentile Christians saved them from destitution, especially in a time of famine (Acts 11:27-30).[26]

Was the church's administrative procedure for the distribution in Jerusalem simply taken over by the congregation of 1 Timothy? Financial problems arose for the church because all widows were eligible for the distribution. It would seem that there were no modifications by the Gentile churches of the Christian distribution system of the Jerusalem church which took account of the social ethos of the secular community from which converts came. There appears to have been adoption with no adaptation. The injunctions in 1 Timothy 5:3-16 aim to modify existing procedures which had included no means test.[27]

III. Avoidance of Benefactions by Children and Grandchildren

In 1 Timothy 5:4 the matter of religious duty is spelled out for children and grandchildren. The households of converts were to be the first place where 'godliness' (εὐσεβία) was expressed in practical help to the resident widows. It was to be seen as the first place where the primary lesson in godliness was to be learnt (μαθανέτωσαν πρῶτον). This godliness was not expressed in worship or personal piety, but in the household. For the Christian church it was the first commandment 'with a promise'.[28]

This filial piety was seen in financial terms in verse 4b.[29] Christians were told that they were under a clear obligation to support

---

[26]Cf. Acts 24:17, 1 Cor. 16:1ff., 2 Cor. 8-9 and Rom. 15:25-27, although in these instances there is no indication of the famine situation referred to in Acts 11:27-30. For a discussion of the famine and its effects see p. 35ff.

[27]J.M. Bassler, 'The Widows' Tale', 34, citing in support of J. Müller-Bardorff, 'Zur exegese vom 1 Timotheus 5,3-16', *Gott und die Götter: Festgabe für Erick Fasher zum 60. Geburtstag* (Berlin: Evangelische Verlagsanstalt, 1958) 113-33.

[28]Cf. Eph. 6:2 citing Ex. 20:12.

[29]C. Spicq, *Les Épitres Pastorales, Études Bibliques* (Paris: Gabalda, 1969[4]) 525.

the widow as compensation for the care and financial cost formerly expended upon them as children and grandchildren (v. 4b). In a society where the meeting of obligations was of paramount importance, failure to do so would have constituted a very serious social breach indeed. The injunction is further supported by the statement that this conduct is acceptable in the sight of God (v. 4c).[30]

In verse 8a there is reference to those who sought to avoid πρό-νοια, i.e. providentia: 'if anyone does not provide for his own, especially those of his own household' (εἰ δέ τις τῶν ἰδίων καὶ μάλιστα οἰκείων οὐ προνοεῖται). The comment was directed towards the heads (κύριοι) of the Christian households (οἶκοι). There is a diversity of opinion about to whom precisely the terms 'own' (ἴδιος) and 'own household' (οἰκεῖος) refer. Commentators have regarded ἴδιος in verse 8 as a reference either to slaves and freedmen or to one's relatives in general, while οἰκεῖος could refer either to blood relatives or to members of one's immediate family.[31]

In verse 8, ἴδιοι could be a general reference to those belonging to a household and encompass one's freedmen who may not necessarily live at home, but to whom one had obligations, especially if he were to find himself impoverished. The attempt to avoid benefactions for one's slaves by making them freedmen was certainly a known reason for granting manumission.[32] It enabled the slave-owner to retain his services part-time without the cost of his upkeep. Slaves so manumitted took responsibility for finding their own lodgings. If ἴδιοι covers those belonging to this group to whom there were still obligations owed by the κύριος, then it would follow that οἰκεῖοι refers specifically to the family who lived at home, and among them was the widow who was residing with the κύριος of the dowry.[33]

---

[30]τοῦτο refers back to the imperatives in that verse.

[31]See Spicq, Les Épitres Pastorales, 531; J.N.D. Kelly, A Commentary on the Pastoral Epistles (London: A. & C. Black, 1963) 114-15; and Verner, The Household of God, 138 for a summary of opinions.

[32]The Lex Aelia Sentia of AD 4 required a patron, on pain of losing the right to the operae, to provide food for his freedman. This is generally thought to mean that 'he had to prevent a freedman from dying of starvation, just as a freedman had to support his patron if he had fallen into need', Duff, Freedmen in the Early Roman Empire, 48. S. Treggiari, Roman Freedmen during the Late Republic (Oxford: Clarendon Press, 1969) 16, states that 'the freedman would usually support himself, taking the burden of finding food and lodging from the shoulders of his patron'.

[33]χωρὶς οἰκοῦντες refers to those who were not part of their master's household in the narrow physical sense according to Harrison, The Law of Athens: Family and Property I, 167 n. 5.

If verse 8a ἴδιοι is a specific reference to widows, then the term embraced a widow who was not living at home.[34] The κύριος had a Christian responsibility towards her, based on the Decalogue. οἰκεῖος would still refer to the widow residing at home and for whom legal responsibility had been assumed with the acceptance of the dowry. There was then a specific legal commitment for a widow living at home and less of a legal obligation towards one residing away from the household. As the overall context of verses 3-16 is the issue of widows, it is suggested that ἴδιοι could refer to those widows residing away from households. It must be remembered that the number of widows in a family household could be at least two so that the widow not living at home was encompassed in this verse.[35]

The condemnation in verse 8b is twofold. One relates to the OT commandment and the other to the legal situation outlined above. First, in verse 8b there is the serious charge of the denial of the faith (ἡ πίστις) which encompassed the important commandment to children to honour parents, but which the church shouldered when there were no others to fulfil it (v. 16). The use of the imperative τίμα in verse 3 indicates that it is the fifth commandment from the Decalogue that rests behind the discussion. This avoidance of 'providence' (πρόνοια) by the κύριος was seen as a denial of the faith by those who had widowed mothers and grandmothers. It comes within the same category, condemned in the teaching of Jesus, of the convention whereby one claimed *corban*,[36] which was criticised because it set aside the command of God. The neglect of a widow, whether she lived at home or away from home, would come under this condemnation, be she mother or grandmother (v. 3).[37]

Secondly, the offender was declared to be 'worse than' an unbeliever (ἄπιστος) which is an exceedingly strong charge to bring

---

[34]Verner, *The Household of God*, 138 rightly sees that this possibility is difficult to explain, as widows away from home 'would be in greater danger of neglect'. However, if the responsibility for the dowry was assumed by another, then the statement is explicable; as it applies to widows living away from those Christian households being addressed in v. 8. Verner's objection thus disappears.

[35]It ought not to be assumed that the Christian families being addressed were either all nuclear families or all extended families. D.C. Barker, *New Docs* 4 (1988) 89 and 93, has shown from a survey of Egyptian census returns that 53.4% were households with offspring and unmarried siblings, while the remainder were either more than one nuclear family or relatives living with the nuclear family.

[36]Mk. 7:9-13.

[37]This commandment was certainly interpreted to include more than parents by Philo, *Dec.* 165-7.

against any member of a Christian congregation (v. 8).[38] Why would this be said of the heads of households? It refers to the fact that while holding the dowry, the head was not fulfilling his legal responsibility to support the widow. Harrison notes that by remaining in her late husband's house, 'her sons were κύριοι of the dowry, being charged with her maintenance out of it'.[39] Furthermore the preceding verse, 'Command this so that they may be without reproach (ἀνεπίλημπτοι)' suggests a condemnation from society which was already happening, for such offensive behaviour was in clear breach of the law (v. 7).[40]

It would seem that at least some Christians were not supporting their widows, whether they were residing in their households or elsewhere. As a result they were cast upon the strained financial resources of the church, even though Christians as individuals were bound to support them on legal and/or religious grounds. This would suggest that the church's general distribution to widows enabled some of the members of the Christian ἐκκλησία conveniently to evade obligatory benefactions, *i.e. providentia.*

Epigraphic evidence from a Christian tombstone shows how Christian children of a later generation obeyed 1 Timothy 5:16.

> To well-deserving Rigina her daughter beautifully fashioned this tombstone. Rigina, mother, widow who remained a widow sixty years and never burdened the church; a *univera* who lived eighty years, five months, twenty-six days.[41]

IV. Benefactions by the Believing Women

In an endeavour to provide for the 'real' widow, a 'believing woman' (ἡ πιστή) must support any relatives who were widowed (v. 16). To whom does this refer? It has been suggested that this verse means 'If any man or woman is converted and brings with him into the church his household (with his sisters and cousins and aunts), he or she is to continue to support them and not burden the local congregation'.[42] It

---

[38]J.N.D. Kelly, *A Commentary on the Pastoral Epistle,* 115, 'even pagans. . . recognize and set store by the obligations of children to parents'.
[39]Harrison, *The Law of Athens: Family and Property* I, 57.
[40]The plural ταυτα is meant to cover the instructions in v. 4 as well as v. 8. ἀνεπίλ-ημπτοι means 'not censured', 'not culpable'.
[41]E. Diehl, *Inscriptiones Latinae Christianae Veteres* (Berlin: Weidmann, 1967) 1581, cited by M. Lightman and W. Zeisel, '*Univira*: An Example of Continuity and Change in Roman Society', *Church History* 46 (1977) 29.

has further been argued that 'The false teachers were also urging these widows not simply to avoid the married life, but to abandon the support of their elderly mothers and grandmothers as well'.[43]

The injunction, however, appears to have been an innovation which had neither legal nor ecclesiastical precedent.[44] Christian women were being called upon to relieve the church of the burden to support their widowed relatives. There is no censure in verse 16, but a call to shoulder responsibility for kinship relationships so that the church can adequately support widows who are without relatives.[45]

V. Benefactions for the 'Real' Widows

There is great care taken in 1 Timothy 5:3-16 to define precisely whom the church should support. The passage begins with the imperative addressed, presumably, to the one who has the congregation's oversight. He is to honour the widow who is a real widow, *i.e.* make sure that the church provides for her needs (v. 3).[46]

The 'real' widow is defined in verse 5a as a person 'without relatives' (μεμονωμένη).[47] Because of the situation in which she finds her-

---

[42]F.C. Synge, 'Studies in texts: 1 Timothy 5.3-16', *Theology* 108 (1968) 200-1. He accepts the reading πιστὸς ἤ πιστή which is usually rejected, see B.M. Metzger, *A Textual Commentary on the Greek New Testament* (London and New York: United Bible Societies, 1971) 642.

[43]A. Padgett, 'Wealthy Women at Ephesus: 1 Timothy 2:8-15 in Social Context', *Interpretation* 41 (1987) 21.

[44]In the context it seems clear that 'having widows' refers to relations *contra* Verner, *The Household of God*, 139, who suggests that αἱ πισταί were probably women like Tabitha in Acts 9:36ff. who have taken widows under their protection. The verb 'to have' describes relatives, *cf.* 1 Cor. 7:2. The argument of 1 Tim. 5:3-16 is about the need to secure support for widows with kinship relationships in the congregation, in order for the church to care for its real widows.

[45]Later evidence in the Christian church in Egypt shows that there were αἱ πρὸς χήραις, but it is not clear that they were relatives of the widows or women appointed by the church to care for them. See E. Wipszycka, *Les ressources et les activités des églises en Égypte du IVe au VIIIe siècle*, Papyrologica Bruxellensia 10 (1972) 114 for the discussion of 'les femmes chargées de s'occuper des veuves' and the evidence cited.

[46]Hence the use of a second person singular present imperative.

[47]The perfect participle should be so interpreted and could be translated as 'left all alone', *i.e.* without relations. See P.G. Duncker,'". . .*quae vere viduae sunt*"(1 Tim. 5.3)', *Angelicum* 35 (1958) 121-38 for a discussion of distinguishing characteristics of the true widow in the OT and the Semitic world, and of the real widow as μεμονωμένη.

self she is like the widow in the OT who is cast upon God alone (ἤλπικεν) and is therefore given to supplication and prayer, day and night, for her needs (v. 5b).[48] This is the 'real' widow for whom the church must take financial responsibility because there is no other person to care for her.

She is described as being 'not less than sixty years of age'. The precise reason for the restriction of age is uncertain. Had it been over fifty years, then it would have been explicable in the light of the fact that Roman law required a woman under fifty to remarry because she was still regarded as being of child-bearing age and, as a financial disincentive, was precluded from obtaining any inheritance until she attained that age.[49] The reason may simply have been that women under sixty years were considered capable of working.[50]

She is also designated 'the wife of one husband'. If one adopts the interpretation that this refers to a woman who has married only once, then it poses problems for those young widows who obey the injunction of verse 9 to remarry. In old age they could be disqualified from assistance in the church on the sole grounds that they are not 'a wife of one husband'. There is no reason to argue that here is a prohibition on a second marriage. On the contrary, women of marriageable age were instructed to marry again.[51]

Her proven record of Christian benefactions, *i.e.* good works, is outlined. She is to be 'well attested for her good deeds (ἐν ἔργοις καλοῖς) having brought up children, shown hospitality, washed the feet of the saints, relieved the afflicted and devoted herself to good works in every way' (παντὶ ἔργῳ ἀγαθῷ, vv. 9-10). It is important to note here that the hallmark of the Christian widow is her benefaction

---

[48]The perfect indicative also indicates her state or, better, her status, for she has none other than God in whom she can put her confidence to meet her material needs.

[49]A. Wallace-Hadrill, 'Family and Inheritance in the Augustan Marriage Laws', *Proceedings of the Cambridge Philological Society* 207 (1981) 59.

[50]Our contemporary societies see no reason to justify the fixing of the age when a woman can receive a pension in some countries at the age of sixty other than that she is not expected to work beyond that age. For the activities of working women, see S. Treggiari, 'Jobs for Women', *AJAH* 1 (1976) 76-104, N. Kampen, *Image and Status: Roman Working Women in Ostia* (Berlin: Gerb. Mann Verlag, 1981) and J.N. Bremmer, 'The Old Women of Ancient Greece', in J. Blok and P. Mason (eds.), *A Sexual Asymmetry: Studies in Ancient Society* (Amsterdam: J.C. Gießen, 1987) 196f.

[51]ἡ ἑνὸς ἀνδρὸς γυνή cannot mean that she was married once, but rather she did not commit adultery; *cf.* M. Dibelius and H. Conzelmann, *The Pastoral Epistles*, (Philadelphia: Fortress Press, 1972) 75, who argue that it refers to chastity, whether married once or twice.

which was a requirement of all Christians, as the discussion in the previous chapter has argued.

The 'real' widow is defined in 1 Timothy 5 as being sixty years old, having neither children nor grandchildren nor a 'believing' woman to 'honour' her with support, a chaste Christian lady with true spirituality who has been given to good works, *i.e.* has been a benefactor.

VI. Disqualifying Young Widows from benefactions

It was expected in the ancient world that a widow would remarry. Augustus, in the *lex Papia Poppaea* of AD 9, actually legislated for this after a husband's death if the widow was still of child-bearing age, *i.e.* under fifty.[52] The period during which she could remain a widow was finally set at two years. This was the legal position in the empire in the first century, even if it was not observed by all.[53] There was also a very strong conviction that the Greek woman would remarry 'so that she be not left a widow', a thought abhorrent to the Greeks.[54] 'There can be little doubt that young widows, even if they had children, were expected to remarry', for remarriage provided a secure option for the younger widow.[55]

The discussion of the young widows in 5:11-15 contains descriptive and evaluative, as well as prescriptive, elements. An examination of all three helps to reconstruct the problem which the young widows posed for the church.

The descriptive elements in verses 11b-12 are joined with verse 13 by the important connective 'and at the same time' (ἄμα δέ) which denotes the coincidence of actions.[56] The text indicates that the young widows now desired to remarry (v. 11b). They may have taken a vow of *univera* in response to the false teaching of others in the church who forbade marriage and, naturally, remarriage.[57] Had they dedicated themselves to God in prayer and supplication? This would have

---

[52]Wallace-Hadrill, 'Family and Inheritance in the Augustan Marriage Laws', 59; see also J.F. Gardner, *Women in Roman Law and Society* (London and Sydney: Croom Helm, 1986) 178-9.

[53]B. Rawson, 'The Roman Family', in B. Rawson (ed.), *The Family in Ancient Rome: New Perspectives* (London and Sydney: Croom Helm, 1986) 31.

[54]Schaps, *Economic Rights of Women*, 41 and (for sources cited) 127 nn. 105-6.

[55]Lacey, *The Family in Classical Greece*, 108.

[56]BDF 425,2.

expressed confidence in the God who cares for the needy and
epitomised the godly widow? Whatever is meant by the expression, it
is certain that there was now seen as a departure from ἡ πρώτη πίστις.[58]
'At the same time' (ἅμα) there was a change in lifestyle with the
emergence of the 'merry' widow who is learning to be idle, going from
house to house not for the benefit of the inhabitants but simply to
engage in 'public' gossip.[59] She was also discussing matters deemed
to be inappropriate to the Christian profession (v. 13). The nexus
between verses 11b-12 and 13 is related to the decision to remarry. The
unbecoming behaviour may be linked to the way another marriage is
being sought by the young widow.

The conduct of the widows is evaluated as 'running riot' against
Christ (v. 11b) and is thus condemned because of their abandoning of
another way of living.[60] Some of the widows have already committed
apostasy (v. 15).[61] It is clear that their conduct differs from that of the
true widow because nowhere are benefactions mentioned as the hallmark of their lives, as was the case with the 'true' widow.

The solution is laid out in verses 11a and 14. In the latter case the
use of 'therefore' (οὖν) indicates that the prescription which follows is
meant to remedy the unsatisfactory conduct already described. The
young widows are to remarry, but there is an explanation of what
marriage is from a Christian perspective. They are to have children,
rule their own households and conduct themselves in such a way that
they do not bring the Christian faith into disrepute, i.e. 'give the enemy
no occasion to revile us' (v. 14).

The refusal of the church to enrol young widows in verse 11 must
be judged in the light of the implications of the requirement to remarry
in verse 14, an injunction prescribed by Roman law. Such a call to the
young widow rightly presupposes that the widow has a dowry. There
must therefore have been a person in charge of it and thus legally

---

[57]See Lightman and Zeisel, 'Univira,' 119ff. for a discussion of this in secular
Roman society.
[58]See A. Sand, 'Witwenstand und Ämterstrukturen in den urchristlichen
Gemeinden', Bibel und Leben 12 (1971) 196, who argues that it refers to a vow of cel-
ibacy for devotion to God. Cf. Rev. 2:4, ἡ ἀγάπη ἡ πρώτη.
[59]On the role of gossip in politeia see Hunter, Policing Athens, 106-119 esp. 111-
116.
[60]καταστρηνιάω does not occur elsewhere in Greek but the meaning is clear from
στρηνιάω = 'to run riot', 'become wanton' and the use of κατά simply intensifies it.
[61]Verner, The Household of God, 165-6, cites similar expressions in 1 Tim. 1:6, 6:20
and 2 Tim. 4:4 and shows that the reference is to following false teachers.

responsible for her maintenance in her present status as a widow. The church does not have to support her.

VII. 1 Timothy 5:3-16 and its Social Context

1 Timothy 5:3-16 answers important questions for the church as it seeks to fulfil its benefaction commitment to widows. Should a local congregation continue to draw on its resources to support widows *per se* when there existed a legal mechanism for their financial provision? Furthermore, should the church assume responsibility for widows if there were children or grandchildren or female relatives in the same congregation who could support them? If it was the custom or the law for young widows to remarry and there was the requisite dowry, the governing body of that church should not support one who refused to do so, especially if the objection was based on a misplaced belief that there was a Christian prohibition of marriage or remarriage.

This is addressing the very important issue of the church and its members fulfilling the fifth command by honouring the widow (v. 4). It was to be done by its members resuming their legal responsibility imposed by the custody of the dowry, and by Christian women assuming responsibility for any widowed relatives (v. 16). Children and grandchildren were also to care for widows for whom they may have had no legal dowry responsibilities (v. 4). Kinship relationships were still to be paramount in the Christian community. Not providing for 'one's own' (ἴδιος) when there were legal obligations assumed with the taking over of the dowry was condemned in the strongest language as 'apostasy' and being 'worse than' pagans (v. 8). The young widow could not draw upon the resources of the church, for she must remarry in accordance with the legal or quasi–legal conventions of the society of her day.

The overall concern in redefining the eligibility of widows for financial support is also clearly spelt out in 1 Timothy 5:3-16. The church must be able to fulfil its rôle to care for the widow who was on her own and unable to care for herself. If she was a 'real' widow, then the church would come to the rescue by providing benefactions for the 'widow of God'.[62] The subsequent history of the church shows that this did happen, for there are extant records of the administration of

---

[62]For the Christian inscription 'To the matron Octavia, a widow of God' see H.E. Fox, *Christian Inscriptions in Ancient Rome* (London: Morgan and Scott, 1920) 45.

distributions which read 'Provide for Sophia, widow, from the coats you have, one coat for good use'; 'to the widows. . .one double jar of wine'.[63]

The concept of an ecclesiastical 'order of widows' is supported neither by one particular text in 1 Timothy 5:3-16 nor by the passage taken as a whole. It is not necessary to postulate such an order to make sense of it. Recent discussion which looks at later periods of history where such 'orders' existed, may well have retrojected that phenomenon into the first century when reconstructing the situation behind the text in 1 Timothy.[64] In fact such an approach appears to have caused key elements in the discussion of 1 Timothy 5:3-16 to be overlooked. For the purposes of the present investigation, because the dowry was in effect synonymous with marriage and widowhood in the first century, the passage is better understood in the light of this legal reality and the stipulations concerning the remarriage of the younger widows rather than as a search to find the genesis for a later 'order of widows'.

VIII. 1 Timothy 5:3-16 and Benefactions

The concept of benefactions is central to our understanding of this passage and furthers our investigation of social ethics in the early church. Christian social ethics in this passage were concerned with justice for widows (v. 8). Those who failed to fulfil their responsibilities to the widow as custodians of her dowry were not only accused of denying the faith, but also described as 'worse than unbelievers', *i.e.* their fellow citizens, because they were knowingly breaking the law. In the public place the non–Christians would have condemned their avoidance of this legal obligation. Christian social ethics were also concerned with the needs of the widow to whom one was related, even if there were no legally binding obligations. Thought was also to be taken for providing for her needs (v. 8).

Social ethics were equated with 'piety'. Children and even grandchildren must express Christian 'piety' towards their own parents and, given the context of 1 Timothy 5:3–16, widows in their family. While 'piety' is not defined in verse 4, it was by implication to be taken

---

[63]*P.Wiscon.* 64 and *P.Oxy.* 1954 cited in *New Docs* 2 (1982) 192-3.

[64]See Thurston, 'The Origins of the Widow's Order', ch. 3 esp. 46. This comment is in no way meant to detract from the important treatment given to the later period of the church's 'order of widows'.

up with proper support, *i.e.* the relieving of their needs. This was the first step in godliness, for charity or benefactions began at home with one's own widows.

The godly widow's conduct is described in terms of benefactions. It is important for our enquiry to note that the hallmark of the Christian widow who qualified for support by the church was a life which had been given to benefactions—'well attested for her good deeds (ἐν ἔργοις καλοῖς)' and someone who 'devoted herself to good in every way (παντὶ ἔργῳ ἀγαθῷ)', is how she is described in 1 Timothy 5:9-10.

Social ethics were seen as a way of bestowing honour. The discussion of widows begins with the commandment to 'honour the widows who are widows indeed' (χήρας τίμα τὰς ὄντως χήρας, 1 Tim. 5:3), and the way this was to be done is indicated at the very end of the discussion in verse 16. They are to be honoured clearly by the church giving support to them, 'that it [the church] may relieve those who are widows indeed (ἵνα ταῖς ὄντως χήραις ἐπαρκεσῃ)'. In the terminology of benefaction language, just as the ' the Council and the People' of the [secular] ἐκκλησία were required to honour the civic benefactors, so too were the members of the Christian ἐκκλησία. Because these widows had a proven track record of benefactions, they were to be duly recognised by the Christian community as, in effect, 'good and noble'. Their 'praising' comes by way of tangible support by the community from their sixtieth year onwards in clear recognition of their 'good deeds'. Having met the needs of others with their benefactions, they are now duly honoured with support from the church. They 'crown' the widows, to use another benefaction metaphor. This benefaction was not to be seen not so much as a sign of her need but rather as the way of 'honouring' her.

There appears to have been no private/public divide in benefactions by Christian widows (v. 10). The benefactions which were spelt out related to the family, the Christian community and others in need. She 'brought up her children', 'used hospitality to strangers', 'washed the feet of the saints', and 'relieved the afflicted'. The listing of these benefactions suggests that there were no demarcation lines at all in reflecting on the widow's benefactions as she 'diligently followed every good work'. It would seem that 1 Timothy 5:3–16 was not about 'the order of widows' or the restriction of their ministry, but was concerned with their activity as benefactors domestically, ecclesiastically and publicly.

In concluding this major section on benefactions, it should be noted that the honouring of the benefactor/widow who is the 'true' Christian widow further substantiates the finding of previous chapters that benefactions were obligatory not just for the Christians who were wealthy, but for all Christians capable of earning money or undertaking good works such as widows were meant to do. This move 'downwards' on the social scale of those who were now to seek the welfare of the city as its benefactors would have given the Christian message its most distinctive social ethic and indeed its unique characteristic in *politeia*.

PART TWO

EARLY CHRISTIANS AS CITIZENS

CHAPTER FIVE

CIVIC RESPONSIBILITY

Philippians 1:27–2:18

A citizen of the early empire who read Philippians 1:27–2:18 might be forgiven for identifying it as a summary of the standard discussion of the well-known problem of discord and concord among citizens in the public domain. The only basic difference would have been its appeal to unity, which was not related to the 'goddess of unity' (Ὁμονια, *Concordia*), but was based on the example of the humiliation and subsequent exaltation of Jesus as Lord. He would have been struck immediately by the use of a constellation of terms or synonyms usually connected with πολιτεύεσθε (Phil. 1:27ff.) which were drawn from activities in *politeia*. These would have helped him to identify the problem as that of disunity in an 'association', the difficulties this could create in the wider context of *politeia* and the call to concord within its ranks. Would this identification have been correct? What is being proposed in this chapter is that it would have been an accurate understanding of the Christian community's problem as it faced life in the Roman colony of Philippi.

Paul's lengthy discussion in Philippians 1:27-2:18 concerns the obligation of Christians 'to live as citizens' (πολιτεύεσθε) in the world of *politeia* in a way that is worthy of the gospel—*i.e.* in concord and not discord, to borrow the terminology of those who wrote on the subject in the early empire. However the few attempts to argue that the term in 1:27 means 'to live as citizens'[1] have not generally commended themselves[2] nor has the overall discussion been seen to relate to *politeia*.

There are reasons why 'to live' rather than 'to live as citizens' has become the preferred option, even with those commentators who cite primary texts which discuss *politeia*. Their interpretation in Philippians has been narrowly based linguistically. Insufficient attention has

---

[1]For a discussion of the injunction 'live as citizens' see E.C. Miller in Πολιτεύεσθε in Philippians 1.27: Some Philological and Thematic Observations', *JSNT* 15 (1982) 86–96 who discusses the normal terminology Paul uses in ethical and religious injunctions and rightly asks why such terminology was not invoked by him in 1:27. He suggests that its use only here means that it is a *terminus technicus* referring to their obligations as citizens of Philippi, 81. See also the earlier argument of R. Roberts, 'Old Texts in Modern Translation: Philippians 1.27', *ET* 49 (1937-38) 325-6, where the imperative is translated as 'behaving as a citizen should'. For a discussion arguing that the injunction means 'live as citizens' see R.R. Brewer, 'The Meaning of *politeuesthe* in Philippians 1:27', *JBL* 73 (1954) 76–83, who cites Xenophon's *Cyropoedia* I, 1:1, 'people who preferred to live under any form of government', and Thayer, *Greek English Lexicon of the New Testament*, 77. S. Cipriani, 'Saint Paul et la "Politique"', in L. De Lorenzi (ed.), *Paul de Tarse: apôtre du notre temps* (Rome: Abbaye de S. Paul, 1979) 596-618 offers no discussion of Phil. 1:27ff. at all.

been given to the possibility that the specific meaning of the word is to be located in the context of *politeia*. The institutions covered in the ancient world by the term *politeia* (πολιτεία), how they functioned, and the way in which similar problems were also discussed by secular writers, have not been sufficiently understood by commentators.

A consideration of these factors is important because New Testament semantic studies can be afflicted with 'tunnel vision'. That is, linguistic studies often look only at lexicographical references in non-Biblical texts in order to see if the actual word which occurs there could support the consensus rendering of a specific word in the New Testament. With the advent of the Ibycus scholarly computer and its equivalents, and the gathering together for the first time on CD ROMs of the vast body of ancient Greek literature in the *TLG* and the comparable project begun for non-literary sources, Biblical scholars have been given access to the Greek corpus of some sixty million Greek words from Homer to the sixth century A.D. This means that a far broader linguistic base now exists for word studies.

At the same time such evidence calls for a more sophisticated method of arriving at a decision on the meaning of at least some words. Attempts ought to be made to find comparable contexts in ancient literature to the passage in the New Testament which uses the actual term or synonyms—Biblical studies can also unwittingly give the impression that *koine* Greek had no wide range of synonyms. Scant attention, or none at all, may be paid to the fact that a term might be an 'umbrella' one in a semantic field. It could harbour other words which also have a variety of meanings. When the latter are seen to be standing under a particular semantic shelter, then the meaning of the term can be quickly identified.

For example, in a discussion of twentieth-century Christian social ethics, if an instruction was given that Christians were 'to live their lives as citizens worthily of the gospel', precisely what this meant would need to be explored, as in Philippians 1:27ff. How would uncertainties about the actual situation to which the passage is referring be resolved? There would be at least two ways. It could be explained

---

[2]The major translations over the past one hundred years give no specific sphere of reference for this injunction in 1:27—'Only let your manner of life be worthy of the gospel of the Messiah', RV; 'Only conduct yourselves in a manner worthy of the gospel', NASV; 'Whatever happens let your conduct be worthy of the gospel', REB; 'Whatever happens, conduct yourselves in a manner worthy of the gospel', NIV; while only the RV provides an alternative translation 'Only behave as citizens worthily of the gospel'.

by seeing if there were actual prohibitions countering inappropriate or unworthy conduct given the nature of the Christian gospel. It could also be discerned from positive imperatives, spelling out what was appropriate Christian conduct in this situation. Both approaches might be used by the author, as was the case in Philippians. It could also be understood from examples or the use of a constellation of terms which appeared after the main instruction as an explication of its meaning.

In addition, the person issuing these directives would need to take note of the characteristics of the particular society in which his discussion of *politeia* was taking place. The political structures in which citizens lived varied from society to society and these variations would need to be taken into account. Reverting to a first-century example, cognisance would need to be taken of the peculiar status of Philippi as a Roman colony and the civic status of those who lived there. It might determine in part the author's choice of key terms. What was meant by the command 'to live as citizens worthily of the gospel' would be explained by some or all these factors. Similarly, for any secondary reader of the text it would be necessary for that person to appreciate the above in order to have a measure of certainty concerning the concrete application of the particular imperative 'to live as a citizen'.

It is suggested that the approaches outlined above point the way forward to an understanding of the problem dealt with in Philippians 1:27ff., and can resolve whether the main verb is an exhortation for a specific area of life, *viz. politeia,* or simply a general injunction regulating any area of Christian relationships. Discussions of Philippians 1:27–2:18 generally proceed on the assumption that it concerns corporate Christian relationships outside the actual church gathering. It is not usually seen to be about how the people of God should face life corporately in the public place *(politeia)* where they would find a fairly antagonistic situation. The impression is given that in Philippians 1:27–30, the problem is primarily about 'outsiders' being a threat to the Christian gathering or community, while 2:1-14 is related to internal difficulties. This still leaves some uncertainty as to how 2:15-16 is to be understood, and why the focus appears to return to that of 1:27-30.

However, if Philippians 1:27–2:18 has a single focus, does the previous discussion in the letter in any way help to confirm this? Having already thanked the Philippian Christians for their fellowship in the gospel (1:3–11), Paul recounts how his own difficult personal circumstances had fallen out for its progress (1:12–26). These related specifically to his 'bonds' as he awaits the hearing of his court case.

Courts were regarded as part of *politeia* in the first century. There 'envy and strife' also played a significant rôle. Subsequent discussion will show that there is a connection between Paul's experiences and the situation in Philippi which is more specific than simply common suffering (1:30). Their sufferings and difficulties were part of Christian existence and occur in the same broad area, *viz. politeia*.

When understood against the first-century background of the public life of citizens, as against the private domain, 1:27-2:18 and 1:12ff. could be said to address the issue of Christians operating in *politeia*, and their witness was potentially or actually threatened by internal strife which may in part be related to 4:2–3. The problem for Christians might differ little from that of their non–Christian compatriots. They too faced discord within the committed relationships of their particular associations. They could also experience pressures from outside groups or administrative tribes in the realm of *politeia*.[3] Furthermore, individual private differences in these associations in the first century had a habit of quickly spilling over into *politeia* and causing havoc in the political assemblies. More often than not, they ended in a civil action in court. Evidence for this can be found in the first century A.D. writers, Plutarch and Dio Chrysostom, and other ancient authors all of whom can help illuminate the problem in Philippians 1:27ff. and 4:2–3—one that was endemic in *politeia*.[4]

It will be argued, then, that Philippians 1:27-2:18 deals with this single but highly complex situation, beginning with a sustained exhortation relating to the civic responsibility of Christians in the public place (1:27-28), concluding with an injunction to shine as lights in *politeia* (2:14-16a), and sandwiching the discussion in between the two imperatives.[5]

This will be done by exploring (I) the meaning of functioning with discord and concord or 'unworthy' and 'worthily' in *politeia* in Plutarch and Dio Chrysostom, (II) Paul's own problems in Philippians 1:12ff. in relationship to *politeia*, (III) how 'living as citizens' in concord and not discord in 1:27–2:18 is to be understood in the light of a similar discussion in the non–literary and literary sources, (IV) the importance of the Philippians resolving the problem in 4:2–3 which could easily

---

[3]Jones, *The Roman World of Dio Chrysostom*, 80 for discussion.

[4]Because of Paul's methods of discussing complex relational issues elsewhere, the difficulties in 4:2-3 can be demonstrated to be connected with and even central to, the discussion in 1:27-2:18. See p. 89.

[5]See P.T. O'Brien, *Commentary on Philippians*, NIGTC (Grand Rapids: Eerdmans, 1991) 143ff.

spill over into *politeia* as a civil action, and (V) what 'living as citizens worthily of the gospel' meant.

I. Functioning in *politeia* in Plutarch and Dio Chrysostom

(i) Plutarch

Plutarch's 'Precepts of Politics' (πολιτικα παραγγελματα) is a discourse on the theme of how to function appropriately, or, to repeat Paul's word, 'worthily', in *politeia*. It arises out of a request by a young man seeking advice about entering public life and is illuminating in its discussion.

First he defines for this young man what a politician is:

A speaker of speeches, and also a doer of actions.

μύθων τε ῥητῆρ ἔμεμαι πρηκτῆρά τε ἔργων.

This citation, appropriately taken from that touchstone for much first-century discussion, Homer's *Iliad* 9.443, makes it clear that the aspiring politician will engage in discussions in the assembly and the undertaking of benefactions. The young man's ambition is judged to be a laudable one and appropriate to his noble birth (498B). Not all were eligible to undertake liturgies, to which one could be elected on an annual basis, or even to vote in the assembly. Some citizens lacked even the necessary 500 drachmae which enabled them to exercise their civic responsibilities.[6]

Plutarch warns the young man of the ease with which those who possess the financial qualifications could slip into public affairs, but also warns him of the great difficulty in disengaging oneself from them, presumably because of the enormous social pressure to continue to costly public liturgies. He writes critically of these 'busybodies'

because they have no business of their own that is worth serious attention, they throw themselves into public affairs (δημόσια πράγματα) treating political activity as a pastime, and many having

---

[6]For a discussion of this in relation to Tarsus, see Jones, *The Roman World of Dio Chrysostom*, 80–81who cites Dio Chrysostom, *Or.* 34.21-3. Jones feels this qualification is 'a less well-known feature of Greek city life'.

engaged in public affairs by chance and had enough of them are no longer able to retire from them without difficulty (798D).

High standards were expected from those with public leadership rôles. 'Small faults appear great when observed in the lives of leaders. . .on account of the opinion which the majority has of governing and public office' (οἱ πολλοὶ περὶ ἀρχῆς καὶ πολιτείας ἔχουσιν). No clear distinction was drawn between the private and public spheres of life, for Plutarch observes

> people see through the character, counsels, acts and lives of public men,. . .they love and admire one man and dislike and despise another quite as much for his private as for his public practices (ἀπὸ ἰδιων ἢ τῶν δημοσίων ἐπιτηδευμάτων, 800F–801A).

Plutarch records that Livius Drusus, the tribune, 'gained in reputation because, when many parts of his house were exposed to the view of his neighbours. . .[he] made the whole house open to view, "that all the citizens may see how I live"' (800F). By contrast 'the people' have been known to reject a motion because of the character of the mover, and ask another to move it so that it could pass (801B-C). Plutarch cites Menander 'The speaker's lifestyle, not his speech persuades' (τρόπος ἐσθ' ὁ πείθων τοῦ λέγοντος ὁ λόγος). Plutarch criticises those who subordinated the affairs of the community and the public to private favours and interests (τὰ κοινὰ καὶ δημόσια ταῖς ἰδίαις χάρισι καὶ σπουδιᾶς ὑφιέμενος, 807B).[7]

Supervision was expected of the person holding a public liturgy but not required of private citizens. On standing and watching tiles being measured and stores delivered Plutarch opines

> a man would be paltry and sordid who managed them for himself and attended to them for his own sake, but if he does it for the public and for the State's sake, he is not ignoble, on the contrary his attention to duty and his zeal are all the greater when applied to little things (811C-D).

The demands of a high-profile public life are not portrayed to this young man as easy options. He is warned that there are dangers and difficulties attached to public office—'those who hope for glory, fall into disgrace and are drawn into offices which involve danger and

---

[7]Cf. Phil. 2:4 where Paul commands that each of the Christians 'must look not only to their own things, but also to the things of others.'

public disorder' (εἰς πράγματα κινδύνους ἔχοντα καὶ παραχας ἄγωνται, 798D).[8] So much for Plutarch's discussion of the responsibilities and pitfalls of the life in *politeia* for this young man.

Plutarch proceeds to deal with a much wider concern in *politeia*. As he enumerates the greatest 'good' or blessings which cities can enjoy as 'peace, liberty, plenty, abundance of men and concord' he deals with all except the last succinctly in one paragraph. The issue of 'concord' which is described as 'the equal of any of the other blessings' will occupy the remainder of the discussion in this treatise. He defines concord as working with, rather than against, others. It means '. . .(to) pay the highest honour to one who holds office, but the honour of an office resides in concord and friendship with one's colleagues much more than in crowns and purple bordered robes' (816A). For Plutarch the reason that this should be so is clear. The *task* of the politician is 'to see in advance that factional discord shall never arise among them and to regard this as the greatest and noblest function of what may be called the art of statesmanship' (τέχνη τῆς πολιτικῆς, 824C).

The task of the statesman is 'always to instil concord and friendship in those who dwell together with him and to remove 'strife' (ἔρις), 'discord' (διχοφροσύνη) and all 'enmity' (δυσμένεια)' (824D). In the matter of 'quarrels' (δισφοραῖς) among friends, he must seek to help those who feel wronged, trying to 'mollify and teach' them

> that those who let wrongs go unheeded are superior to those who are quarrelsome and try to compel and overcome others, not only in reasonableness and character, but also in wisdom and greatness of spirit. . .it is best for wise men to accept one advantage—a life of 'harmony and quiet' since Fortune, has left us no prize open for competition (824E).

Plutarch also observes

> disorder in a State is not always kindled by contentions about public matters, but frequently differences arising from private affairs and offences pass thence into public life and. . .private troubles become the causes of public ones and small troubles of great ones (825A).

In civil actions he cautions against treating others with 'contentiousness, anger or any other passions which inject harshness and bitterness into unavoidable disputes' (825E). He rejects the 'sharpen-

---

[8]D.F. Epstein, *Personal Enmity in Roman Politics 218–43 BC* (London and New York: Routledge, 1987).

ing' and 'poisoning matter, as if they were darts and arrows, with bad words, malice, threats, to make them incurable, great, and of public importance, if they are overlooked and do not in the beginning receive treatment or smooth counsel' (825A).

He suggests that the best way to do this is not to ignore them, but 'by taking hold of them, suppress them, and cure them. For by attention, as Cato says, the great is made small and the small is reduced to nothing' (825D). Plutarch rightly epitomised political life as 'dealing with affairs of state and public conflicts. . .' (798B).

Here he gives advice to a young man whose status would qualify him for quite specific functions in *politeia*. The information shows how one should handle concord and discord which was part and parcel of *politeia* in cities of the Roman empire. That discord should be regarded as an inevitable characteristic indicates how typical it was in the first century. The use of the term πολιτεία in this discourse and Plutarch's discussion of 'Precepts of Politics' reflect Paul's similar concerns about concord and discord in Philippians 1:27ff.

(ii) Dio Chrysostom

Dio Chrysostom devotes thirteen of his eighty orations to the political theme of 'concord'. He does so out of a concern for the destructive effects of 'discord' in *politeia* both among citizens of a city and between cities themselves.[9] Four of the orations carry the word 'concord' in the title. The remainder concern his native city, Prusa, where he was embroiled in the problems of local politics and experienced their debilitating effect on himself and the body politic. There are other orations which have a bearing on political life, *e.g.* 'On Reputation' and 'On Popular Opinion' (66, 67). These writings date from *c.* A.D. 70 to 110.[10] Together they provide an important insight into the problems in *politeia* in the East.[11]

---

[9]For example Dio Chrysostom deals with the problem of discord and concord in the following orations: 'To the Nicomedians, on concord with the Nicaeans' 38, 'On concord in Nicaea' 39, 'On concord with Apameia' 40, 'To the Apameians, on concord' 41. This is certainly not the sum of his discussion. The series of orations to his native city, Prusa, shows that Dio himself is embroiled in the local politics and experiencing the debilitating effect of discord, 42-50.

[10]For dating see Jones, *The Roman World of Dio Chrysostom*, 134f. *Or.* 38, 39 (*ca.* 98), 40, 41, 42 (*ca.* 101), (*ca.* 106-7) 43.

Dio states that 'concord (ὁμονοία) is a fine and salutary thing', even though the sophists can perversely argue the opposite. He believes in the divine origin of concord uniting, as it was thought, the basic elements of the universe, *i.e.* fire, air, water and earth, and embracing 'friendship, reconciliation and kinship' (38.10-11, *cf.* 40.35-37). In his estimate, the reason that mankind falls short of the blessedness of the gods is because of insensitivity to concord.

Discord is often contrasted with concord. Dio explains that some 'actually love the opposite, strife' (στάσις). 'Discord results in wars and battles and is continuously at work in communities, the *demoi* and nations like disease in our bodies' (38.11). In the same oration he contrasts 'wars, factions, diseases' with their opposites—'peace, concord and health' and argues that no person can really regard the former as good. It is 'envy and rivalry' (φθόνος καὶ φιλονικία) which create this strife. He indicates what he means by 'envy and strife'—'your plotting against one another, your gloating over the misfortune of your neighbours, your vexation at their good fortune' (38.43). He sees the opposite as 'sharing things that are good, unity of heart and mind, rejoicing of both peoples in the same things' (κοινωνίαν, ἀγαθῶν, ὁμοφροσύνην) (38.43).

'Roman' eyes see discord as a particularly Greek problem according to Dio, and it occurs when men seek 'first place'. On those who seek the 'marks of distinction', Dio observes that not only are they 'the objects of utter contempt in the eyes of all persons of discernment, but also in Rome they excite laughter and, what is still more humiliating, are called "Greek failings"' (Ἑλληνικα ἁμαρτήματα, 38.38).

How can discord be remedied? In an attempt to deal with the long standing discord between the cities of Nicomedia and Nicaea, Dio provides an example as he addresses the former in the hope of bringing about concord. First he outlines the structure of the speech. He will address the matter of 'concord' in general, informing his audience where the concept comes from and what it achieves, and then 'over against that to set off strife and hatred in contradistinction to friendship' (ἐξ ἐναντίας τὴν στάσιν καὶ τὴν ἔχθραν διακρῖναι πρὸς τὴν φιλίαν). He believes that once one has demonstrated the universal benefits of concord, then it will be possible to show how indispensable it is for the two cities. He also outlines the benefits which accrue. (38.8).

---

[11]See the discussion by Jones, 'Concord' and 'Local Politics', *The Roman World of Dio Chrysostom*, chs. 10 and 11.

From the beginning Dio wants it to be understood that his purpose in addressing this topic is for the goodwill of his audience alone
and rejects the possibility that he is seeking his own glory or any advantage that might result from reconciliation, stating that he is
concerned for the 'advantage of the state city. . .your advantage' (ὑμᾶς.
. .τὰ συμφέροντα) (38.9) because political motives were always
suspected.

As he discusses the divine origin of concord Dio argues that it
embraces friendship, reconciliation and kinship (φιλία, καταλλαγή συγ-
γένεια) and it unites the foundational elements of the universe i.e. fire,
air, water and earth, a theme repeated in *Orations* 40.35-37. The reason
that mankind falls short of the blessedness of the gods is insensitivity
to concord. In fact, there are those who 'actually love the opposite,
strife' (στάσις) in cities and nations (38.11).

Individuals or groups of people would universally agree on
what is 'evil' (κακία) and what is 'good' (καλός), Dio argues. Under the
first category come terms such as 'wars, factions and disease', and
under the second, the opposites 'peace, concord and health'. Given
this agreement, what infuriated Dio was that there are 'some among
us—or rather a good many—who delight in the things that are admit
tedly evil' (38.14).

The oration then turns its attention to the other community in the
city *viz.* the household whose safety depended not only

> on the like–mindedness (ὁμοφροσύνη) of master and mistress but also
> upon the obedience of servants, yet both the bickering (στάσις) of
> master and mistress and the wickedness of servants (κακοδουλία)
> have wrecked many households (38.15).

Concord holds together the good marriage, discord does not save bad
one. It is the virtue of concord that holds together all the relationships
of life, parents and children. 'What is fraternity (ἀδελφότης) save concord of brothers (38.15)?'

Dio reminds his audience that there are times when people
choose war rather than peace. On other occasions they have pursued
the path of peace even when the spoils of war were so great because
they prefer the things of the highest value. Waging war for no reason
is likened to the remorseless fighting of wild beasts and yet he notes
that 'many even of us treat human beings too as wild beasts and take
pleasure in the conflict waged with those of our own kind' (38.17).

Dio suggests that the gods attempt to teach 'us to live on good
terms with one another' (ἡμᾶς ὁμονοεῖν αὐτοῖς) by giving us 'all those

signs and omens' which men deliberately ignore. These omens are said to be divine signs, be they heralds proclaiming peace or unarmed envoys confidently going into enemy camps to sue for peace as messengers of the gods. There can also be 'an omen from heaven' or an earthquake which is seen as a heavenly sign that the gods are telling armies about to fight not do so. These, together with the customary celebration of peace with garlands, sacrifices and 'high festivals' are the signs and omens which are divine lessons on concord (38.18-19).

Why then are the Nicomedians contending with the Nicaeans, Dio asks? It is not a dispute over revenue. He outlines everything they have in common—mutual trade, intermarriage, personal friendships, common customs, the worship of the same gods and similar religious festivals. All this ought to be the occasion for 'friendship and concord'. There are no grounds for claims and the men of Nicaea have not issued counterclaims. At stake is the title of primacy for Nicomedia. 'We are contending for the primacy' (ὑπὲρ πρωτείων ἀγωιζόμεθα) over the Nicaeans (38.21-24). The dispute is whether the Nicomedians can call themselves 'first' (πρῶτοι) and be able to put it on their monuments and inscriptions (38.28). As Jones notes

> A vivid illustration of the jealousy such inscriptions awakened in other cities is given by the east gate of Nicaea, on which the words 'the first of the province' have been erased. . .Nicodemia was at last able to have the offending phrase erased from its rival's monuments.[12]

In order for the individual to occupy first place, according to Dio one must become wealthy, great or powerful. He sees this activity as the struggle for supremacy and calls it 'vainglory' (τὸ κενοδοξεῖν). He observes that it 'has come to be regarded as a foolish thing even in private individuals, and we ourselves deride and loathe and end by pitying those persons above all who do not know wherein false glory differs from the genuine' (38.29). He makes an ironic comment to those in his audience who are educated and leaders of the city —'besides no educated man has such a feeling about glory as to desire a foolish thing'. In the same discussion he notes of others that 'their doings were not mere vain conceit (κενόδοξα) but a struggle for real empire' (38.38). There is no denial that a person may wish to be designated 'first'.[13] Dio

---

[12]Jones, *The Roman World of Dio Chrysostom*, 87.
[13]Jones, *The Roman World of Dio Chrysostom*, 85, 'Desire for honour and glory was ubiquitous. . .individuals struggle to the "first men" of their city or to wear the gold crown and purple robe of office'.

saw nothing intrinsically wrong with that because in life 'someone really is first, and no matter if another wears the title, first he is. For 'the titles are not guarantees of facts but 'facts of titles' (38.40).

For Dio concord is, in effect, a synonym for unity. He says,

> I myself rejoice at the present moment to find you wearing the same costume, speaking the same language, and desiring the same things. Indeed what spectacle is more enchanting than a city with singleness of purpose, and what sound is more awe–inspiring than its harmonious voice?. . .What city acts more smoothly than that which acts together? To whom are afflictions lighter than to those who bear them together, like a heavy load? (39.3).

A prayer for unity concludes his discourse 'On concord in Nicaea on the Cessation of Civil Strife'

> that from this day forth they [the gods] may implant in this city yearning for itself, a passionate love, a singleness of purpose, a unity of wish and thought: and, on the other hand, that they cast out strife and contentiousness and jealousy' so that the city may be numbered among the most prosperous and the noblest for all time to come (39.8).

Concord was such a prized feature of private and public life, that it was deified as the goddess, *Homonia* or *Concordia*. That divinity has to be invoked in the hope of securing and retaining unity shows its importance for the stability of *politeia*.

II. Paul's own problems with *politeia* in Philippians 1:12ff.

Paul's own detention in 1:12ff. had been made more difficult by the conduct of some from the city from which he wrote his letter. It is normally assumed that his problems had nothing to do with *politeia*. However, that is to misunderstand its extent in the first century. In an important chapter on 'local politics' in the Roman world of the early empire, C.P. Jones has observed that they

> were not conducted only in the council and assembly, but spilled over into another area of public life, the courts. Though the power of the city courts was limited, they were the arena for political rivalries. . .the problems of Prusa [Dio Chrysostom's city of birth]. . .recall those of republican Rome.[14]

Paul, in bonds awaiting trial, speaks of the difficulties he experienced which were deliberately created by others. He reports that some are preaching 'the Messiah' for the purpose of creating 'strife and envy' (φθόνος καὶ ἔρις) and doing so out of 'faction' (ἐριθεία) in order to make his pre-trial detention even more difficult—'thinking to raise up affliction for me in my imprisonment' (1:15, 17).

In order to piece together the situation, it is helpful to explore the terms he uses to describe precisely what was happening. A careful survey of the first term 'envy' (φθόνος) has concluded

> To judge from the frequency with which *phthonos* and the terms that we rather inadequately render by hatred and enmity are found together in Greek, it was widely assumed that the ill-will of *phthonos* was likely to be intense; hatred and enmity are inadequate precisely because they lack the element of active ill-will. . .The *phthoneros*, then, in his ἐχθρά not only dislikes the object of his *phthonos*, but wishes actively to see him harmed.[15]

Dio confirms this when, in his oration devoted to an analysis of 'envy' (φθόνος), he indicates that one expressed it against ones adversaries by 'plotting against them in every way' (ἐπιβουλεύοι πάντα τρόπον) and praying for their ruin' (77/78.29).

The meaning of this term can now be evaluated in Paul's own discussion. He recounts that when his bonds became 'manifest in Christ' it opened up unprecedented access to 'the whole praetorian guard and the rest' (1:13). He saw from this that his imprisonment had actually resulted in progress for the gospel, because of the doors it had opened (1:12). The other knock-on effect had been the renewed confidence of most Christians to preach (1:14). The way some expressed their envy was to undertake the extraordinary action of 'proclaiming the Messiah' with the intention of actively harming Paul. This is the meaning of 'envy'—doing something that would be highly prejudicial to the outcome of his case when he came to trial.

---

[14]Jones, *The Roman World of Dio Chrysostom*, 99.
[15]K.M.D. Dunbabin and M.W. Dickie, '*Invidia rumpantur pactora*: Iconography of Phthonos/Invidia in Graeco–Roman Art', *JbAC* 26 (1983) 10. See also Epstein, *Personal Enmity in Roman Politics*, 48ff. on envy as a source of enmity. A specific term διαβολή was coined to described the prejudice created by circumstances preceeding a trial. See Aristotle, *Rhetoric* 3.15 and *Rhet. ad Alex.* 29.61.11-64.23 and discussion in T. Cole, *The Origins of Rhetoric in Ancient Greece* (Baltimore: John Hopkins University Press, 1991) 6.

The term 'strife' (ἔρις) encompasses the idea of partisan behaviour which was also connected with *politeia*.[16] Did these opponents wish to split the association of which they were part, and make Christians take sides for or against Paul? Bearing in mind the guilt by association of the treason trials under Tiberius where friends were implicated with the accused,[17] and the danger of associating with a prisoner (especially one whose case had not been resolved),[18] taking Paul's side could have seriously affected his supporters if the case went against him.

The terms 'strife and envy' appear together in lists which have to do with activities in the public arena—'arousing strife or greed or contentions or jealousies and base desires for gain' (77/78,39). Dio Chrysostom also speaks of 'jealousy and envy' (φθόνος καὶ ζηλοτυπία) and notes that this results 'in the desire that no one else shall ply the same trade'. While he applies this to potters, butchers, and more suitably brothel–keepers in his informative oration on 'Envy' (77/78.3-4), it could well illustrate the situation that Paul had faced in his missionary journeys with respect to the Jews. Dio provides an example of what 'envy and strife' meant—'your plotting against one another, your gloating over the misfortune of your neighbours, your vexation at their good fortune' (38.43).

Paul proceeds to indicate the actual motivation of his opponents which provoked them into creating jealousy and strife. He says it arose 'out of faction' (ἐξ ἐριθείας) (1:17a). This third term carries a variety of meanings in *politeia* including 'political manoeuvres' or 'election intrigue',[19] and was also used to refer to 'party spirit', 'faction'.

The result they hoped to achieve is also spelt out (1:17b)—'hoping to raise up trouble' for the purpose of complicating his case, or 'defence' (ἀπολογία) as he calls it (1:7). When Paul reports that they are 'hoping' (οἰόμενοι) to create complications for him, it is clear that their present activities have a future goal. Thus the stirring up of trouble was meant to prejudice the outcome of his case when it came to court. At least this much can be said—that Paul's opponents engaged in an activity that was calculated to aggravate his difficulties at his trial.

---

[16] It actually became the name of the goddess of strife, Ἔρις.

[17] B. Levick, 'Tiberius and the Law: The Development of *maiestas*', *Tiberius the Politician* (London: Thames and Hudson, 1976) ch. 12.

[18] For evidence of this see B. Rapske, 'The Importance of Helpers to the Imprisoned Paul in the Book of Acts', *Tyn.B.* 42 (1991) 1-30 esp. 23-9.

[19] Aristotle, *Politics* 1302b.

However, his detention had created an unparalleled opportunity for him among 'the whole of the Praetorium guard and the rest' (1:13).

Isocrates spoke of the misfortune of his life—'false reports which are spread about me, of the calumny and prejudice (διαβολὴ καὶ φθόνος) which I suffer' (12.21). Elsewhere he recorded 'I observe that you are being painted in false colours by men who are jealous of you. . .in the habit of stirring up trouble in their own cities' (5.73). Paul could readily see the same happening in what might be called his 'misfortune', but in what would turn out in the end to be his deliverance *i.e.* 'salvation' (1:19). The term here does not refer to the Christian's salvation, but is used in a secular context to refer to the successful outcome of his trial (*cf.* 1:25). For this he seeks the Philippians' prayers and the 'supply' of the Spirit of Christ overruling in his situation (1:19).

Who were 'the rest' (1:13)? If Paul means the bureaucracy of Rome, then one could understand that his opponents were those who had brought the charge against him in Caesarea. They had to appear in Rome, given the public affirmation of forensic procedure which had been specifically reiterated at Paul's trial in Acts 25:16. They would have been resentful, indeed agitated, by what appeared to be Paul's favoured access to the seat of power.[20] The Jewish 'lobby' had always actively cultivated relations with Rome for Judaea and elsewhere. In spite of their difficulties early in the reign of Claudius, they continued to make a comeback through their imperial connections.[21]

If the situation does not refer to the criminal proceedings instigated in the Roman provincial court adjourned to Rome, (Acts 24ff.) the same situation may well apply, for the Jews also courted city authorities (*e.g.* Acts 13:50). We know that Roman governors brought officials with legal expertise with them and the reference to 'the rest' could be to them.[22] Wherever the location of this particular imprisonment, Paul indicates elsewhere in the letter that those of 'Caesar's household'[23]

---

[20]For a discussion of Jewish accusations against Paul see my 'Official Proceedings and Forensic Speeches in Acts 24–26', in A.D. Clarke and B.W. Winter (edd.), *The Book of Acts in its Ancient Literary Setting*, The Book of Acts in its First Century Setting (Grand Rapids and Carlisle: Eerdmans and Paternoster, 1993) 322ff.
[21]Levick, *Claudius* 179ff.
[22]J.A. Crook, *Law and Life of Rome, 90 B.C.–A.D. 212* (London: Thames and Hudson, 1967) 73. On the governor's retinue see B. Levick, *The Government of the Roman Empire: A Sourcebook* (London: Croom Helm, 1985) 13 and A. Lintott, *Imperium Romanum: Politics and Administration* (London: Routledge, 1993) 50–52.
[23]See Weaver, *Familia Caesaris: A Social Study of the Emperor's Freedmen and Slaves* on the extent of Caesar's household.

who were Christians sent the Philippians their greetings (4:22). So his access to 'the guards and the rest' had definitely been fruitful for the gospel.

If the opponents were Jewish preachers, then the way to harm Paul most was 'to proclaim'—a word not only used in Christian preaching, but also of imperial decrees, etc.—'the Messiah' (1:15, 17, 18). If the preachers were Paul's opponents from the Christian community, then their behaviour is explicable from the perspective of any association or *politeia* in general. As will be seen (p. 100ff.), small issues could become big issues spilling out into *politeia* and creating havoc. Litigation was one route whether in a civil or a criminal case.

Whether the opponents were Jews or Christians, they behaved in a way that was typical of citizens in *politeia* who manoeuvred in litigation to prejudice its outcome. This sort of behaviour was condemned by secular writers as it bred discord and fuelled animosity even further.[24]

While Paul genuinely rejoices that the Messiah is being proclaimed, he notes that it is being done by some whose motives are impure (οὐχ ἁγνῶς, 1:17) and whose public activities are nothing more than a 'sham', 'pretext' (πρόφασις, 1:18) because they aimed at stirring up 'trouble', 'tribulation' (θλῖψις) for Paul (1:17). They actively pursued this by creating 'envy' and 'strife', deliberately working against him. If they are other Christians, then their disaffection with Paul had already been carried beyond 'the association' or Christian community into the secular sphere where those who had scores to settle with him were now doing so.

Whether or not hostility and difficulties for Paul had originated from the Christian ἐκκλησία and emerged in a subset of *politeia*, viz. the courts (1:12ff.), they provide an example of what discord and its attendant evils could do. This sort of behaviour was condemned by Plutarch and Dio Chrysostom as discordant and counter–productive to the 'welfare' of others (cf. *Or.* 38.9). For Paul it provides an illustration of what unworthy gospel behaviour meant among those operating in *politeia* and hence an appropriate prelude to his subsequent discussion of worthy behaviour among the Philippians in 1:27ff.

---

[24]For examples of this in civil cases by Christians see ch. 6.

III. Christians and *politeia* in Philippians 1:27–2:18

Paul is concerned that the Christian community will experience the same troubles as he did when in Philippi in the legal area of *politeia* (Acts 16:19ff.), and which they hear he is now experiencing (1:30). It is suggested that the language he uses in 1:27–2:18 indicates that their problems are related to *politeia*. There is also the danger that they would perpetuate the same discord in Philippi as Paul's opponents did for him in his detention. He addresses the Christians as they face the world of *politeia* by invoking the mind-set of Christ which was able to motivate them to concord. The implication of this would be that, as the people of God, shining as lights in their day, they must live in accordance with the gospel they proclaimed (2:15–16).[25]

In 1:27 Paul stresses the importance of the Philippians' conduct with the use of 'only' (μόνον). When he emphasises 'your' manner of life, he may well be contrasting it with that of his opponents whose behaviour stands condemned. O'Brien notes the significance of verse 27 because 'the subsequent admonitions and statements expand and explicate what is involved in living worthily of the gospel'.[26] This admonition stands as a heading for the whole section as Paul underlines his primary concern that Christians should 'live as citizens' or in public in a way that is worthy of that gospel (1:3-11, 12–26, 27ff.).

He issues the following instruction, 'Do nothing through factions and vainglory' (μηδὲν κατ' ἐριθείαν μηδὲ κατὰ κενοδοξίαν). In 2:3 Paul condemns the same motivation which created difficulties for him in 1:17a. As noted, the term has strong overtones of factionalism *politeia*, *viz.* out of 'faction' (ἐριθεία) normally translated 'strife' or 'factionalism' (*P.Sorb.* 1. 34, 230 BC). The other motivation of the Philippian church was 'primacy' which is called 'vain glory' (κενοδοξία). This unfortunate feature of the secular ἐκκλησία was also sadly manifested

---

[25]The passage is a unity. The five sentences comprising 1:27-2:18 are connected either by particles, γάρ, διὸ καί, ὥστε or by parallel thoughts (2:2, 3 *cf.* 2:5ff.). Christ's mind-set is to be reflected in his followers' attitudes in 2:14ff. 1:27-2:18 begins and ends with a command to live in *politeia* worthily of the gospel, shining as lights in the world with the gospel. Most recently O'Brien, *Philippians,* 143ff. argues for the unity of this passage under the heading of 'Conduct worthy of the gospel: Exhortations and an example to the community (1:27-2:18)'.

[26]O'Brien, *Philippians,* 143. This is 'one highly significant demand in v. 27. . . which stands as a heading to the whole section 1:27–2:18', citing D.F. Watson, 'Rhetorical Analysis of Philippians and its Implications for the Unity Question', *NovT* 30 (1988) 79.

in its Christian counterpart (2:3). The push for primacy not only characterised cities but also individuals, as Dio Chrysostom noted.[27]

These two terms placed together suggest a division in the church and a struggle for primacy by an individual or leader. Who was involved is uncertain, but it could be related to the discord which had developed between the two women in 4:2-3 over some unspecified issue. In the same discussion Paul appeals for concord, based on the enormous benefits of God's covenant with his people (2:1). With a synonymous expression for 'concord' from the semantic field of *politeia* (2:2ff.), he urges them 'to be of the same mind' (τὸ αὐτὸ φρονεῖτε, 2:2) *cf.* 4:2.[28] He explicates this in 2:5, 'have this mind among you which was also in Christ Jesus' calling on them to live in concord as citizens with the mindset of Christ (2:5-8).

He proceeds to argue that Jesus did not grasp at his primacy *i.e.* his equal status with God. He took upon himself a non-status posture, submitting himself with the attitude of a slave to condemnation and death in *politeia* before a Roman court. He refused the escape rightly available to him on the grounds of his rights as one equal with God.[29] His obedience has resulted in a title consistent with God's exaltation of him. He has been given a primacy which all creation will have to acknowledge (2:9–11).[30] In the words of Dio Chrysostom, 'titles (τὰ ὀνόματα) are not guarantees of facts but facts of titles' (*Or.* 38.40).

The consequences of Christ's obedience are spelt out with an injunction to work out the consequence of the gospel's salvation with reverence and trembling, and that all things are to be done without discord (2:14). The two terms have connotations of *stasis*, 'murmuring' (γογγυσμός) and 'disputing' (διαλογισμός) (2:14). The language is drawn from the semantic field of politics, even though there are Old Testament resonances of the challenge of Yahweh's lordship over his people by their attitudes and behaviour both to him and their leader, Moses.[31] The discussion reflects discord in the Christian community as it did in the Old Testament incidents alluded to by Paul. The benefit

---

[27]See pp. 92-3.

[28]S.K. Stowers, 'Friends and Enemies in the Politics of Heaven: Reading Theology in Philippians', in J.M. Bassler (ed.), *Pauline Theology* (Minneapolis: Fortress Press, 1991) 1, 112 identifies this with *homonoia* citing Dio Chrysostom, 'Second Tarsic Oration', *Or.* 34.20, but overlooks the discussion of concord and discord in his orations devoted to that subject.

[29]D.W.B. Robinson, 'The Deliverance Jesus Refused', *ET* 80 (1969) 253–4.

[30]*Cf.* Dio, *Or.* 38.41, 'the titles are not guarantees of facts, but facts of titles'.

[31]Ex. 16:7ff. and Num. 14:27.

of conduct that is undertaken without discord is specified—'so that' (ἵνα) the Philippian Christians will bear a credible witness as lights that shine in their own generation and hold out the word of life *i.e.* the gospel (2:15-16a.) As has been already noted, Paul begins with the over-arching injunction to live as citizens worthily of the gospel and concludes with the Christians shining in their world by their conduct as they hold out the gospel in *politeia*.

IV. Potential Problems in *politeia* in Philippians 4:2-3

In 4:2–3 Paul urgently appeals to the community to help resolve the dispute between Euodia and Syntyche, fellow workers with Paul in his gospel endeavours. Disagreements were not uncommon in the Roman colonies. As Epstein in his discussion of '*Inimicitiae* and the Courts' has shown, personal falling-out could result in open and long-lasting enmity in the secular ἐκκλησία which frequently resulted in civil litigation.[32] Aristotle noted in his discussion of the phenomena of factions:

> Factions arise not about but out of small matters; but they are carried on about great matters. And even small ones grow extremely violent when they spring up among men of the ruling class.[33]

Plutarch also observed the capacity of private matters to spill over into the realm of *politeia* and create major difficulties (825A).[34] This is why he insisted that one of the tasks of the statesman was to resolve tensions immediately. Discord which arose from litigation continued to surface in the secular ἐκκλησία.

In another Roman colony Christians were caught up in internal 'strife and jealousy' (1 Cor. 1:10, 3:3) and some had gone to the secular court on 'trifling matters' (1 Cor. 6:2)—the two were not unconnected in a struggle for primacy in the congregation.[35] Paul was likewise concerned that the dispute between the two women in Philippi be resolved with help from other Christians. He exhorted them to be of the same

---

[32]'*Inimicitiae* and the Courts', Epstein, *Personal Enmity in Roman Politics,* ch. 5 esp. 96ff. on litigation as a manifestation of personal enmity.

[33]*Politics* 1303b.

[34]Epstein, *Personal Enmity in Roman Politics,* 90–6.

[35]On the latter matter see chapter 6 and a discussion of the background to this problem among the Corinthian Christians see A.D. Clarke, *Secular and Christian Leadership in Corinth: A Socio–Historical and Exegetical Study of 1 Corinthians 1–6* (Leiden: E.J. Brill, 1993).

mind in the Lord (τὸ αὐτὸ φρονεῖν ἐν κυρίῳ) Philippians 4:2 which is similar to the call for concord made in 1:27 and 2:2.

Does this mean that private disagreement between two women was in danger of spilling over into the public place through their spokesmen?[36] This could well be at the heart of Paul's concern about their unworthy behaviour as citizens in Philippians 1:27ff. D.E. Garland concluded that Paul 'wrote primarily to defuse the dispute between these two women as it was having disastrous repercussions for the unity of the church'. This is the climax of his letter.[37] Garland's view concerning the climax of Philippians can be endorsed because of the Pauline technique of deferring the important implications of central issues to later in the letter. Again there is a parallel in Paul's dealing with a complex relationship issue in another Roman colony. In handling the problem of internal strife over leading teachers in the Corinthian congregation (1 Cor. 1:10–4:21), he did not address the future implications of the problem of rallying behind Apollos over against Paul (4:6) at the end of the discussion. It is not until 16:12, after dealing with other issues, that the request to have Apollos come back is refused. Garland's line of argument, which was recently rejected on the grounds that 'it seems to infer too much',[38] has a clear precedent in a touchy situation in Corinth.

What should not be assumed is that the discord had internal implications only. Here is the very warning which Plutarch gave against allowing personal enmity to continue so that it becomes a 'public matter',—'differences arising from private affairs and offences pass thence into public life (ἴδια κοινῶν καὶ μικρὰ μεγάλων) and. . .private troubles become the causes of public ones and small troubles of great ones' (825A). There is a clear nexus between the two passages in this letter with the same exhortations to unity in 1:27ff. and 4:2. Are the women struggling for 'primacy' (κενοδοξία) through their connections

---

[36]On the obligations to pursue litigation on behalf of the family see Epstein, *Personal Enmity in Roman Politics*, 93. See also J.F. Gardner, 'Gender: the Independent Woman' *Being a Roman Citizen* (London: Routledge, 1993) ch. 4.

[37]'Composition and Unity of Philippians: Some Neglected Literary Factors', *NovT* 27 (1985) 173. While Garland's conclusions are accepted, his reasons are not for they are based on the thread he sees in the argument in 1:27–4:3, at 162–72. This possibility has been recently argued by J. Hainz, *Ekklesia*, 216 and B. Mengel, *Studien zum Philipperbrief: Untersuchungen zum situativen Kontext unter besonderer Berücksichtigung der Frage nach der Ganzheitlichkeit oder Einheitlichkeit eines paulinischen Briefes* (Tübingen: J.C.B. Mohr [Paul Siebeck], 1982) 279–80, although no literary or non–literary sources are cited to support the connection.

[38] O'Brien, *Philippians*, 479.

either in the Christian community or in the public place? While the former is more likely, the other is not beyond the realms of possibility. Whatever their falling out was about, it had severe implications for the gospel in which cause they had once been united. Does it mean that they have sought to polarise the congregation? They are behaving in such a way that they will discredit the gospel publicly by their internal discord. How will it reach the public place? In the same way it had in Corinth, with vexatious litigation before secular judges and juries arbitrating and awarding financial damages to the winning party. There would be no winners but a divided church was inevitable, for those who supported one of the litigants automatically opposed the other.[39]

Even if the discord did not finally result in civil litigation, it was unacceptable that such a dispute, which was obviously known to the Christian community, should be allowed to continue unresolved or to spill over into the public place.

V. Live in *politeia* worthily of the Gospel

A survey of the use of πολιτεύομαι 'in the political or civic discussions in inscriptions and papyri shows how widespread the meaning 'to live as citizens' was. What also emerges is that it was aligned with terms from *politeia*. From an investigation of over 250 of its occurrences in a limited selection of inscriptions and papyri there emerges a constellation of 'political' terms which stand alongside this word. They deal with the theme of *politeia*. In a number of inscriptions this word is linked with 'concord' (ὁμόνοια) and means functioning in harmony in public life (μεθ' ὁμονοίας τὰ πρὸς αὐτοὺς πολιτεύωνται).[40] Epigraphic material elsewhere refers to those who 'by means of concord save the cities'.[41] In addition 'concord' is linked with other words, one of which is highly significant in the 'politics of friendship'—acting 'towards others with concord and friendship' (μεθ' πρὸς ἀλλήλους ὁμόνοιαν καὶ φιλίαν).[42] Concord is also placed alongside freedom, (εἰς ὁμόνοιαν καὶ ἐλευθερίαν ἀποκαταστήσαντα, το πολίτευμα)[43] 'health' (*i.e.* politically of a city) and safety and harmony'

---

[39]Epstein, *Personal Enmity in Roman Politics*, 94–5.
[40]Caria, Iasos 78 . Iasos 13 and 4, 56, 67, 43 for other examples. Also 1 Priene 54 Iona Pri. 8, 9, 52, 53, 63.
[41]Attica IG II (2) 687.
[42]*IG* II (2) 1006, 1027, 1039, *SEG* 15, 104; 17, 32; 21, 451.
[43]IG II (2) 3218.

(περὶ ὑγιείας καὶ σωτηρίας καὶ ὁμονοίας).[44] The use of this meaning of πολιτεύομαι was highly 'visible' because it was displayed on public inscriptions which drew attention to those who functioned actively as citizens. Concord and other civic virtues also commended in our literary sources are the antidote for that discord which hounded life in *politeia*. This meaning would have occurred to any reader of the Philippian letter in the first century and been re-enforced by the constellation of terms drawn from *politeia*.[45] Following the above examination of the comparable secular discussion and the light it throws on Philippians 1:27–2:18, should we not translate this 'one highly significant demand'[46] which stands as a heading to the whole section 1:27-2:18 'live as citizens worthily of the gospel'?

When the secular discussion of concord[47] and discord in *politeia* is incorporated into the discussion of Philippians, it helps to illuminate certain aspects of Paul's instruction. In particular it draws attention to the concern that small private disputes quickly became big matters that spilt over into *politeia* with debilitating and on–going consequences for the credibility of the gospel. In 1:27 Paul relates in the same sentence the injunction 'to live worthily of the gospel as citizens' to unity in a community as it strives to give credibility in the public place to the implications of the faith created by the gospel—'that I may hear of your state, that you stand fast in one spirit, with one soul striving for the faith of the gospel' (1:27). What Paul is driving at becomes explicable in the light of the discord between the two women whom Paul describes as having 'laboured with me in the gospel' (4:3). The poten-

---

[44]*Attica Tort Rham.* 17 (225/4 BC).

[45]Paul's use of a cognate πολίτευμα in Phil. 3:20 does not influence the translation of the verb in 1:27. In 3:20 the contrast is being drawn between the 'earthly' minded false teachers who are driven by self-seeking and self-centred motives and Christians whose conduct is to be determined by 'heavenly commonwealth' values. See A.T. Lincoln, *Paradise Now and Not Yet: Studies in the Role of the Heavenly Dimension in Paul's Thought with special Reference to his Eschatology*, SNTSMS 43 (Cambridge: CUP, 1981) 97ff. who rightly points out the reference is not to them as a colony of heaven on earth. For the Jewish discussion of the use of πολίτευμα see G. Lüderitz, 'What is the Politeuma?' in edd. J.W. van Henten and P.W. van der Horst *Studies in Early Jewish Epigraphy* (Leiden: E.J. Brill, 1994) 183-225.

[46]Watson, 'Rhetorical Analysis', 79.

[47]M.M. Mitchell, *Paul and the Rhetoric of Reconciliation*, HUT 28 (Tübingen: J.C.B. Mohr [Paul Siebeck], 1991) 76–7 rightly argues that the term was not used by Paul because of the goddess, *Homonia* or *Concordia* but 'being of the same mind', 1 Cor. 1:10 is its NT synonym which in the political field referred to political unity and stability in contrast to *stasis* 'discord'. While the application of this to 1 Cor. 1:10 is not certain, her comments are apposite for Philippians.

tial for small disputes between two of his gospel–related fellow workers to become big disputes and spill over into the secular courts and thus create lasting discord in the association and *politeia* has a long history. Once discord was manifested in public, then the leading members of the Roman colony would need to declare their loyalty to one at the expense of the other.[48] How could the gospel flourish in such a situation? That was not fulfilling the Christian responsibility to live as a citizen worthy of the gospel.

E.C. Miller has recently drawn attention to the fact that the normal terminology used by Paul in ethical and religious injunctions has not been invoked in 1:27 when discussing Christian ethics.[49] When Paul calls upon the Christian community to live as citizens always worthy of the gospel (πολιτεύομαι, 1:27) one might expect a discussion similar to that of Romans 13:1-7. There the worthy Christian citizen pays his legal dues and renders customary honour to those in public office. He also calls upon those who operate within the field of *politeia* to do good *i.e.* to be a public benefactor and thus earn the due public honours given to such.[50]

Surprisingly, worthy citizenship in the context of the Roman colony of Philippi does not cover the same ground as Romans 13:1-7.[51] The above discussion explains why this is so while preventing us from simply concluding that Paul is not dealing with *politeia*. Rather he addresses a pattern of conduct endemic in that area of life which has infiltrated the Christian community and threatens to do great harm to the gospel. He sees similar complexities based in part on his own situation in *politeia* being replicated in the colony of Philippi with Christians being motivated by factions (ἐριθεία). Whereas Christians in *politeia* were meant to be beacons in that world as they lived 'blameless, harmless and unblemished lives', one way to undermine all this was to engage in the murmuring and disputing that was endemic in *politeia* and to allow a private dispute to emerge in the civil courts. The significance of what this would have meant in practice will be explained in the following chapter.

---

[48]Epstein, *Personal Enmity in Roman Politics,* 80ff.
[49]*E.g.* E.C. Miller, 'Πολιτεύεσθε in Philippians 1.27', 93ff.
[50]See ch. 2.
[51]It cannot be denied that it may not have been part of his political παράδοσις in churches within his apostolic jurisdiction.

CHAPTER SIX

CIVIL LITIGATION

1 Corinthians 6:1–11

1 Corinthians 6:1–11 discusses civil litigation in Corinth with Christians taking Christians to court over the 'smallest causes'.[1] The purpose of this chapter is to explore why Paul prohibited Christians in the Roman colony of Corinth from engaging in this area of *politeia viz.* civil litigation, when he was to give such a high rôle to judges in criminal actions in Romans 13:1–7. He teaches that there is no 'public place' for Corinthian Christians in the civil courts. Paul's statements about the character of civil litigation and civil courts in Corinth will be assessed in the light of extra–biblical evidence. They help to explain why he procribes civil actions between Christians.[2]

It has been argued that 1 Corinthians 6:1–11 reflects a situation in Corinth where Christians were submitting their cases to Jewish judges to arbitrate in their disputes.[3] In the words of H. Conzelmann, that conclusion is 'misguided'.[4] This interpretation arose in part because the verb used in 6:4 can mean 'to appoint a judge' (καθίζειν). However, an example is provided by G.D. Fee where it was used for the convening of a court to hear arguments. In addition, Dio Cassius records that a group involved in a disagreement demanded that their rights be recognised and a court be convened 'in order to hear the case' (ἵνα καθιζήσῃ).[5] So the statement in 6:4 refers to the convening of a court to hear a dispute between Christians. Linguistic issues apart, it

---

[1] κριτήριον = 'a legal cause': ἐλάχιστος = 'smallest'. See n.7.

[2] For the most recent discussion see E. Dinkler, 'Zum Problem der Ethik bei Paulus: Rechtsnahme und Rechtsversicht, I Kor. 6,1-11', *ZThK* (1952) 167-200, reprinted in *Signum Crucis: Aufsätze zum Neuen Testament und zur christlichen Archäologie* (Tübingen: J.C.B. Mohr [Paul Siebeck], 1967) 204-240: L. Vischer, *Die Auslegungsgeschichte von 1 Kor. 6.1-11* (Tübingen: J.C.B. Mohr [Paul Siebeck], 1955); D.W.B. Robinson, 'To Submit to the Judgement of the Saints', *TynB* 10 (1962) 1-8: A. Stein, 'Wo trugen die korinthischen Christen ihre Rechtshandel aus?', *ZNW* 59 (1968) 86-90: M. Delcor, 'The Courts of the Church of Corinth and the Courts of Qumran', in J. Murphy-O'Connor (ed.), *Paul and Qumran: Studies in New Testament Exegesis* (London: Geoffrey Chapman, 1968) ch. 4; S. Meurer, *Das Recht im Dienst der Versöhnung und des Friedens: Studien zur Frage der Rechts nach dem Neuen Testament* (Zürich: Theologischer Verlag, 1972) 141-56; R.H. Fuller, 'First Corinthians 6:1-11—An Exegetical Paper', *Ex Auditu* 2 (1986) 96-104; J.D.M. Derrett, 'Judgement and I Corinthians 6', *NTS* 37 (1991) 22–36 and A.J. Mitchell, 'Rich and Poor in the Courts of Corinth: Litigiousness and Status in 1 Corinthians 6.1–11', *NTS* 39 (1993) 562–586.

[3] Stein, 'Wo trugen die korinthischen Christen ihre Rechtshandel aus?', 87-88.

[4] *A Commentary on the First Epistle to the Corinthians* (ET Philadelphia: Fortress, 1975) 105, n. 23.

[5] *The First Epistle to the Corinthians* (Grand Rapids: Eerdmans, 1987) 236. Josephus, *Ant.* 13.75, Dio Cassius, *Roman Histories* 37.27.1 *cf.* LS 'to cause an assembly or court', *i.e.* to institute proceedings.

is extremely unlikely that Christians would have gone for arbitration to a Jewish court which operated under the aegis of the synagogue and was presided over by a Jewish ḥākām, an official one step below a rabbi in status.[6] In Acts 18:12ff. the Jews had already dragged Paul before Gallio seeking to initiate a criminal hearing. The animosity engendered by that unsuccessful attempt and the successful evangelism among Jews made for a lasting break with the synagogue in Corinth, and would have ruled out access to the Jewish arbitration system.

There is important background evidence which explains why Paul condemned Christians who took fellow Christians to civil courts in 1 Corinthians 6:1-11 and thereby further clarifies our understanding of the public place of Christians. The discussion will proceed with an examination of (I) the nature of civil litigation in Roman Corinth, (II) judges and 'the unrighteous', (III) the powerful and 'the unrighteous', (IV) enmity and civil litigation, (V) the *arbiter* and litigation, and (VI) those 'least esteemed in the church'.

I. Civil Litigation in Roman Corinth

In the first century there were specific offences covered by civil as against criminal actions. The former related to claims concerning legal possession, breach of contract, damages, fraud and injury.[7] As the breach of the law in 1 Corinthians 6:2 is described as 'the smallest or trivial cases' (κριτήριον ἐλάχιστον), it is right to regard the actions initiated by a Christian against his fellow believer as coming within the scope of civil and not criminal law.

The right to prosecute was not granted to all. If the defendant was a parent, a patron, a magistrate, or a person of high rank, then charges could not be brought by children, freedmen, private citizens

---

[6]See Dinkler, 'Zum Problem der Ethik bei Paulus', 171-208 on the Jewish official. On the legal problems raised by A. Stein, 'Wo trugen die korinthischen Christen ihre Rechtshandel aus?', 88-89, see the most recent treatment by P. Garnsey, 'The Civil Suit', *Social Status and Legal Privilege in the Roman Empire* (Oxford: Clarendon Press, 1970) Part III.

[7]P. Garnsey, *Social Status and Legal Privilege in the Roman Empire* (Oxford: Clarendon Press, 1970) 181. Criminal cases included high treason, embezzlement of state property, bribery at elections, extortion in the provinces, murder by violence or poisoning, endangering of public security, forgery of wills or coins, violent offences, adultery and seduction of reputable unmarried women. See W. Kunkel, *An Introduction to Roman Legal and Constitutional History* (ed 2; Oxford, Clarendon Press, 1973) 66.

and men of low rank respectively.[8] Generally, lawsuits were conducted between social equals who were from the powerful (οἱ δυνατοί) of the city, or by a plaintiff of superior social status and power against an inferior.[9] The reason for these proscriptions was to avoid (i) insulting the good name of the person concerned or (ii) showing lack of respect for one's patron or superiors. 'Discriminatory rule or discriminatory practices, then, protected members of the higher orders from being taken to law in some circumstances' and 'the evidence shows that a humble prosecutor might be rejected merely because of the quality of his opponent'.[10]

Augustus declared that 'except in capital cases the provincial governor must himself act and judge or appoint a panel of jurors (αὐτὸς διαγεινώσκειν καὶ ἱστάναι ἢ συμβούλιον κριτῶν), but with the rest of such affairs it is my wish that Greek jurors be appointed'.[11] 'In Cyrene, a "province of the Roman people", under Augustus, iudices were normal for all civil suits'.[12] The governor left much of the minor litigation of a province to local municipal courts, for his concern was with matters which related to public order.[13] This would have been no less true in the Roman colony of Corinth. Certainly in the early years of the empire, minor civil actions were left to the local courts and could be tried by judges or juries.[14]

The civil case began in the court of the law officer. In Corinth he was one of two honorary magistrates (duoviri) who were chosen from among leading citizens. The office was undertaken for the year, and among the duties to be performed was the administration of justice.

The plaintiff, when petitioning the magistrate, explained the grounds for the charge, and if there was a case to answer, a private

---

[8]Garnsey, Social Status and Legal Privilege, 182.

[9]J.M. Kelly, Roman Litigation (Oxford: Clarendon Press, 1966) 62ff. Exceptionally, there were cases where a patron took up the cause of his client: see P. Garnsey, Social Status and Legal Privilege, 216 n. 4.

[10]Garnsey, Social Status and Legal Privilege, 187.

[11]SEG IX. 8, IV ll. 67-69 cited by V. Ehrenberg and A.H.M. Jones, Documents Illustrating the Reigns of Augustus and Tiberius (Oxford: Clarendon Press, 1976) No. 311, IV ll. 66-68; D.C. Braund, Augustus to Nero: A Sourcebook on Roman History 31 B.C. - A.D. 68 (London and Sydney: Croom Helm, 1985) No. 543, D; and for discussion see A.H.M. Jones, The Criminal Courts of the Roman Republic and Principate (Oxford: Blackwells, 1972) 98-100.

[12]J. Crook, Law and Life in Rome, 86.

[13]A.N. Sherwin-White, Roman Society and Roman Law in the New Testament (Oxford: Clarendon Press, 1963) 14.

[14]Crook, Law and Life in Rome, 79. See the Lex Irnitana Chs. 86-89 on the iudex, arbiter and recuperatores.

summons was issued requiring the other party to appear in court.[15]
When the parties came to court, the preliminary pleadings were
entered into, and the official declared the parameters within which the
case was to be heard. It could then be tried by a single judge or argued
before a jury which was chosen from among well-to-do citizens.[16] The
task of the magistrate hearing a case in Corinth was to preside, to
inform the court of the verdict and to decide the penalities.

II. Judges and 'the Unrighteous' of 1 Corinthians 6:1

Who were 'the unrighteous' (οἱ ἄδικοι) in v. 1? One solution has been
to equate them with 'the unbelievers' (οἱ ἄπιστοι) in v. 6 and not to
regard the comment in v. 1 as 'a moral judgement'. Paul is not said to
be implying that 'the Corinthian courts were corrupt', nor did he
'intend to demean the Roman courts, to which he himself had recourse
more than once, as if they were corrupt'.[17] Is that judgement correct or
does it refer to 'judges whose judgement is unjust'?[18]

It is suggested that 'the unrighteous' referred to the character of
the judges or the juries who pronounced verdicts in civil cases.

---

[15]At times, compelling an opponent to appear in court could be an extremely difficult task and it was not until the principate of Trajan that penalties were used to
ensure that the accused appeared, Garnsey, *Social Status and Legal Privilege*, 170-1,
193. See *P.Oxy.* 2852 (A.D. 104/5) for a summons and the initiating of a civil action
and 726 (A.D. 135) *ll.* 17-20 where a representative was appointed to make the journey to the assize centre because of illness. The substitute was to represent him
whether the case was heard before the prefect, the *epistrategus*, or 'other judges'
(ἕτεροι κριταί).

[16]Garnsey, *Social Status and Legal Privilege*, 6 and Crook, *Law and Life in Rome*, 78-79.
Dio Cassius, *Roman Histories* 52.7.5, notes that 'when one is accused of committing
a private wrong, one is made a defendant in a private suit before a jury of one's
equals. . .they shall sit in judgement of one'.

[17]Conzelmann, *A Commentary on the First Epistle to the Corinthians*, 104 n. 12 and
Fee, *The First Epistle to the Corinthians*, 232. See also H.H.B. Ayles, 'I Corinthians
VI.1', *ET* 27 (1915-16) 334, 'the prevailing idea of ἄδικος is not of one who acts
unfairly to others, but of one who breaks the law of God', C.K. Barrett, *The First
Epistle to the Corinthians* (London, A. & C. Black, 1971) 135, ἄδικος = 'non-Chris-
tians' and ἅγιος = 'Christians', L. Vischer, *Die Auslegungsgeschichte von 1 Kor. 6.1-
11*, 9, 'Das Wort ist nicht im moralischen Sinne gemeint', R.H. Fuller, 'First Corinthians 6:1-11', 98, 'Neither word ἄδικος nor ἅγιος is intended in a moralizing sense.'
Paul's use of ἀδικέω in conjunction with ἀποστερέω in vv. 7-8 would suggest that
the cognate has a moral sense. Certainly in v. 9 the ἄδικοι are connected with
moral conduct.

[18]Robinson, 'To Submit to the Judgement of the Saints', 3.

Evidence warrants such an adverse evaluation of those engaged in resolving civil actions in the empire. The edict of Augustus of 7-6 B.C. clearly shows that injustices were being perpetrated by the jury-courts in Cyrene. Augustus refers to Roman 'jurors' (οἱ κριταί) who have formed certain 'cliques' (συνωμοσία) and who act oppressively against Greeks on capital charges with the same people (*i.e.* the cliques) taking it in turns to act as prosecutors and witnesses. The emperor states, 'I have learnt that innocent individuals have been oppressed in this way and have been consigned to the ultimate penalty'. The personal knowledge of Augustus suggests the problem of corruption was not confined to Cyrene.[19]

There is other non-literary evidence which confirms that juries could not be relied upon to administer justice impartially. In Egypt a former *exegetes* of the city of Arsinoïtes was taken to court by a money lender who was charging 48% (double the current rate) on a debt. A petition had originally been sent to the prefect of Egypt who passed the case on to a judicial adviser so that it would be heard before a jury. The plaintiff then sent a further petition arguing that the jury would be open to the influence of a person of more senior status and therefore could not act impartially.[20]

An edict of A.D. 111 from the prefect of Egypt, dealing with judicial procedures of a *conventus*, adds further support for the view that there was substantial corruption in the judicial processes. He 'absolutely prohibits the receiving of bribes, not now for the first time forbidding this evil'.[21]

Corinth differs little from elsewhere. Dio Chrysostom records *c.* A.D. 100 that there were in Corinth 'lawyers innumerable perverting justice'.[22] A decade later Favorinus refers to the unjust treatment which he has received at the hands of the leading Corinthian citizens.

---

[19]SEG IX. 8, A *ll.* 11-12. V. Ehrenberg and A.H.M. Jones, *Documents Illustrating the Reigns of Augustus and Tiberius*, 99.

[20]*P.Fouad*. 26 (A.D. 157-159).

[21]*P.Oxy*. 2745 *ll.* 7-8. It is of interest that many of the cases were referred to the friends, φίλοι, of the prefect, *i.e.* his legal advisers who act as judges (κριταί).

[22]*Or*. 8.9. 'to twist' (στρέφειν) was used of a wrestler trying to avoid an adversary and metaphorically of arguments. On the use of the wrestling image for demonstration pieces or declamations see also Philo, *Det*. 41 'they will be exhibiting the prowess of men sparring for practice [declamations], not that of men engaged in real combat [actual debates]'. The young men were declaiming forensic pieces in the courtyard of Poseidon's temple during the Isthmian Games in the hope of securing a case from a plaintiff. For the dating see Jones, *The Roman World of Dio Chrysostom*, 136.

He contrasts that with the actions of their forefathers in pre–Roman days who were themselves 'lovers of justice' (φιλοδίκαιοι) and showed to be 'pre-eminent among the Greeks for cultivating justice' .[23] Those in Roman Corinth were obviously not. Later in the second century, Apuleius inveighs against the Corinthians alleging that 'nowadays all juries sell their judgements for money'.[24]

III. The Powerful and the 'Unrighteous'

The powerful in the city exercised a number of unfair advantages in the judicial system of the first century. These included financial qualificat-ions for jury service, influence over honorary magistrates and judges, and the importance given to social status in weighing judgements.

Jurors were selected from the highest census group of men, whether Romans or Greeks, 'none having a census rating and property (if there is a sufficient number of men) of less than 7,500 *denarii*'.[25] They also had to be over the age of twenty-five. In the time of Claudius one could be exempted if he had a large number of children. In Rome the list of jurors was revised by the emperor and it was said of Claudius that he struck from the list a man of high birth who was a leading citizen of Greece.[26]

In Nero's reign there was a complaint about the influence of a local power. 'We have therefore been robbed on every side by this man, against whom we made petitions and presented reports many in number, which he scorned in virtue of this superior local power'.[27] A prosecutor believes that his case cannot succeed because the defendant 'possesses great local influence through his insolence and violence' and 'he will be unable to oppose him before a jury of this kind (*i.e.* local), for he is very influential'. In the original petition the prosecutor refers to the fact that the defendant, a former *exegetes*, is 'relying on the prestige of his position. . .possessing great local influence'. He is able to cite a previous case heard against the same defendant before a *strate-gus* in which the son of a gymnasiarch instigated proceedings against the same defendant who 'behaved insolently, and the *strategus* made

---

[23]*Or.* 37.16-17. The contrast is between Greek Corinth and Roman Corinth.
[24]*Metamorphoses* or *The Golden Ass* IX.33.
[25]*SEG* IX. 8, A *l.* 18. See also the *Lex Irnitana* ch. 86 where 5,000 sesterces was specified.
[26]Suetonius, *Claudius*, 15.16.2.
[27]*P.Ryl.* 119 (A.D. 54-67).

an entry about him in his memorandum-book'. The fact that, in a former case , the defendant cites a person of status, the son of a gymnasiarch, demonstrated that the jury could not be trusted to be impartial in the face of the powerful. This accounts for the attempt of the prosecutor to have the case heard by the prefect and not a jury.[28]

Seneca's case of a rich and powerful man daring a poor man to institute proceedings provides an apt illustration of the problem which the powerful created in the judicial processes. 'Why don't you accuse me, why don't you take me to court?' was his taunt, and Seneca comments, 'This rich man was powerful and influential, as not even he denies, and thought he never had anything to fear, even as a defendant'. The poor man's response epitomizes the reality, 'Am I, a poor man, to accuse a rich man?' The rich man all but exclaimed, 'What would I not be ready to do to you if you impeached me, I who saw to the death of a man who merely engaged in litigation with me?'[29]

Even the veracity of a witness was determined by his status and wealth. Juvenal was to complain

> At Rome you may produce a witness as unimpeachable as the host of the Isaean Goddess...the first question asked will be about his wealth, the last about his character: 'how many slaves does he keep? how many acres does he own?'...A man's word is believed to be in exact proportion to the amount of cash he keeps in his strong–box'.[30]

Another unjust influence on the outcome of judicial decisions was the payment of bribes. The edict of A.D. 111, cited above, deals with judicial procedures of a *conventus* and adds further support to the view that there was substantial corruption in the judicial process. The prefect 'absolutely prohibits the receiving of bribes, not now for the first time forbidding this evil'.[31] The jury in civil litigation could be bribed to return a 'guilty' or a 'not guilty' verdict.[32] This may have been the reason why some had a passion for jury service.[33]

Finally, the relative importance of the social status of the prosecutor and the defendant was considered by the magistrate who

---

[28]*P.Fouad.* 26 *ll.* 21-24.
[29]Seneca, *Controversiae* 10.1.2 and 7.
[30]Juvenal, *Satire* III.136-44.
[31]*P.Oxy.* 2745 *ll.* 7-8. On the similar problem of the bribery of juries in Greece, see E.S. Staveley, *Greek and Roman Voting and Elections* (London: Thames and Hudson, 1972) 108ff.
[32]Garnsey, *Social Status and Legal Privilege,* 4 and 199ff.
[33]Suetonius, *Claudius* 15.1.

undertook to see that the law was administered.[34] He decided whether or not to carry out the sentence and fixed the fine. Social status and legal privilege were clearly connected in the Roman empire.[35]

There were, of course, exceptions and the very recording of one such case in an unknown town near Spinx, Egypt proves the rule. The city fathers expressed their gratitude for having been blessed with an honest *strategus* and specifically mention that 'in his judgements he always dispenses justice correctly and without bribery' (δίκαιος καθαρῶς καὶ ἀδρωροδοκήτως).[36]

Cicero's observation of his own day also sums up the problems with litigation in the civic courts in the East. He declared that there were three major hindrances in civil litigation: 'excessive favour' (*gratia*), 'possession of resources' (*potentia*) and 'bribery' (*pecunia*).[37] 'The unrighteous' were susceptible to all these pressures.

IV. Enmity and Civil Litigation

Litigation caused personal enmity and litigation was used to aggravate personal enmity.[38] The proceedings were not conducted dispassionately by the parties but with great acrimony.

> What the Romans called *reprehensio vitae* or *vituperatio*—a personal attack on the character of one's opponents—was taken as absolutely normal; and manuals of rhetoric dealt in great detail with the most effective ways to construct a *vituperatio*. . .[it] was the rule also in ordinary civil cases.[39]

What has been observed of Roman Greek litigation had been no less true in the Hellenistic period .[40]

---

[34]Crook, *Law and Life in Rome*, 74.

[35]Garnsey, *Social Status and Legal Privilege*, 4.

[36]*SEG* VIII 527 (A.D. 22-23) *ll.* 9-10.

[37]Cicero, *Pro Caecina* 73.

[38]'Litigation as a Source of *inimicitia*' and 'Litigation as a Manifestation of *inimicitia*', Epstein, *Personal Enmity in Roman Politics*, 90-100. *Cf.* Dio in his Alexandrian oration where he portrays the character of the first-century judicial scene in the East with 'a multitude of quarrels and lawsuits, harsh cries, tongues that are mischievous and unrestrained, accusers, calumnies, writs, a hoard of professional pleaders [forensic orators]', *Or.* 32.19.

[39]J.M. Kelly, *Studies in the Civil Judicature of the Roman Republic* (Oxford: Clarendon Press, 1976) 98-9.

The prosecutor, with his hostile speeches and the damaging evidence of his witnesses, caused great personal resentment with loss of dignity for the defendant. No areas were immune from ferocious attacks. 'The advocate. . .was permitted to use the most unbridled language about his client's adversary, or even his friends or relations or witnesses.'[41] No rules of evidence guarded against this, and defendants were subjected to muck-raking and fabrication. This lack of legal restraint helps to explain why prosecutor and defendant could so rarely avoid lasting animosity.[42] It could also be the motivation for instituting legal proceedings.[43]

Furthermore, young men were keen to display their talents as orators by taking well-known citizens to court.[44] They were greatly admired for successful prosecutions because such success meant that they were undeterred by the enduring enmity which that created. This enmity was not restricted to the prosecutor, but included the presiding honorary magistrate, the witnesses and even jury members. All could be the objects of the defendant's fury.[45] Cicero notes that jurors 'consider the man they have condemned to be their *inimicus* [enemy]'.[46]

Was the enmity evident in the Corinthian church caused by civil litigation or was litigation used to express publicly personal or household enmity in 1 Corinthians 6?[47] It is clear that it had developed in the church because of personal loyalty to Christian teachers. This 'strife and jealousy' arising out of the issue of Christian leadership is also

---

[40]J.W. Jones, *The Law and Legal Theory of the Greeks* (Oxford: OUP, 1956) 151, comments on 'bitter wrangling rather than calm judicial inquiry'.

[41]Jones, *The Law and Legal Theory of the Greeks*, 98.

[42]Epstein, *Personal Enmity in Roman Politics*, 91. See also Kelly, *Studies in the Civil Judicature of the Roman Republic*, 102. 'In Quintilian's manual on rhetoric. . .we are expressly told that the beginning of a court speech should contain a consideration of the persons involved: and this must involve blackening (*infamandam*) the person on the other side'.

[43]In Roman society, enmity 'could be the major impetus of a trial', D.F. Epstein, *Personal Enmity in Roman Politics*, 102 -103.

[44]Epstein, *Personal Enmity in Roman Politics*, 90.

[45]Epstein, *Personal Enmity in Roman Politics*, 90.

[46]Cicero, *pro Cluentio* 116; D.F. Epstein, *Personal Enmity in Roman Politics*, 95.

[47]Marshall's important work *Enmity in Corinth*, ignores 1 Cor. 6 although that passage fits well into his *hubristic* thesis and shows that the attitudes and actions of those who were 'wise in this world' were not only reserved for the apostle. L.L. Welborn, 'On the Discord in Corinth: 1 Corinthians 1-4 and Ancient Politics', *JBL* 106 (1987) 85-111, whose starting point is politics rather than the model of sophistic leadership as it related to μαθηταί in παιδεία, also ignores 1 Cor. 6 where his suggestion has most relevance.

expressed in litigation with one of the leading Christians taking another leading Christian to court. If in 1 Corinthians 3:1-4 'strife' (ἔρις) and 'jealousy' (ζῆλος) were signs of an 'immature person' (σαρκικός) and that they were 'walking in a secular fashion' (κατὰ ἄνθρωπον περιπατεῖν), as sophists and their μαθηταί did in Corinth,[48] then the litigation of 1 Corinthians 6 was a reflection of the same problem, but manifested this time in the secular courts rather than the Christian congregation.[49]

It should be remembered that if some had already successfully prosecuted fellow Christians, then the person who won the action would have been awarded financial compensation. This would have only aggravated the problem of strife within the Christian community as the contestants would then appear in church together. If the jury took sides, then would not the members of the church be tempted to do the same? Whether one lost or won, the effect could only be harmful to relationships in the congregation.

V. The *Arbiter* and Litigation

'Is there no wise man among you who is able to judge?' (v. 5). Is Paul's question full of irony?[50] There were wise men 'according to this age' who were members of the congregation (1 Cor. 1:20, 26; 3.18). Their secular education consisted not only of intensive instruction in literature but also of training in oratory, including forensic skills. They engaged in declamation pieces before their fellow pupils and were also taught to evaluate court cases.[51] Reference has already been made to the desire of young men—those under twenty-five who were not eligible to enter into debates in the official meeting of citizens (ἐκκλησία)—to practice their forensic abilities after completing their formal training by initiating a court action. Is Paul making a reference to them?

---

[48]For evidence see my *Philo and Paul among the Sophists: a Hellenistic Jewish and a Christian Response* 177-195.

[49]The basis for this argument is the established nexus between the various branches of oratory, in particular declamation and forensic oratory, at the highest level of παιδεία and therefore in the life of secular Corinth. For a general discussion see M.L. Clarke, *Higher Education in the Ancient World* (London: Routledge & Kegan Paul, 1971) 39ff.

[50]It is 'biting sarcasm' according to Fee, *The First Epistle to the Corinthians*, 237, where he argues for Paul's use of irony is seen in the series of questions in this passage.

Provision existed in Greek, Roman and Jewish legal systems for the use of arbitrators who acted in a legal capacity with the agreement of the defendant and the plaintiff.[52] Why had some in the church not used their gifts and training in a profitable way by acting in an extra-judicial capacity as an arbitrator, *i.e. arbiter ex compromisso*?[53] Christians who were wise were 'capable' (δύνασθαι) of actually applying the fruits of their secular education in disputes which could normally be settled by a civil action. Paul's question in v. 2, 'Are you not competent to judge a minor case?' may be a reference to such people. Those who boasted of their secular wisdom and who had clearly been the source of disaffection particularly against Paul, had dissipated their energies in the wrong direction creating havoc and disunity within the church.[54] They could have helped settle minor legal disputes. Paul's preference is that they do not engage in such disputes among themselves,[55] but rather be prepared to suffer wrong even from other Christians (v. 7).

VI. Those Least Esteemed 'in the Church'

Is the comment concerning those 'least esteemed' another case of Paul's use of irony or does it refer to Christian Jews as 'competent

---

[51]For a good example of a handbook of legal cases prepared for pupils by Quintilian, see A. Winterbottom, *Declamationes pseudo-Quintilianeae: Declamationes minores* (Berlin and New York: de Gruyter, 1984). It was used by English pupils of the seventeenth century: see J. Taylor, *The Minor Declamations of Quintilian: Being an Excitation or Praxis upon his XII Books, Concerning the Institution of the Orator* (London, 1686).

[52]See P.J. Rhodes, 'Political Activity in Classical Athens', *JHS* 106 (1986) 137 and Crook, *Law and Life in Rome*, 78-79, for the Roman period. For Judaism, see Fuller, 'Judicial Practices in Judaism', 103-4 and Delcor, 'The Courts of the Church of Corinth and the Courts of Qumran', ch. 4.

[53]Crook, *Law and Life in Rome*, 78-79 citing as an example the Herculaneum Tablets where a person was to be 'arbitrator by agreement' between X and Y and was 'to give a decision'. See also the *Lex Irnitana* ch. 86 where the parties by agreement could also have access to an *arbiter* who was appointed on an annual basis.

[54]*Contra* Robinson, 'To Submit to the Judgement of the Saints', 4ff., where he suggests that the Jewish Christians had the right to act as judges in the congregation because they were 'the saints', *i.e.* the faithful Jews who had the scriptures.

[55]His instructions cannot be construed to mean that he was setting up a quasi-permanent court parallel to the Jewish ones. *Contra* Delcor, 'The Courts of the Church of Corinth and the Courts of Qumran', 71, although he is careful to argue that similarity does not imply dependence.

judges in the church who have been ignored and despised by those whom Paul is addressing'?[56] In 1 Corinthians 1:26ff. Paul has dealt with the way in which those 'least esteemed' in society (v. 28), had been chosen by God.[57] In the on-going discussion in 4:6ff. Paul uses with great irony the technique of 'covert allusion', deliberately applying the high-status terms to the Corinthian Christians.[58] The low-status term of a person who is 'least esteemed' is then applied to himself as an apostle of the crucified and humiliated Messiah who has been called to follow in his steps. He summoned the Corinthians not to imitate their teachers in the way secular followers of their sophist did, but to follow him in his non-status position. The comment in 1 Corinthians 6 about those least esteemed in the ἐκκλησία should be seen as a continuation of Paul's use of irony, and not as a reference to Jewish Christian teachers.

Does Paul's question concerning those 'least esteemed' reflect the Corinthians' attitude or his own? At least some, if not all, Corinthian Christians were conscious of the importance of secular status. This status would express itself in the activities of the secular ἐκκλησία of Corinth, and was epitomized by facility in rhetoric. The boasting which Paul confronts in 1 Corinthians 1–5 appears also to have spilt over into the issue of the successful litigant scoring a victory. It does not seem that the Corinthian Christians felt a sense of disgust at the way in which the local legal system operated. On the contrary, they endorsed it by taking cases to it. The question reflects Paul's concept of status in the Christian ἐκκλησία as against the city's ἐκκλησία. For him, those who had status by reason of their birth, wealth and position in the latter context did not thereby gain any special status in the Christian ἐκκλησία. He had already stressed that what men are in Christ gives them status (1:30). Paul indicates that the social class from which secular Corinthian judges and juries were drawn had no status *per se* within the actual meeting of the Christian assembly (*cf.* 5:4). Christians needed to be reminded of that reality, hence his description of the judges and juries as 'those least esteemed in the [Christian] ἐκκλησία'.[59]

---

[56]Robinson, 'To Submit to the Judgement of the Saints', 6.

[57]Paul uses the same verb, ἐξουθενεῖν in 1:28 and 6:4. For comments on the sophists' use of a similar *syncrisis* see Philo, *Det.* 32-34 and my discussion *Philo and Paul among the Sophists*, 104ff.

[58]B. Fiori, ' "Covert Allusion" in 1 Corinthians 1-4', *CBQ* 47 (1985) 85-102. See further the discussion in *Philo and Paul among the Sophists*, 206ff., which shows how Paul deliberately negates the covertness of that rhetorical device.

The issue of status also lies behind the comment 'To have lawsuits at all is a defeat for you. . . You do wrong, you defraud and that [action against] brothers (τοῦτο ἀδελφούς)' (vv. 7-8).[60] The action of taking a brother to court which may have resulted in a successful prosecution was seen by Paul as a defeat. Why is this? The decision to institute proceedings was determined by the social status of the one against whom the initiator of litigation proposed to proceed. The plaintiff had to take into account the enmity arising from the actual court proceedings, or he might wish to express his existing personal enmity by means of civil litigation. The awarding of financial damages as an additional penalty may well have been what Paul had in mind when he wrote of 'defrauding' a brother. The initiating of legal proceedings against a brother was thus seen as a sign of defeat in relationships long before the verdict was pronounced in court.[61]

VII. Conclusions

Paul's condemnation of Christians appearing before 'judges' or 'juries' (κριταί) who were patently unjust in the way they arrived at judicial decisions is explicable, given the difficulties of civil litigation in the first century.

It has also become clear that the strife and jealousy over teachers in 1 Corinthians 1:11ff. had spilt over into the area of seemingly minor disputes which were being settled by civil action. The power struggle in the church was not restricted to 1 Corinthians 1-4. Enmity in the *politeia* characterized those relationships in the secular ἐκκλησία in Corinth which were not based on 'the politics of friendship'. Those in the 'church of God' (ἐκκλησία τοῦ θεοῦ) who belonged to the class of

---

[59]In this passage Paul uses the term ἐκκλησία to mean the actual gathering of Christians in the same way as it was used to refer to a recognised gathering in the secular world, *cf.* Acts 19:39.

[60]The place of τοῦτο ἀδελφούς in the whole sentence lays stress on the Christian status of the defendant. Fee, *The First Epistle to the Corinthians*, 239, n. 4 believes that the use of τοῦτο combines the wronging and cheating. The continuative use of the single neuter demonstrative pronoun which points to a previous action suggests that the reference is to a single act of wronging.

[61]For an interesting example of Christians resolving a claim and counter-claim involving a large sum of money and garments in A.D. 481, see H.B. Dewing, 'A *Dialysis* of the Fifth Century A.D. in the Princeton Collection of Papyri', *AJP* 53 (1922) 113-127. They signed a *dialysis*, which was a legal contract recording the settlement between a bishop and two presbyters and a deacon.

the wise, the powerful and the well-born allowed that secular phenomenon to surface in their dealings with one another, especially in the area of civil law.[62]

In presenting his argument, Paul not only referred to the important issue of the future rôle of the saints in judging the world. He also asked ironically about 'the wise man in your midst' and those 'least esteemed'. The former was clearly represented in the Christian community by the 'wise among you in this age' (3.18). The latter group was readily recognised in the city of Corinth in stark contrast to those 'most esteemed' in the secular 'Council' (βουλή) and the city's official gathering of citizens (ἐκκλησία). Those most esteemed in Corinthian society had no special standing in the Pauline doctrine of the church by reason of that secular status cf. 1 Corinthians 1:26ff.

Paradoxically, the Corinthian church had judged the outsider in politeia when they had no right to do so (5:12) but failed dismally to judge the insider when they should have done so (5:13). On the other hand, they had allowed the unrighteous outsiders to judge the insiders (6:1) when they should have resorted to the use of a fellow Christian from their number who, by reason of his legal training,[63] would have had the requisite qualifications to act as a private arbitrator.

The difference in attitude on the part of Paul between 1 Corinthians 6:1-8 and Romans 13:1-7 is clear.[64] In the latter he discusses the attitude of the Christian citizen and the legitimacy of criminal procedures because of the divine imperium held by government. Civil litigation in Corinth came within the purview of the local honorary magistrates. They acted as judges or appointed them and the juries, who comprised the well-to-do in that city. They could not be trusted to resolve matters solely on the grounds of civil law.[65]

The exclusive commitment to various Christian teachers was a not unusual secular response by 'followers' in Corinth.[66] The working out of enmity between the élite members of the community in the

---

[62]Cf. 1 Cor. 3:4, κατὰ ἄνθρωπον περιπατεῖν.

[63]See my 'Philo and Paul among the Sophists', 209.

[64]E. Käsemann, Commentary on Romans, 345-357, 'From an apocalyptic standpoint secular courts, thus political authorities, are disparaged and rejected when it is a matter of settling disputes within the community.'

[65]Contra A. Robertson and A. Plummer, A Critical and Exegetical Commentary of the First Epistle of St Paul to the Corinthians (Edinburgh: T. & T. Clark, 1914) 110, who suggested that a 'fair, if rough summary' of Paul's teaching in the two passages was 'obey the criminal courts, but do not go out of your way to invoke the civil courts'. However, Paul forbids the use of the latter.

[66]See my Philo and Paul among the Sophists, ch. 8.

public place in this Roman colony was also perfectly acceptable in society.[67] Epstein observes of the peculiar rôle played by enmity.

> Roman society was unusual in allowing *inimicitiae* to compete along with other more conventional values such as patriotism and humanity in guiding a public figure's conduct. A reputation for successfully pursuing *inimicitiae* was a vital asset to a Roman politician seeking to establish and maintain an influential voice.[68]

1 Corinthians 6:1-8 then reflects a typical, first-century struggle for power among the élite.[69] This time it was not one arising out of a dispute between citizens who were politically active in the city's gathering (ἐκκλησία) or some local association but from within the Christian gathering (ἐκκλησία). What they had in common with the public arena in which such clashes occurred was that their struggle was also between the élite who were social equals or near equals. The contest which had surfaced in jealousy and rivalry between factions in the Christian meeting had also spilt over into in the secular courts of Corinth in civil actions.

The presence of Christians in civil courts taking actions against fellow members of their 'association' was prohibited. Their conduct had nothing to do with benefactions or gospel concerns. It was simply a spill-over of divisive behaviour from the Christian ἐκκλησία into the civil courts which were regarded as a legitimate sphere in struggles for primacy in *politeia*.[70] Relationships were tense because in the syndrome litigation that prevailed in Corinth, Christians had not abandoned the use in order to gain primacy in their particular association. It is therefore right to argue that the problems Paul faces in 1 Corinthians over strife and jealousy must not be restricted to the first

---

[67]For a discussion of this group in the church see Clarke, *Secular and Christian Leadership in Corinth*, ch. 5 and D.W.J. Gill, 'Acts and Urban Élites', *The Book of Acts in its Graeco Roman Setting*, ch. 5.

[68]Epstein, *Personal Enmity in Roman Politics*, 127. It is interesting that Martial, Epigrams X, 47 declared that one of the things that made life enjoyable was 'no lawsuits'.

[69]For a critique of Mitchell, 'Rich and Poor in the Courts of Corinth' who argues that rich Christians were taking poor Christians to court see my 'Civil Litigation in Secular Corinth and the Church: The Forensic Background to 1 Corinthians 6:1–8', in B. Rosner (ed.), *Understanding Paul's Ethics: Twentieth Century Approaches* (Grand Rapids: Eerdmans, forthcoming 1995) 101–3.

[70]Jones, *The Roman World of Dio Chrysostom*, 99, notes that local politics 'were not conducted only in the council and assembly, but spilled over into another area of public life, the courts'.

four chapters of the letter, as traditional exegesis has often done.[71] In this Roman colony the nature of society was such that those who belonged to its upper echelons were given over to seeking primacy in *politeia* by using vexatious litigation as an acceptable means of doing so. Rajak and Noy have noted that in the proliferation of associations in Graeco–Roman cities there was 'a tendancy to replicate in miniature the organization and government of the cities themselves. Not only names and methods are transferable, however, but, more importantly, an ethos'.[72] This was certainly true in Corinth where there was the inherent danger of importing the litigatious spirit of the world of *politeia* into the Christian association—a major term from the world of *politeia*, ἐκκλησία, had such currency in their midst.[73] Christians had no problems adopting the ethos of *politeia* at this point, for this was how leading citizens had operated in the secular ἐκκλησία for generations. Christians sadly did 'undertake everything as citizens' in this area of *politeia*.

---

[71]See the discussion of the struggle over the leadership issue which goes beyond 1 Cor. 1-4 in Clarke, *Secular and Christian Leadership in Corinth*.

[72]T. Rajak and D. Noy, 'Archisynagogoi: Office, Title and Status in the Graeco–Roman Synagogue' 89.

[73]See my discussion of this point in 'The Problem with "Church" for the Early Church' *In the Fullness of Time: Biblical Studies* 205ff. and the recent comment of Meeks, *The Origins of Christian Morality*, 45. 'It is remarkable that the Christians. . .did seize on the term [ἐκκλησία] that had been adopted by the Bible translators for the sacral assembly of Israel and applied it to themselves. . .[and] was the preferred self–designation of Christian groups in the cities of the Roman provinces'.

CHAPTER SEVEN

CIVIC OBLIGATIONS

Galatians 6:11–18

Roman citizens living in the Provinces had a civic obligation to worship 'the Divine Julius (*Divus Iulius*) and Roma', while ordinary provincials were committed to the worship of 'Augustus and Roma'.[1] Given this fact, one of the enigmatic features of early Christianity in the Julio–Claudian period is the apparent absence of any interaction with the imperial cult.[2] However, from the very beginning of the empire this religious phenomenon grew more spectacularly than did the Christian movement in its first century. 'The diffusion of the cult of Augustus and of other members of his family in Asia Minor and throughout the Greek East from the beginning of the empire was rapid, indeed almost instantaneous.'[3] How this came about and the particular consequences of this civic obligation for early Christians will be explored in this chapter.

Contrary to a common perception in New Testament studies, the imperial cult had been firmly established at both local and provincial levels before Christ's birth and continued to expand during the first wave of Christian missionary activity. From Augustus onwards, veneration was not restricted to deceased emperors, but included reigning ones and living members of their family. The central place of the imperial cult in *politeia* created an enormous problem for early Christians because they were part of *politeia*.

The purpose of this chapter is (I) to rehearse the evidence for, and nature of, the imperial cult, (II) to examine Christian teaching concerning the worship of imperial figures who were 'gods. . .on the earth' (1 Cor. 8:4–6) and (III) to explore the responses by Christians to the civic obligation of imperial veneration, especially in the province of Galatia where local Christians took evasive action in order to overcome this requirement for members of their community.[4]

---

[1] Dio Cassius 51.20.6-7.

[2] Christianity's confrontation with the cult has been recorded in apocalyptic language at the time of the writing of the Book of the Revelation presumably in the Principate of Domitian. For example see S.R.F. Price, *Rituals and Power: The Imperial Cult and Asia Minor* (Cambridge: CUP, 1984[2]) 196-8 for a succinct discussion of the cult and its clash with Christianity in Rev. 13. For an important refutation of any wholesale persecution of Christians in that period based on the limited extant evidence see the biography of Domitian by B.W. Jones, *The Emperor Domitian* (London and New York: Routledge, 1992) 114-7.

[3] S. Mitchell, *Anatolia: Land, Men, and Gods in Asia Minor* (Clarendon: Oxford, 1993) I. 100.

[4] I am grateful to Dr. Walter Hansen for drawing my attention to literary conventions concerning Gal. 6:11ff. Professor Paul Trebilco also made a number of helpful observations which have enhanced the argument.

I. The Presence and Nature of the Imperial Cult

Nicholaus of Damascus, a contemporary witness, said of Augustus

> because men call him by this name[5] as a mark of esteem for his hon-
> our, they revere him with temples and sacrifices, organised by islands
> and continents, and as cities and provinces they match the greatness
> of his virtue and the scale of his benefactions to them.[6]

In the major provinces where a Christian presence had been
established in the Claudian principate, the imperial cult had long
existed. As visitors approached the gateway to Judaea through the
harbour of Caesarea Maritima they were confronted with the
enormous temple to Augustus and Roma which had been built by
Herod the Great before the birth of Christ.[7]

Some seventy years before the arrival of Christianity the provincial imperial cult for Augustus and Roma was founded in the Roman
province of Galatia in 25 B.C.[8] Its grow was rapid and Galatia provides
'much the most detailed evidence for the spread of emperor worship
in the central Anatolian provinces.'[9] On one of the three important
excavation sites in Galatia a major imperial temple which dated from
the middle to late Augustan period has been uncovered. This is in the
Roman colony of Pisidian Antioch where a Christian community
existed. A cult site also existed in another Christian centre, Iconium,
which had its own priest for Tiberius.[10]

In the Province of Asia, the imperial cult and temple in
Aphrodisias were established at the time of the formal deification of
Augustus in A.D. 14, having been preceded there by the cult of *Thea
Roma* from the second half of the first century B.C.[11]

The imperial cult also existed in the province of Achaea. In
Corinth there was the veneration of Julius Caesar who had authorized

---

[5]In 27 B.C. Octavian took the name 'Augustus' = Σεβαστός meaning 'reverenced',
'august' with its strong religious overtones.

[6]*F.Gr.* 90 F 125.1.

[7]D. Fishwick, *The Imperial Cult in the Latin West* (Leiden: E.J. Brill, 1987-1992) I.1 and
II.2, 129, 147, 521.

[8]S.J. Friesen, *Twice Neokoros: Ephesus, Asia and the Cult of the Flavian Imperial Family*
(Leiden: E.J. Brill, 1993) 27.

[9]See S. Mitchell, 'The Imperial Cult', *Anatolia: Land, Men, and Gods in Asia Minor*,
(Oxford: Clarendon Press 1993) 1, ch. 8, esp. 100, 102.

[10]Mitchell, *Anatolia*, I. 104. See A.N. Sherwin–White, *The Roman Citizenship* (ed 2;
Oxford: Clarendon Press, 1973) 403 on the importance the cult of Augustus and
Roma assumed in this period.

its founding as a Roman colony.[12] A statue, possibly of the deified
Julius Caesar, has been located.[13] The temple of Octavia which was the
site of the imperial cult in Corinth was dedicated to the sister of
Augustus who was also deified in Athens.[14] A provincial imperial cult
for member cities of the Achaean league was established in Corinth c.
A.D. 54, soon after the arrival of Christianity. This would have had an
annual imperial festival accompanied by wild beast shows.[15] The first
high-priest of the provincial, in contrast to the local, imperial cult was
the great benefactor of Corinth, C. Julius Spartiaticus whose title indicates that he was the priest of deified (deceased) and living members of
the imperial house (*domus divina*).[16] This was 'an elastic term that
included all the members of the Imperial house'[17] The forerunner to
the provincial cult was the celebration of imperial festivals on the
accession of Gauis and Claudius by the Panachaean assembly.[18] From
the very beginning of the century, a Roman official, P. Cornelius Scipio,
had sought to promote the cult in Messene and other provincial
cities.[19]

It is popularly believed that in the early stages of the Julio–
Claudian era, the imperial cult venerated only the deceased emperor.
There was, however, the deification of Julius Caesar in his life time.[20]
Living members of the imperial family also received veneration in the

---

[11]J.M. Reynolds, 'The Origins and Beginnings of the Imperial Cult in Aphrodisias',
Proceedings of the Philological Society 206 (1980) 70-82, 'New Evidence for the Imperial Cult in Julio-Claudian Aphrodisias,' *ZPE* 43 (1981) 317-27, and 'Further
Information on Imperial Cult at Aphrodisias', *St. Cl.* 24 (1986) 109-117. R. Mellor,
ΘΕΑ ΡΩΜΗ: The Worship of the Goddess Roma in the Greek World, Hypomnemata 42
(Göttingen: Vandenhoeck & Ruprecht, 1975).
[12] '[sacred] to the deified Julius Caesar', J.H. Kent, *Corinth*, 8.3. No. 50.
[13]This is in the Museum of the American School of Archaeology in Corinth.
[14]The second-century traveller to Corinth, Pausanius recorded 'above the market
place is a temple of Octavia the sister of Augustus', 2.3.1. The question of the use
of the 'Octavian' temple in Corinth for the imperial cult has been re-opened for discussion by M. Wallbank, 'Pausanias, Octavia, Temple E', *Annual of the British School
at Athens* 84 (1989) 361–94. For Octavia's deification in Athens see A.E. Raubitschek, 'Octavia's Deification at Athens', *TAPA* 77 (1946) 146-50.
[15]A. Spawforth, 'Corinth, Argos, and the Imperial Cult: A Reconsideration of
Psuedo–Julian, *Letters* 198', *Hesperia* 63.2 (1994) 211–32.
[16]For a discussion of the inscription in West, *Corinth*, 8.2. No. 68 *archieri domus Aug.
[in] perpetuum, primo Achaeon* 'high-priest for life of the Augustan house, the first of
the Achaeans to hold this office', *ll.* 8-9 see Spawforth, 'Corinth, Argos, and the
Imperial Cult', # V.
[17]Fishwick, *The Imperial Cult,* II, 425 and 422 for discussion of the term.
[18]Spawforth, 'Corinth, Argos, and the Imperial Cult'.
[19]*SEG* XXIII. 206 cited by Fishwick, *The Imperial Cult*, I. 514.

early empire. In the province of Galatia there was an imperial sanctuary in Apollonia with the text of the *Res Gestae* and statues of the divine Augustus, Julia Augusta, Tiberius, Germanicus and Drusus. It is known that these were set up during the Principate of Tiberius between A.D. 14 and 19. While it has been thought that Tiberius shunned the imperial cult, Mitchell plots something of its development in Galatia during his principate through a leading provincial family. Its members undertook two embassies to Augustus in Rome and another to Germanicus when he himself was in the East *c.* A.D. 18–19. Mitchell suggests that as a result of such meetings the cult of Rome, with its republican origins and the worship of the imperial family, was further cemented.[21] Such an expansion of the cult in Galatia received the endorsement of Rome both in the time of Augustus and Tiberius.

In major centres in Galatia the first building of the Romanizing presence was that of the imperial temple. It was not simply added to an existing temple dedicated to the local pantheon but was located at the very centre of the new Augustan cities.[22] This location epitomises the place the imperial cult occupied in the minds of the provincials, uniting *politeia* with religious veneration. The imperial temples at the three major sites in Galatia have been excavated.

> [The temples] are the best evidence for the purely physical impact that emperor worship had on provincial cities; they also evoke patterns of public life and religious activity which are more fully defined by documentary evidence. Inscriptions associated with the imperial cult show the changes brought to society.[23]

In addition, the list of extant priests of Tiberius in Galatia reveals the imperial connection with its leading families and the extensive nature of the benefactions. The latter included banquets and gladiatorial spectacles, wild beast shows, athletic, horse and chariot races, and also grain distributions. Tacitus recorded of imperial priests in Britain that they poured out their entire fortunes under the guise of maintaining the imperial cult,[24] may also have been true of those in Galatia.[25]

---

[20]Fishwick, 'Divus Iulius' *The Imperial Cult* I.a, ch. 6 traces the deification of Julius Caesar in his lifetime.
[21]Mitchell, *Anatolia*, I. 104.
[22]Mitchell, *Anatolia*, I. 107.
[23]Mitchell, *Anatolia*, I. 107.
[24]Tacitus, *Ann.* 14.31.
[25]For a helpful discussion of this point together with a list of priests and their benefactions see Mitchell, *Anatolia*, I. 107–112.

The priests of Tiberius, by means of benefactions, expressed the nexus between the cult and civic institutions. The wealthy fulfilled their civic obligations in Galatia in part by undertaking an annual public office but also by carrying out the functions of priests of the imperial cult.

The deification of the living grandmother of Claudius dates from A.D. 18 when a coin was struck designating her 'goddess Antonia' (θεὰ 'Αντωνία), and divinity was also ascribed to her and to Gaius while they were alive.[26] The connection of her veneration to the wider imperial cult is recorded c. A.D. 18 in 'a group portrait inscription' to Rome and Augustus, Tiberius, Julia Augusta, Antonia and Agrippina.[27] A cult was established to her during her life time at Ilium (c. A.D. 18), and at Athens, the place of her conception (A.D. 18-37).[28] She was seen to personify various goddesses, and was specifically linked to *Venus Genetrix*. This reflects the popular perception of her as 'the mother of the Imperial *gens*', and 'presumably metaphorically [as] "the mother of Rome"'.[29] In the Principate of Claudius there was renewed interest in Aphrodite and a marble statue of Antonia in the form of Venus (Aphrodite) has been found.[30] Some eleven members of the imperial family received priesthoods.[31]

Why did the cult establish itself as it did? Its central rôle in Galatia related to the fact that, just as with Britain, the introduction and propagation of the cult came at a time of integration into the empire. The Celts found a new identity with the civilising influence of Rome. Added to this, there was the dominant influence in Galatia of those with Roman origins. They were keen to replicate in this outpost of empire, 'things Roman'.

> This was one reason why the cult became central in the minds of its citizens. Emperor worship was not a political subterfuge, designed to elicit the loyalty of untutored provincials, but was one of the ways in which Romans themselves and provincials alongside them defined their own relationship with a new political phenomenon, an emperor whose powers and charisma were so transcendent that he appeared to them as both man and god.[32]

---

[26]*E.g.* Gaius *IGR* iv 145 and his living grandmother, Antonia Augusta as θεὰ Αντ-ωνία *IK* 3, no. 88.

[27]N. Kokkinos, *Antonia Augusta: Portrait of a Great Lady* (London: Routledge, 1992) 45, 110.

[28]Kokkinos, *Antonia Augusta*, 158.

[29]Kokkinos, *Antonia Augusta*, 162.

[30]Kokkinos, *Antonia Augusta*, 115ff.

[31]Price, *Rituals and Power*, 57.

In the cities it achieved 'rapid, indeed almost instantaneous' growth at a local level.[33] For a substantial fee freedmen could secure the prized liturgy of priests of Augustus by holding the office of *serviratus Augustalis*. It had been established as a means of securing the loyalty of wealthy freedmen by appealing to their ambition to secure their place in Roman society. It meant that, as former slaves in Roman households who were manumitted, they obtained not only Roman citizenship as freedmen, but also the honour of becoming priests of Augustus.[34] With the active involvement of free men and freedmen, the cult quickly took hold.

In addition, in Narbonne (Narbo) in Gaul, the inscription on the altar specifies that three *equites* and three freedmen were each to sacrifice an animal twice a year and provide incense and wine for 'the colonists and residents' four times a year in connection with the cult. The liturgy could not be held consecutively by the same families which meant that direct involvement in the imperial cult quickly grew, as a different families participated over a period of time in this office.[35] This inscription also records that veneration was undertaken on 24th September (possibly part of the New Year celebrations which began the previous day on the birthday of Augustus),[36] 1st and 7th January, and 31st May—'worship of the Roman emperor was based on an official calendar applicable with local variations throughout the empire and a variable date of the *natalis* of the reigning emperor.'[37] Because it involved 'the colonists' (Roman citizens) and the residents, leading families and provincials were thus drawn into this aspect of the Romanising processes of Galatia.

What was actually involved in imperial veneration? P. Cornelius Scipio directed that 'sacrifices be offered in cities of the provinces and crowns worn for the ceremony'.[38] Incense was burnt with obeisance before a statue of the imperial figure. The cult was often observed by colourful processions carrying candles and torches as the images were carried from the imperial temple by the 'imperial priests'

---

[32]Mitchell, *Anatolia,* I. 103.

[33]Mitchell, *Anatolia,* I. 100.

[34]See pp. 156-7.

[35]*CIL* XII 4,333. The translation is derived from N. Lewis and M. Reinhold, *Roman Civilization I: The Republic* (New York: Colombia University Press, 1990) 622. I am grateful to Dr. David Gill for this point.

[36]Mitchell, *Anatolia,* I. 101.

[37]Fishwick, *The Imperial Cult,* 588.

[38]*SEG* XXIII no. 206 and Fishwick, *The Imperial Cult,* 514.

(σεβαστοφόροι). The honour accorded to the image was not dissimilar
to that accorded to an imperial visit; imperial ceremonial was observed
as if the emperor himself were present.[39] In Gyntheum 'once the
procession had entered the theatre, incense was offered up before the
images of Augustus, Livia and Tiberius'.[40] Music accompanied the
procession and choral hymns specifically composed for the purpose
were sung by youths.[41] An inscription of the provincial council of Asia
at Hypaepa records 'the choir of Asia' celebrating 'the birthday of
Tiberius with hymns and sacrifices and holding banquets'.[42] Speeches
were delivered on these occasions and like the priests who bore the
imperial image, the orators were given a special title (σεβαστολόγος) in
keeping with the importance attached to the cult.[43]

Games were also part of the celebrations. These were to become
associated traditionally with gladitorial combats, athletic competitions
in the circus and theatrical performances as well as blood sports and
the execution of criminals.

Banqueting followed the return of the statues to their permanent
place. This feasting near the imperial temple gradually became an
essential part of cultic celebrations, as it also did in the provincial
imperial cultic sites of Galatia.[44] Temple feasts were not open to everyone and could be restricted to the magistrates and the priests of
Augustus.[45]

The cost of these celebrations was enormous and it did not come
from the public purse. 'To provide feasts and distributions on imperial
days was a benefaction that came to be expected of rich men in general
and of imperial priests in particular'.[46]

While members of the local élite were at the forefront of the liturgy, others also participated. On the evidence of a later Christian
writer, it has been deduced that 'in principle everyone was expected to
take part but all that was required was to wear festival attire, notably
crowns and to hang the door of one's house with laurels and lamps'.[47]
Earlier evidence shows that individuals did participate by making sac-

---

[39]Fishwick, *The Imperial Cult*, 533.

[40]Fishwick, *The Imperial Cult*, 563, citation at 564.

[41]Cite Fishwick, *The Imperial Cult*, 566ff.

[42]IGRR 4. 1608c, Fishwick, *The Imperial Cult*, 586.

[43]For evidence under Gaius in Asia see Fishwick, *The Imperial Cult*, 571–2.

[44]Price, *Rituals and Power*, 109.

[45]Fishwick, *The Imperial Cult*, 585.

[46]Fishwick, *The Imperial Cult*, 587.

[47]Fishwick, *The Imperial Cult*, 529 citing Tertullian, *De corona* 1.1.13, *cf. Apol.* 35.

rifices and worshipping before images.[48] 'Wine and incense may also
have been distributed to the townsfolk to enable them to perform private acts of devotion, conceivably wearing a wreath'.[49]

It has generally been thought that the sacrifices were directed
only to the emperor as a god, but evidence suggests that sacrifices were
also performed to the gods for the emperor.[50]

> the double prayer—*to* the emperor and to the gods *on behalf* of the
> emperor—does not reveal a deep–seated ambivalence at the heart of
> imperial cults. Rather, the twofold prayer accurately reflected imper-
> ial policy: the gods looked after the emperor, who in turn looked after
> the concerns of the gods on earth to the benefit of humanity.[51]

However adherents conceived of their imperial worship, Christians were not in a position to offer up sacrifices to the emperor or even
for him as Jews did daily.[52] Christians possessed no sacrificial system
and therefore could only offer up prayers for him (1 Tim. 2:2).

II. Christian Teaching on 'Gods on the Earth'

Of the many Christian documents from this period, one reveals the
Christian attitude towards religious pluralism and, it is suggested,
directly to the imperial cult. It was written to the Roman colony of
Corinth and therefore is all the more important as it helps focus on this
civic obligation. Nowhere more than in a Roman colony would loyalty
to Rome express itself by means of ardent devotion to the cult.

> we know that an idol is nothing in the world, and that there is no God
> but one. For even though (γὰρ εἴπερ) there are the so–called gods,
> whether in heaven or on earth; as (ὥσπερ) there are many gods and
> many lords; but (ἀλλά) for us there is one God, the Father from whom
> all things derive (ἐξ οὗ τὰ πάντα) and for whom we live (ἡμεῖς εἰς
> αὐτόν) and one Lord, Jesus Christ, through whom are all things (δι' οὗ
> τὰ πάντα) and through whom we live (ἡμεῖς δι' αὐτοῦ) 1 Cor. 8:4-6.

---

[48]Fishwick, *The Imperial Cult*, 530ff.
[49]Fishwick, *The Imperial Cult*, 588.
[50]Fishwick, *The Imperial Cult*, 565.
[51]Friesen, *Twice Neokoros: Ephesus, Asia and the Cult of the Flavian Imperial Family*,
152.
[52]Price, *Ritual and Power*, 220–22 and Goodman, *The Ruling Class of Judaea*, 3.

The description of the gods and lords as 'so-called' means that they are popularly but erroneously so designated. The participial construction 'the so–called' (οἱ λεγόμενοι) was used of kings, philosophers and sophists who, some thought, made false claims. Others had inappropriately designated the religious phenomena as gods and lords.[53] The old English term 'commonly' meaning 'normally but incorrectly' serves as a comparable example for this Greek conventional phrase.[54] The *Hermetic Writings* reflect the Pauline convention 'neither other so–called gods. . .only God'[55] and Tertullian wrote, 'The so–called gods are of course mere names'.[56] In the clause 'For even though (γὰρ εἴπερ) there are the so–called gods', 'even though' (εἴπερ) can be used to imply that the statement is contrary to fact,[57] while the use of 'as' (ὥσπερ) in 'as there are many gods and many lords' can be translated 'just as indeed' which indicates the existence of many gods and many lords in Corinth.[58]

This is the one passage in the Pauline corpus where he refers to gods 'on the earth'. The deified living emperor and members of the imperial family would have been identified as divinities 'upon the earth' in contrast to 'those in the heaven'.[59] The lack of gender references would not invalidate the title for female members of the imperial family, for Aphrodite was sometimes addressed as 'lady' or a goddess and likewise as god or lord.[60] While Paul nowhere refers to goddesses or ladies, his statement would clearly include Aphrodite, the 'patroness' of the colony. Therefore deified emperors and living members of the imperial family were identified among the 'so-called gods' (λεγόμενοι θεοί) *i.e.* popularly but erroneously called gods.

---

[53]*E.g.* Epictetus 4.1.51 and synonymous 'so–called' statements in Dio Chrysostom 31.11, 77/78.34. On the discussion of the construction in the latter writer see J.L. Moles, 'The Career and Conversion of Dio Chrysostom', *JHS* 97 (1978) 91.

[54]The term 'so-called' cannot be taken to mean 'a concession of the existence of many gods and lords [which] was not necessarily incompatible with Jewish monotheism', P.A. Rainbow, *Monotheism and Christology in 1 Corinthians 8:4–6* (Oxford University D.Phil., 1987) 132, or as 'emphatic a qualification of the monotheism of [v. 4] as Paul could have made as a Christian', J.C. Hurd, *The Origins of 1 Corinthians* (London: SPCK, 1965) 125.

[55]*The Hermetic Writings* 2.14.

[56]Tertullian, *De idolotria* xv.

[57]Liddell and Scott.

[58]Pausanius, the second-century traveller of religious sites, who visited Corinth records the proliferation of statues and temples, 2.3.1.

[59]For discussion of this point see p. 126ff.

[60]See my 'Theological and Ethical Responses to Religious Pluralism: 1 Corinthians 8-10', *Tyn.B.* 41 (1990) 214 for evidence.

The strong adversative statement makes the exclusivism of the Christian confession more stark as it is formulated in contra-distinction to the religious pluralism of the era and to the imperial cult in particular. The claim of origin and dependence concerning the one God, the Father 'from whom all things derive' (ἐξ οὗ τὰ πάντα) and 'for whom we live' (ἡμεῖς εἰς αὐτον) and the one Lord 'through whom are all things' (δι' οὗ τὰ πάντα) and 'through whom we live' (ἡμεῖς δι' αὐτοῦ) contradicted the imperial claims.[61]

Unlike some Stoic and Epicurean philosophers in the Claudian period who permitted their adherents to participate in popular cultic activities in spite of their teaching in *De natura deorum*,[62] Paul forbade Christians to participate in such pagan cultic activities (1 Cor. 10:21).[63] This would have included the civic obligations towards the imperial cult.

III. Avoidance of a Civic Obligation

Judaism was recognised by the Romans as a *religio licita*. What was Rome's attitude towards a new movement which sprang from it? It is difficult to see on what grounds Gentiles who became Christians could *ipso facto* claim exemption from participation in the cult. We know in the provinces of Asia, Bithynia, and Galatia, that Roman citizens had a civic obligation to venerate the cult of Rome and *Divus Iulius*, and local inhabitants the cult of Augustus and Roma.

> He (Augustus) commanded that the Roman residents in these cities should pay honour to these two divinities; but he permitted the aliens. . .to consecrate precincts to himself. . .this practice, beginning under him, has been continued under other emperors, not only in the case of the Hellenic nations but also in that of all the others, in so far as they are subject to the Romans.[64]

---

[61]See N.T. Wright, *The Climax of the Covenant: Christ and the Law in Pauline Theology* (Edinburgh: T. & T. Clark, 1991) 125ff. for an important discussion of the application of Deut. 6:4 to this passage.

[62]See my 'In Public and in Private: Early Christianity and Religious Pluralism', in A.D. Clarke and B.W. Winter (edd.), *One God and One Lord: in a World of Religious Pluralism* (ed 2; Grand Rapids and Carlisle, Baker and Paternoster 1992) ch. 6.

[63]B. Rosner, '"No Other Gods": The Jealousy of God and Religious Pluralism' in *One God and One Lord: in a World of Religious Pluralism*, ch. 7.

[64]Dio Cassius, 51.20.6-7.

Would there now be any change in the religious status of Christian Jews in the eyes of Rome, the emperor's vicegerent, and more
immediately, those who exercised local power in these cities? If they
were no longer perceived to be adherents of a legal religion in Roman
eyes, then this would place Jewish Christians under the civic obligation
to participate in the imperial cult.

Christianity's self–description before the Roman authorities in a
court case was that of 'a party' (αἵρεσις) within Judaism whose beliefs
were grounded only in the Jewish scriptures (Acts 24:14, 26:6-7, 22-23).
On the other hand, the term 'Christians' (Χριστιανοί) appears to have
been coined by the Romans in Antioch as a description of this new
movement, according to E.A. Judge.

> [The term] can hardly be invented by orthodox Jews since it concedes
> the messiahship of Jesus. Its suffix implies the word was coined by
> speakers of Latin. . .The suffix–*ianus* constitutes a political comment.
> It is not used of the followers of a god. It classifies people as partners
> of a political or military leader, and is mildly contemptuous.[65]

The Christians could be seen by the Romans in different parts of the
empire as either followers of a political or military leader or basically
Jewish; by the Jews as members of a *religio illicita*; and by themselves as
those who were part of a *religio licita* because they had embraced the
promise made in the Jewish scriptures.

The Jewish leaders in Roman Galatia seem to have had no
difficulty persuading the civic authorities that Christian missionaries
were not entitled to operate under their aegis. In Pisidian Antioch
when Paul and Barnabas accepted an invitation from the rulers of the
synagogue to preach (13:15) a large number of Jews and God-fearers
responded positively to it and followed Paul and Barnabas. The
following Sabbath day 'almost the whole city' turned out to hear Paul
and Barnabas, and, moved by jealousy, the Jews publicly contradicted
Paul and Barnabas, but to no avail for the message spread throughout
the region (13:49). However, 'devout women of high rank and chief
men of the city' (τὰς σεβομένας γυναῖκας τὰς εὐσχήμονας καὶ πρώτους τῆς
πόλεως) were urged by Jews to persecute the preachers and they were
cast out (13:50). In the next centre, Iconium, the inhabitants were

---

[65]E.A. Judge, 'Judaism and the Rise of Christianity: A Roman Perspective', *Tyn.B.*
45.2 (1994) 363. See also J. Taylor, 'Why were the Disciples first called "Christians"
at Antioch? (Acts 11:26)', *Revue Biblique* 101 (1994) 75–94 who argues for Jewish agi-
tation in the background at Antioch.

divided between the Jews and the apostles—the latter were ejected by both Gentiles and Jews with 'their rulers' (14:4-5). At Lystra Jews arrived from Pisiadian Antioch and Iconium to pursue the missionaries who moved on to Derbe (14:20). It is of interest that in this province the Jews could be in league with the city authorities over a matter which related to their *religio licita*.

This coalition of Jews and city authorities was all the more significant given the fact that imperial policy towards Diaspora Jews was unfavourable at the time when these incidents occurred. Some were seen to have fomented trouble, especially 'certain Jews who came from Syria'.[66] The letter of Claudius to the Alexandrians at the beginning of his Principate specifically mentions the latter, and the subsequent eviction of Jews from Rome in A.D. 49 reflects further alienation.[67] An alliance in this period of local Jewish/Roman authorities, especially in the Roman colony of Pisidian Antioch, would ease the situation. If the rulers of the Jews succeeded in disowning this 'sect', then the only tangible way loyalty to Rome could be expressed by the latter would be by observation of the cult. Fergus Millar, in a discussion on the imperial cult and Christians, has raised the matter, not in relation to Jewish but pagan concerns.

> But when gentiles began to convert to Christianity, might we not expect that the pagan communities in which they lived would begin to use against them the accusation of not observing the Imperial cult?[68]

If the evidence of Acts is used, then Jewish leaders are seen linking hands with the civic authorities and the leading women against Christian missionaries (Acts 13:50). Other evidence confirms the close relationships that Jews had with Gentiles and the important rôle women of distinction played in priestly and other offices.[69]

---

[66]*P.Lond.* 1912 *l.* 96.

[67]For a discussion of the Alexandrian letter *P.Lond.* 1912 see most recently A. Kasher, *Jews in Hellenistic and Roman Egypt* (Tübingen: J.C.B. Mohr, [Paul Siebeck], 1985) 310ff. and on the eviction of the Jews from Rome, B. Levick, *Claudius* (London: Batsford, 1990) 183ff.

[68]F. Millar, 'The Imperial Cult and the Persecutions', in W. den Boer, *Le Culte des Souverains dans l'empire romain*, 163 (Geneva: Vandoeuvres, 1972) 163.

[69]P.R. Trebilco, *Jewish Communities in Asia Minor*, SNTSMS 69 (Cambridge: CUP, 1991) chs. 1-5 and R. Gordon, 'The Veil of Power: Emperors, Sacrificers and Benefactors', *Pagan Priests: Religion and Power in the Ancient World* , in M. Beard and J. North (edd.) (London: Duckworth, 1990) ch. 8.

Given the exclusion from the Jewish synagogues, how would rank and file Christians cope with the cult? It is being suggested that, from within the ranks of the Christian communities in Galatia, there were Jewish Christians who counselled evasive action. They sought to place all Christians, whether Jew or Gentile under a Jewish, as distinct from a synagogue, umbrella. Some may have been tempted to portray the house church in which they met as a Christian 'place of prayer' (προσευχή).[70] There was, in the end, a clear way for the Christian community to escape the obligation of the imperial cult *viz.* by appearing to be wholly Jewish. As in the time of Domitian,[71] so too in the Principates of Claudius and Nero, it was circumcision that identified a person as Jewish.[72] If Christian Gentiles underwent circumcision they would be Jewish proselytes. If they also observed the Jewish law, as did their Christian Jewish brethren in Jerusalem (Acts 21:20), then in the eyes of the outside world they belonged to a *religio licita*. The social identification of Jews by the Gentile world was their observation of the law.

Do we have evidence of a cross–cultural move by Gentile Christians in Paul's letter to the Galatians? It needs to be noted that the motivation for the insistence on circumcision and the keeping of the law and the justification for it by Jewish Christians in Galatia are two separate issues. It can be overlooked that Paul has spelt out the theological reasons why the Galatians must not undergo circumcision which aimed to counter the cogent, theological reasons put forward to Gentiles by some Jewish Christians (Gal. 1–5:1ff.). Only at the end of the letter are the Jewish Christians' motives exposed by Paul for compelling male Gentile Christians to look like Jews physically and to keep the Jewish law which would make their Jewish identification absolutely unmistakable (6:11–18). This part of the letter is said by Paul to be in his own hand (6:11ff.) and is in the rhetorical form of the 'conclusion' (*peroratio* or *conclusio*) where such a subscription was highly appropriate.[73]

---

[70]On the use of this term as a Jewish meeting place see Acts 16:13 and for epigraphic evidence see I. Levinskaya, 'The Meaning of προσευχή', *Tyn.B.* 41 (1990) 154–9.

[71]Suetonius, *Life of Domitian* 12. See pp. 148–9.

[72]Martial (A.D. 40 – c. 104) 7.82 'he was circumcised'.

[73]G. Bahr, 'The Subscriptions in the Pauline Letters', *JBL* 89 (1969) 27–41 in which he argues that the subscription commences in 5:2. For a correction of this see G.W. Hansen, *Abraham in Galatians: Epistolary and Rhetorical Contexts*, JSNT Supp. Series 29 (Sheffield: Sheffield Academic Press, 1989) 52 who argues that it is to be found in 6:11-18 because of the rhetorical form.

We are told that Jewish Christians 'compelled' the Gentile Christians to be circumcised (Gal. 6:12). The enormity of this extraordinary step for Gentiles has perhaps not been sufficiently appreciated. Rome equated circumcision with as serious a criminal act as castration. Socially circumcision could only attract derision in the Gentile world. A Jew who wore a *fibula* to disguise his circumcision while exercising in the gymnasium, lost it and was subject to great derision—'he is a Jew' they cried out.[74] The willingness to undergo circumcision was well known as a step towards becoming a proselyte in the ancient world, but 'compelling' others to do so was not. The reason for such pressure on a fellow Christian must have been an urgent and overwhelming one, and the advantages must have been perceived to far outweigh any social stigma it would attract in *politeia*.

Galatians 6:12 indicates why Christian Jews compelled Christian Gentiles to this course of action. They did so 'only that' (μόνον ἵνα) they themselves would avoid persecution 'for the cross of Christ'. Becoming Jewish was the solution that would protect all the Jewish Diaspora Christians from persecution. In the eyes of the authorities of Galatia they would all be Jewish and not a mixed association. Those Gentiles who joined them and observed the Jewish law in daily life would, as Jewish converts, be exempt from the imperial cult.

The intended result of this action is given in 6:12a. 'They [Jewish Christians] wish "to make a fair show" in flesh' (θέλουσιν εὐπροσωπῆσαι ἐν σαρκί). Paul uses the verb εὐπροσωπέω whose cognates have legal connotations, although it has normally been rendered here somewhat enigmatically as 'make a fair show'. However, if its legal meaning is what was meant by Paul, then it would support the contention that Jewish Christians were seeking to confer some [legal] status 'by means of flesh' *i.e.* circumcision.

Examples are to be found which support such a rendering. Lucian states 'I do not know what answer you can make to give you a good face (εὐπρόσωπός σοι) before your accusers' because of the impossibility of defending the indefensible.[75] Liddell & Scott suggest that the term in Plutarch could refer to a legal personality—'Why I thought my face to be handsome' (καὶ ἐδόκοον εὐπρόσωπος εἶναι) which is seen as a pun because of physical deformity (2.458F). Polemon wrote to Menches requesting him to hasten in collecting taxes. 'Regarding the *komogrammateis* whom you mention [a

---

[74]Martial, 7.82.
[75]Lucian, 'Apology for the "Salaried Posts in Great Houses"' 3.

discussion of overcharging for taxes] you will be right in not diminishing the report compared to the first one, in order that we may make a good show'. Given the fact that Polemon was engaged in official business and that his superior had apparently charged more, it is possible that the verb carries the idea of making the report legal.[76]

The idea of 'legal personality', *juristische Person*, (πρόσωπον) is derived from the stem of the word Paul uses in Galatians 6:12.[77] The term 'face' (πρόσωπον) originally carried the meaning of 'mask' but by the time of the early first century it was used to describe the status of a person. Its Latin equivalent was *persona*. Lohse has suggested that the legal use of the term πρόσωπον for 'person' does not occur in the first century.[78] However, Dionysius of Halicarnassus writing in the time of Augustus used it in its legal sense of the persons whom he represented in court.[79] Schlossmann whose work formed the basis of Lohse's word study acknowledged Dionysius of Halicarnassus' use of the term but dismissed it by attributing it to the influence of Latin.[80] That, however, constitutes no reason for rejecting such a meaning in the Graeco–Roman world of the early empire. Nédoncelle, in a careful study on πρόσωπον and *persona*, has shown that the Latin term *persona* has this legal connotation in Cicero (106–43 B.C.), and that the range of Latin meanings in Cicero are already found in the Greek works of Polybius (*c.* 200–*c.* 118 B.C.).[81]

Having 'a good legal face' would be the antonym for having no status at all. For example Bion was by birth a citizen of Borysthenes [Olbia]. His father was a native of Borysthenes (γένος Βορυσθωνίτης) who 'had no face to show' (ἔχων οὐ πρόσωπον) *i.e.* legal status, but only the writing 'on his face' (ἐπὶ τοῦ προσώπου) *i.e.* he was branded a slave. It emerges that Bion's father, as a freedman, had cheated the government of revenue and was sold into slavery. Bion himself was bought by a certain rhetorician whose library he inherited on his death and promptly burnt in order to become a philosopher.[82]

---

[76]*P.Tebt.* 19 *l.* 12.

[77]To cite Preisigke's translation. See Diogenes Laertius 4.46 and also *BGU* 5114 *l.* 49. *Cf.* Aristotle, *Politics* 1263b 15 'Such legislation therefore has an 'appropriate appearance' *i.e.* it was good legislation.

[78]E. Lohse, 'πρόσωπον', *TWNT* VI 770.

[79]Dionysius of Halicarnassus, *Lysias* 24. See also *Demosthenes* 13, *Thucydides* 34, 37.

[80]S. Schlossmann, *Persona und πρόσωπον im Recht und im christlichen Dogma* (Kiel, 1906) 42.

[81] M. Nédoncelle, '*Prosopon* et *persona* dans l'antiquité classique', *Revue des Sciences Religieuses* 22 (1948) 277–99 at 296 citing Cicero, De *Oratore* 2.102.

[82]Diogenes Laertius 4.46.

The phrase 'having a face' (ἔχων πρόσωπον) is widely used in non–literary sources, especially public inscriptions. Of the 674 examples from the Packard Humanities Institute CD ROM which, it must be remembered, contains only a portion of non–literary material, when πρόσωπον was combined with the verb 'to have', the overwhelming majority of references were to those who had 'legal status'. The papyri also use πρόσωπον to refer to legal persons whether in connection with the laws concerning the division of property according to households and 'not individuals' (μὴ κατὰ πρόσωπον),[83] or with the authorized person in a liturgy, *i.e.* someone duly elected to office or 'some other [qualified] person' *i.e.* possessing legal status, a citizen.[84]

The phrase 'having legal status' (ἔχων πρόσωπον) should therefore be seen as being achieved as a result of an activity (*cf.* Gal. 6:12a). The addition of εὐ- to πρόσωπον allows for a good 'legal face' or 'personality' which the Gentile Christians now possess—prior to that their 'legal personality' was uncertain and would have been in conflict with their civic obligation whether they were provincials or Romans. Local Jewish Christians had 'secured good legal status' for the Galatian Christian Gentiles 'by circumcision'. They could now be regarded as 'having Jewish legal status' which would exempt them from participation in the imperial cult. Because the term sometimes had connotations of spuriousness, did Paul use this word as a *double entendre*?[85]

Motives are further exposed in the statement that the Jewish Christians do not themselves keep the law, but only want Gentiles to be circumcised 'in order that they may boast in your flesh'. Does Paul mean by this that they boast about their Jewishness or that they 'have confidence in your flesh' *i.e.* secure their own safety 'by means of your circumcision' (6:13).[86]

If the words discussed above have been correctly identified in terms of form and derivation from the semantic field of legal and quasi-legal terminology, then the passage would read

> 12. As many as wish to give you secure legal status by means of flesh, these people compel you to be circumcised only in order that they may not be persecuted for the cross of Christ. 13. For those who them-

---

[83]*P.Ryl.* 76 *l.* 12 (second century A.D.).

[84]*P.Oxy.* 904 *l.* 8 see also *P.Oxy.* 1033 *l.* 8.

[85]Demosthenes, *De Corona* 149.5, Dionysius of Halicarnassus, *Ant. Rom.* 3.11.3, Lucian, *Herm.* 45.1.

[86]J. S. Bosch, *'Gloriarse' Segun San Pablo: Sentido y teologia de* καυχάομα, Analecta Biblica (Rome and Barcelona: Biblical Institute Press, 1970) 227–8.

selves are circumcised do not keep the law, but only wish you to be circumcised in order that they may have confidence in your flesh.

Betz draws attention to the fact that this conclusion (*peroratio*) contains the *recapitulatio* which sums up and sharpens the case. The *indignatio* was meant to create hostility against those who had made the Gentile Christians Jewish, and the *conquestio* arouses support for Paul's argument.[87] The recapitulation of the case is outlined in 6:12 and the indignation is reflected in the following verse. Paul draws support from the readership by indicating his own source of confidence, and the fact that the Christian faith is about a new creation which is without ethnic connotations.

The possible link between the Galatian Christians' problem and the imperial cult was explored by Lütgert some seventy years ago.[88] Recent evidence on the imperial cult would support the view that external pressure resulted in evasive action by local Jewish Christians. It has been said of Lütgert's thesis that 'it fails to explain, however, how or why such pressure would be exerted: what legal, social and moral authority the synagogue could have had over the Gentile.'[89] The foregoing discussion answers these legitimate concerns and suggests that the pressure was an internal one from Galatian Jewish Christians which came about because of external pressure in *politeia*. The original cause was Jewish antagonism towards the Christian missionary endeavours in Galatia. They linked up with the local civic authorities to drive the leaders of this movement from the city.

In this chapter it has been argued that avoidance of the imperial cult is connected to the central issue in Paul's Galatian letter *viz.* circumcision and keeping the Jewish law. This was done as a means of dealing with the extremely difficult problem of the observation of the imperial cult for Christians in this particular province. With the emergence of Roman Galatia the imperial cult became intertwined with civic life. For local inhabitants, self–definition in *politeia* in this part of the empire was clearly related to Roman culture and rule, and included the veneration of emperors and the imperial family both past and present. Local Jewish Galatian Christians formulated this

---

[87]H.D. Betz, *Galatians: A Commentary on Paul's Letter to the Churches of Galatia* (Philadelphia: Fortress Press, 1979) 312–3.
[88]W. Lütgert, *Gesetz und Geist: Eine Untersuchung zur Vorgeschichte des Galaterbriefs* (Gütersloh, 1919) 94–106.
[89]J. Barclay, *Obeying the Truth, A Study of Paul's Ethics in Galatians* (Edinburgh: T. & T. Clark, 1988) 51–2.

response to an extremely difficult civic obligation, because their own self–preservation and that of the Christian community was seen to be at stake.[90]

Bearing in mind the first-century society's abhorrence of circumcision, the motivation that compelled Gentile Christians to undergo even what was a degrading practice in Roman eyes, becomes explicable. Galatian Christianity had to be seen to be Jewish if Jewish Christians and the movement as a whole, were to survive in this particular province. How could Christians 'avoid persecution for the cross of Christ' to use Paul's description of their action? Undergoing circumcision and keeping the law was one way of convincing the authorities that Christianity was a *religio licita*, for in Galatia these had become its cultural hall–marks.[91]

At the conclusion of his discussion of the extent of the imperial cult in Galatia, S. Mitchell gives his opinion

> One cannot avoid the impression that the obstacle which stood in the way of the progress of Christianity, and the force which would have drawn new adherents back to conformity with the prevailing paganism, was the public worship of the emperors. . .it was not a change of heart that might win a Christian convert back to paganism, but the overwhelming pressure to conform imposed by the institutions of his city and the activities of his neighbours.[92]

The above discussion of the evidence from Paul's letter to the Galatians suggests that the guaranteed progress of early Christianity was seen by

---

[90]While it is generally held that a party from Jerusalem was responsible for the difficulties in Galatia, it would seem that nothing in the text demands that conclusion. *Contra* R. Jewett, 'The Agitators and the Galatian Congregation', *NTS* 17 (1971) 198-212 who argues that circumcision would thwart the zealots' threat which had pushed Jewish Christians into a nomistic campaign among fellow Christians in Palestine. F.F. Bruce, *Commentary on Galatians*, NIGTC (Grand Rapids: Eerdmans,1982) 269 follows Jewett. *Cf.* earlier G.W. Burton, *Galatians* ICC (Edinburgh: T. & T. Clark, 1921) 349 who argued that Christian Jews wished to remain in good standing in the Jewish community by being able to point to converts from the Gentile world who have not only accepted Jesus as the Messiah, but also were observing the Jewish law. For a helpful summary of views stating why this might be so and the deficiencies in their arguments see Barclay, *Obeying the Truth:* 45ff.
[91]*Contra* Judge, 'Judaism and the Rise of Christianity: A Roman Perspective', 82–98 who argues that the Romans perceived Christianity as a separate movement from Judaism from the time of the formation of the church in Antioch. Such a perception would be obscured if the Christian community in Galatia deliberately blurred the distinction. See also the discussion on Corinth on p. 142.
[92]Mitchell, *Anatolia*, II. 10.

Jewish Christians in Galatia to be dependent on finding a way around the vexed problem of this civic obligation.

Do we possess any evidence from other Christian sources of Jewish pressure being exerted on authorities against the new Christian movement? Luke records a move by Jews in another province, Achaea, to do this in order to terminate Paul's missionary endeavours. Unlike in Galatia, they instigated legal proceedings against Christians at the provincial level in Corinth. Elsewhere I have argued that this was an attempt to mount formal legal proceedings before Gallio to rule that Christianity was not Jewish, and therefore by implication, not exempted from the imperial cult.[93] This was a sensitive case to bring before a Roman court, for 'all the Jews' had only recently been ejected from Rome over the 'Chrestus' affair and some Jews had just settled in Corinth from Rome as a result (Acts 18:2). To raise a Jewish issue risked their own ejection from Corinth—this Roman colony like all colonies sought to demonstrate loyalty by acting in concert with Rome. This perhaps explains the treatment meted out to the ruler of the synagogue by those present when the case was dismissed. The case had to be put in such a way that the 'Chrestus' issue was not raised. As they had presented their petition to commence proceedings, it was perceived by Gallio to be 'questions about words and names and your own law' (Acts 18:15). The case was rejected and Christianity was actually ruled to be Jewish (Acts 18:12–17). Christians were thereby exempted from the civic obligation to participate in the imperial cult. Therefore those in Achaea who were Romans and provincials would not be under any pressure to submit to circumcision and observation of the Jewish law. Because the ruling of Gallio was not to proceed with an actual hearing against Paul, it did not have empire–wide force—it only applied to that province. The governor's perception agreed with that presented in Acts 24–26 where the Jewish origins of the Christian faith were rehearsed before another Roman governor in a court of law where criminal proceedings were also undertaken by the Jews. That governor was also a person of ability in legal matters,[94] and the reader of Acts would have perceived that the relationship between the Jewish

---

[93]'Acts and Roman Religion', in D. Gill and C. Gempf (edd.), *The Book of Acts in its Graeco–Roman Setting*, The Book of Acts in its First Century Setting (Grand Rapids and Carlisle: Eerdmans and Paternoster, 1994) 2. 98–103.

[94]For Felix's role in a legal ruling on behalf of the emperor which made such a favourable impression on leading Jews in Rome that they pressed for his appointment as governor, see my 'The Importance of the *captatio benevolentiae* in the Speeches of Tertullus and Paul in Acts 24:1–21', *JTS* n.s. 42 (1991) 515–6.

faith and the Nazarene 'party' was not rejected. Gallio's ruling was a correct one from Luke's perspective.[95]

In conclusion, the civic obligation to the imperial cult of any Roman citizen or provincial Christian posed a major problem in the Julio–Claudian era, and not simply in the Flavian period when Domitian reigned. Because there was as yet no empire–wide ruling on Christianity as a *religio illicita* by the emperors in the fomer imperial dynasty, Christians from one province took evasive action which prevented a provincial ruling being brought against their movement. The pressure on Christians in Galatia to react can be readily understood, given the peculiar circumstance related to Romanization and the imper ial cult in that province. It was providential that early in Paul's evangelistic activities in Corinth a ruling was forthcoming from Gallio which had the effect of exempting Christians from the cult obligations, especially on the eve of making Corinth the centre for the provincial, as against the local imperial cult.[96] The direct representative of Claudius in the province actually made this ruling in their favour.

Therefore the statement in the Epistle to Diognetus that Christians '. . .take part in everything as citizens' did not apply in the first century to the civic obligation to the imperial cult. It was an activity in which Christians could not participate.[97] Later, Tertullian agreed that while Christians participated in civic life they did not worship gods and did not 'offer sacrifices for the emperors' even though this resulted in accusations of sacrilege and treason.[98]

---

[95]It might be thought that Paul's enigmatic comment, 'If after the manner of man (εἰ κατὰ ἄνθρωπον ἐθηριομάχησα) I fought the beasts in Ephesus' refers to some confrontation with the imperial cult (1 Cor. 15:32). 'Wild-beast fighters' (*venatores*) were often freemen from good families who were connected with the provincial imperial cult. For discussion see C. Roueché, 'Gladiators and Wild–beast Fighters', *Performers and Partisans at Aphrodisias in the Roman and late Roman Periods* JRS mono. ser. 6 (1993) ch. 5. The provincial cult which was accompanied by wild beast shows was not celebrated in Ephesus at this time but elsewhere in the province of Asia in the first century so that Paul cannot be referring to this. The reference is likely to be to passions as the immediate context of 1 Cor. 15:32 relates to hedonism, see A.J. Malherbe, 'The Beasts at Ephesus', *JBL* 87 (1968) 71-80.
[96]Spawforth, 'Corinth, Argos, and the Imperial Cult' 226ff. suggests *c.* 54 A.D.
[97]*The Epistle to Diognetus* V.4-5.
[98]Tertullian, *Apology* 10.1.

CHAPTER EIGHT

SOCIAL MOBILITY

1 Corinthians 7:17–24

In the first century securing greater social status in the Graeco-Roman world was high on the agenda of many provincials. Was there a temptation for Christians to aspire to move up the same social scale? We know of some provincials who made various manoeuvres to secure enhanced legal rights, civic office and honours in Eastern cities. There were provincials who went to extraordinary lengths to secure freedman status, Roman citizenship, free born status for their progeny and a place among the ranks of 'the wise, the well-born and the powerful'. In 1 Corinthians 7:17-24 Paul discusses the matter of 'class' or 'status' in society as part of his standard 'teaching' or 'tradition' (παράδοσις) which he gave 'in all the churches'. This points to the fact that, like others in society, some Christians in the East also aspired to higher status. Why was Paul so opposed to such social mobility in *politeia*?

Some of those wishing to be upwardly mobile in the first century are specifically mentioned in 1 Corinthians 7:18–23. The first group were Christian Jews who contemplated, as did other of their compatriots, removing the marks of their circumcision, which was an inhibiting factor in Roman society (v. 18). The second class were Christian slaves who aspired to freedom (vv. 21–23a). The third group were Christian free men willing to sell themselves into slavery for social and financial benefits (v. 23b).

Commentators have found it difficult to understand why a Christian Jew would be tempted to undergo epispasm, a surgical operation for the disguising of circumcision. For example, G.D. Fee acknowledges, 'As difficult as it might be for us moderns to imagine, during the Hellenization many Jewish men had an operation of a kind that concealed their circumcision' but suggests that 'one can scarcely imagine a situation in Corinth where Jewish believers might actually have been [undergoing epispasm]'.[1] As will be shown, the Jews in the prestigious city of Corinth would have been more likely than those in any other place to be so tempted, because of the social status that the city could afford.

The act of selling oneself into slavery has proved just as enigmatic for commentators. Some feel that there could not have been the need for such an injunction.[2] It has therefore become customary not to regard these verses as describing literally what was happening in Corinth but to treat the prohibition metaphorically.[3] Scott Bartchy, who

---

[1]G.D. Fee, *The First Epistle to the Corinthians* 312 n. 27. H. Conzelmann, *1 Corinthans* 126 n. 10, suggests that it is not necessary to assume that circumcision and stretching of the foreskin had taken place in Corinth. He seeks to defend this conclusion on the basis that 'there is no sign of Judaizing demands'.

briefly discusses some of the evidence for the legal convention of 'selling oneself into slavery', draws the conclusion that 'there are good reasons for finding physical and spiritual slavery in 7:23'.[4] By contrast there has been no difficulty in understanding why slaves should wish to become freedmen, although the reasons for the concessive nature of Paul's statement have not always been correctly perceived.

The purpose of this chapter is to explore the background to these three issues, dealing with the evidence and reasons for (I) the removal of the marks of circumcision by Jews, (II) the seeking of manumission, and (III) the voluntary selling of oneself into slavery. It will be argued that (IV) in all instances discussed in (I)–(III) the reason for doing this was to secure enhanced social status, with its attendant financial advantages. Finally (V) the significance of this for Christians in the public place will be explored.

I. Reasons for Removing the Marks of Circumcision

Epispasm, the operation for removing the effects of circumcision, was described in some detail in *De Medicina* 7:25, a medical handbook written during the principate of Tiberius by Aulus Cornelius Celsus. His account suggests that it was a well–known and relatively simple medical procedure performed by doctors in his day. He notes that there were some who underwent the operation 'because it was the custom of certain races to be circumcised'.[5]

The reason for the removal of circumcision was in some way related to the ambivalent official Roman attitudes towards Jews during the principate of Claudius.[6] The problem for young Christian Jews

---

[2]A. Robertson and A. Plummer, *First Epistle of St Paul to the Corinthians* (Edinburgh: T. & T. Clark, 1914) 149, comments, 'It is a mistake to suppose that the words are addressed only to those who are socially free, charging them not to lose their freedom. Such a charge would be superfluous'.

[3]On the latter issue Fee, *The First Epistle to the Corinthians*, 320, concludes that v. 23b is not to be taken as 'literal', ('do not sell yourselves into slavery'), but metaphorical ('do not become slaves of men'). G.W. Dawes, 'But If you Can Gain your Freedom' (1 Cor. 7:17-24), *CBQ* 52 (1990) 691 n. 35, suggests that the statement 'do not be' or even 'do not remain' is a better translation of μὴ γίνεσθε than 'do not become'. He argues that it is very frequently used in this sense in Pauline exhortations, citing Rom. 12:16, 1 Cor. 14:20, Gal. 5:26 and Eph. 5:7,17.

[4]S. Scott Bartchy, *ΜΑΛΛΟΝ ΧΡΗΣΑΙ: First–Century Slavery and 1 Corinthians 7:21*, SBL Dissertation Series 11 (Missoula: Scholars Press, 1973) 182, a point noted by Fee, *ibid*, 320 n. 58, although in effect rejected.

who contemplated epispasm is connected with the wider problem of some Jews attempting to hide their distinctiveness.

Gentile attitudes towards circumcision help explain why some Jews sought to reverse a sign which epitomized their ethnic origins. To pagan minds, circumcision was the mark of racial identity,[7] whether practised by Jews or, on occasion, by other races.[8] It was, however, primarily associated with Jews and was equated with castration by the Romans.[9] Philo of Alexandria notes that the practice of circumcision was in his day 'ridiculed by many', and Josephus also records that his adversary, Apion, 'ridicules our practice of circumcision'.[10] This could be one of the reasons that some Christian Jews sought to disguise their circumcision.

Suetonius writes from first-hand experience in the late first century, 'I remember being present as quite a young man when in a very crowded assembly an old man of ninety was examined by the procurator to see whether he was circumcised'.[11] The reason for this was connected to the diversion of the temple tax from Jerusalem to the

---

[5]Antyllus, a second-century writer, also refers to the operation, commenting that it was performed when the foreskin was shortened 'as a result of some accident', cited by A. Rousell, *Porneia* (Oxford: Blackwells, 1988) 17. In the Hadrianic period it became a common operation and the Rabbis introduced the requirement of laying bare the *glans penis* (cf. 1 Macc. 1:15; Josephus, *Ant.* 12.5.1).

[6]On the ambivalent treatment of Jews in the early days of Claudius' reign, including the closing of the Roman synagogues in A.D. 41, and, despite the warning against interfering in the Greek games, authorisation of their universal rights in the same year, see Kasher, *Jews in Hellenistic and Roman Egypt*. On the expulsion of Jews from Rome by Claudius in 49, see E.M. Smallwood, *The Jews under Roman Rule from Pompey to Diocletian: A Study in Political Relations* (Leiden: Brill, 1981) 211ff. On his execution of leading anti–semitists in 53 when Agrippa II was with him in Rome, see Levick, *Claudius*, 184–5 and more generally her helpful discussion of his provincial policy in ch. 15, 'Claudius and the Provincials'.

[7]The practice was perceived to have arisen from superstition by Strabo, *Geography* 64.3, and to have been instituted 'in order to be recognised by the difference', Tacitus *Ann.* 5.5,8-9. Both comments reflect ignorance as to its origins on the part of these ancient authors.

[8]Philo, *Ques. Gen.* III, 47. Groups within races might undergo circumcision for religious reasons, *e.g.* an Egyptian priest circumcised his son 'because he cannot perform the sacred offices unless this is done', *P.Tebt.* 293 (c. AD 187), but this required the permission of the Prefect of Egypt according to *BGU* 347 (AD 171).

[9]J.P.V.D. Balsdon, *Romans and Aliens* (London: Duckworth, 1979) 216 and 231, describes the latter as 'a practice which Romans thought detestable' and 'popularly associated with the Jews alone'.

[10]Philo, *Spec. Laws* I.2; Josephus, *Contra Apion* 2.13.137; on the irony of his death from an infection of his foreskin see *ibid.*, 2.13.143.

[11]Suetonius, *Life of Domitian* 12.

pagan temple of Jupiter Capitolinus. Vespasian imposed this on Jews after A.D. 70 as punishment for their revolt against Rome.[12] While this may account for Jews at a later stage seeking at all costs to avoid the humiliation of supporting a pagan temple, these circumstances did not apply at the time of Paul's ministry.

In what circumstances, then, did Jews of Paul's day seek to hide their circumcision? Martial (A.D. 40 – c. 104) 7.82 derides an acquaintance in the public baths who sought to disguise his circumcision with a *fibula* which came off in the middle of the exercise ground. It disclosed that the man was not an actor who sometimes wore this device but a Jew—'he was circumcised'.[13] Celsus states that the operation was performed 'for the look of things to have it [*viz.* the glans] covered'. Circumcised Jews would be identified in the public baths and in the gymnasium.

We know from both pagan and Jewish sources that Jews of the Diaspora participated in the gymnasium in the Roman period.[14] As J. Goldstein says of Philo, 'He takes it for granted that the cities contain gymnasia and that parents see to it that their children receive training in one'.[15] He was obviously trained there and his specialised knowledge of its terminology has filled gaps in our knowledge of gymnastic vocabulary.[16] There is evidence that Jews participated in the gymnasia and the schools at Cyrene.[17]

---

[12]Dio Cassius 104, 'From that time a tax to be paid annually on Jupiter Capitoninus was imposed on those who cherish their national custom'. Suetonius, *Life of Domitian* 12 also notes that the victims of the Treasury department in the collection of this tax were the Jews.

[13]E. Schürer, *The History of the Jewish People in the Age of Jesus Christ (175 BC–AD 135)* (Edinburgh: T. & T. Clark, 1973[2]) I. 148–9 n. 28 suggests that it was undertaken in order 'to avoid mockery in public baths and wrestling schools' as part of the process of rapid Hellenization prior to the Hasmonean dynasty. While the enthusiastic response by Jewish Hellenophiles was to be tempered by the revolt of the Maccabees, it was not dampened in the subsequent era of Herod's reign when Greek culture was sponsored even within Palestine.

[14]See Martial 7.82 for Roman evidence.

[15]'Jewish Acceptance and Rejection of Hellenism', in E.P. Sanders, A.I. Baumgarten and A. Mendelson (eds.), *Aspects of Judaism in the Greco–Roman Period*, Jewish and Christian Self–definition (London: SCM, 1981) II. 84, citing *Opif. Mund.* 17, *Spec Leg.* II. 230. Claudius in his famous letter to the Alexandrians, *P.Lond.* 1912, is not proscribing Jews from joining the ranks of the *ephebes*. See Kasher, *Jews in Hellenistic and Roman Egypt*, 320.

[16]H.A. Harris, *Greek Athletics and the Jews* (Cardiff: University of Wales Press, 1976) 51–91.

[17]Kasher, *Jews in Hellenistic and Roman Egypt*, 319.

Furthermore, Celsus indicates that the operation was performed 'more easily in a boy than a man' (*De Medicina* 7.25). This comment may well indicate that in some cases it was performed before puberty, *i.e.* before the age when an eligible Jewish youth enrolled in the ranks of *ephebi*.[18] Jews *per se* were not excluded from entry to these ranks, if eligible. Enrolment in the gymnasium was open to the children of Roman citizens and to those who held local citizenship in cities of the East.[19]

Students trained in various branches of Greek rhetoric joined the ranks of the professions and acted as orators in the political forum of their city.[20] Training in schools of oratory and in the gymnasium equipped young men to become well-paid teachers at the highest level of education (παιδεία), to operate in the lucrative legal profession, especially with the removal of the ceiling on legal fees during Claudius' reign, or to devote themselves to the services of the Roman administration.[21] Such appointments brought not only financial rewards but also status to those who operated in such professional capacities.

Philo records *verbatim* the attitudes of successful contemporaries to their status. They were conscious of the nexus between their wealth and status and the comfortable lifestyle which these secured as they boasted about their wealth, prestige, status and public office (πλοῦτος, δόξα, τιμή, ἀρχή) declaring themselves to be

> men of mark and wealth, holding leading positions, praised on all hands, recipients of honours, portly, healthy and robust, revelling in luxurious and riotous living, knowing nothing of labour, conversant with pleasures which carry the sweets of life to the all-welcoming soul by every channel of sense.[22]

---

[18]The evidence allows this interpretation. Celsus' discussion begins by noting those groups upon whom it is easier to perform this operation. He proceeds to discuss natural deformities which require surgical correction and then deals specifically with techniques for those who have been circumcised. Therefore the mention of the operation on a boy does not imply that it was only performed on those with natural deformities.

[19]For Egypt see C.A. Nelson, *Status Declarations in Roman Egypt*, ASP 19, especially ch. 2; J. Bingen, 'Declarations pour l'Epicrisis', *Chronique d'Egypte* 16 (1956) 116; and for examples of applications by parents or guardians for the *epicrisis* for Alexandrian citizens, see *P.Oxy.* 477, *S.B.* 733.

[20]Epictetus, III.1,34–5, outlines to a student of rhetoric the career opportunities open to him in the city of Corinth in terms of honorary liturgies.

[21]On the revoking of the two hundred and fifty year old law by Claudius which allowing fees up to 10,000 *sesterces* to be charged, see Tacitus, *Ann.* 11.7

They contrasted their successful lives with those of the 'so-called lovers of virtue', *i.e.* the Jews who had not received their education. Their Jewish opponents are described by a series of antonyms as

> almost without exception obscure people, looked down upon, of mean estate, destitute of the necessities of life, not enjoying the privileges of subject peoples or even of slaves, filthy, sallow, reduced to skeletons, with a hungry look from lack of food, the prey of disease, in training for dying.[23]

The sophists' comment that their Jewish opponents were 'almost without exception' obscure people, acknowledges that there were some Jews of note. This may well have been a specific reference to Philo, whose wider family were people of substance and influence in Alexandria and elsewhere.[24] The invectives used by the Alexandrian sophists conveyed the impression of a group which was, on the whole, without social status.

Did Jews seek these career opportunities? Philo complained that fellow Alexandrians pursued a Greek education, but not for the virtue it instilled which was notionally its grand purpose. He argues that they did this 'with no higher motive than parading their superiority, or from desire of office under our rulers'.[25] Hengel also comments that

> the tendency to demonstrate one's superior status by knowledge of Greek and a degree of Greek education and customs continued under the sons of Herod, the Roman prefects and procurators.[26]

Interestingly, the pagan author Petronius, writing during Nero's principate, notes that unless a Jew is circumcised 'he will leave the tribe and emigrate to Greek cities and will not tremble at the Sabbath', *i.e.* he

---

[22]Philo, *Det.* 33, 34b. *Cf.* Aristides, *Or.* 33.19 where the benefits of engaging in oratory are outlined, *viz.* 'wealth, reputation, honour, marriage, or any acquisition'.

[23]Philo, *Det.* 34a. This last reference to 'training for dying' has been seen as equivalent to ἐπιτηδεύει ἀποθνῄσκειν, used of the philosopher in Plato, *Phaedo* 64a. See *LCL* II, 493-4 and Simmias' response that 'this is exactly what my unphilosophical countrymen would say of the philosophers'.

[24]On the question of the wealth and status of his wider family, see J. Schwartz, 'Note sur la famille de Philon d'Alexandrie', *Mélanges Isidore Lévy. Annuaire de l'Institut de philologie et d'histoire orientales et slaves* (Université Libre de Bruxelles) 13 (1953) 591-602 and S. Foster, 'A Note on the "Note" of J. Schwartz', *S.P.* 4 (1976-7) 25-32.

[25]*LA* III. 167 Jews are certainly meant in this passage; see 'our race' in *LA* III.166.

[26]M. Hengel, *The Hellenization of Judaea in the First Century after Christ* (London: SCM, 1989) 40.

will be a non–practising member of that community and possibly become an apostate.[27] Tiberius Claudius Alexander, the nephew of Philo of Alexandria, best illustrates both the career possibilities open to a young Jew who was trained in Greek education and the temptation to apostasize to which he succumbed.[28]

It is clear from the evidence that the purpose of reversing circumcision related to social standing in the Roman empire, and not simply to ridicule that might be experienced in the public baths or the gymnasium. The reason for young Jewish men, (presumably shared by their parents), wanting them to participate in the latter was not solely connected with athletics. It had to do with their status as *ephebi* and the career opportunities that higher education opened for them. Financial success and social status in the Roman world were much coveted, but Jewish Christians of the Diaspora were precluded by Paul from surrendering their national identity for personal advantage.

II. Manumission of Slaves

The one change of social status in 7:17–24 which Paul appears to have accepted was the legal manumission of slaves (v. 21b). This was discussed within the context of a commandment to the household servant who was not to be concerned about his status as a slave (v. 21a). The Christian could be described as 'the Lord's freedman' if a slave, and 'Christ's slave' if a free man (v. 22).[29]

Verse 21b has been read to mean either that those who are slaves should 'keep on in slavery' or that they should take the opportunity to secure their freedom. A secure case can be made from the text itself that the latter is the preferred interpretation apart from the background material. The verb 'to make use of' (χρῆσαι) is an aorist infinitive implying a single action, while the former interpretation that a servant should remain as a slave would require a present tense.[30]

An important observation has been made concerning first-century slavery which should help sever the connection made in the

[27]*Satyricon* fragment 371.

[28]Schürer, *The History of the Jewish People*, I. 456–8. On the prohibition of nudity by Jews and the refusal of Jews to circumcise their sons, see Jubilees 3:31; 15:33ff.

[29]See Scott Bartchy, *First–Century Slavery and 1 Corinthians 7:21*, 180 and more recently Dawes, 'But If you Can Gain your Freedom', 681–697.

[30]See Fee, *The First Epistle to the Corinthians*, 317 and his other cogent reasons.

minds of many between slavery in more recent centuries and that in the early empire.

> Roman slavery, viewed as a legal institution, makes sense of the assumption that slaves could reasonably aspire to being freed and hence to becoming Roman citizens or, at least, that the main rules of the institution were framed with those slaves primarily in mind who could reasonably have such an aspiration.[31]

It has been noted that 'one of the most striking aspects of Roman slavery was the frequency with which slaves were freed by their masters.'[32] The reasons were not primarily humanitarian but arose out of self–interest. Hopkins argues

> Emancipation reinforced slavery as a system because Roman slaves, frequently, even customarily in my view, paid substantial sums for their freedom. The prospect of becoming free kept a slave under control and hard at work, while the exaction of a market price as the cost of liberty enabled the master to buy a younger replacement.[33]

The clause 'but if indeed you are able to become free' indicates that the person might have the capability to do so. The power to become free might be connected with the servant's possession of the requisite sum of money to secure such freedom.[34] The reference may also be in some circumstances to the willingness of the master to manumit the person concerned.

It has not always been understood that the manumitted person had ongoing commitments to his former master who was now that person's patron. These obligations required the person to undertake a certain number of days in service. *The Digest* explains that 'Such days of work are given to the patron as ought to be estimated in accordance with age, dignity, health, needs, and other such factors, with regard to both parties'.[35] In the event of the former master having financial

---

[31] A. Watson, *Roman Slave Law* (Baltimore and London: Johns Hopkins University Press, 1987) 23. A.L. Higginbotham Jr. in his preface to this volume draws attention to the value of this study which helps to draw important distinctions between the two eras: see ixff.

[32] Hopkins, *Conquerors and Slaves*, 115.

[33] Hopkins, *Conquerors and Slaves*, 116 and also K.R. Bradley, *Slaves and Masters in the Roman Empire: A Study in Social Control* (Oxford: OUP, 1987) 108–12.

[34] Bradley, *Slaves and Masters in the Roman Empire*, 110ff. on the *perculium*, the money collected by a slave which gave him or her the ability to secure freedom.

[35] *The Digest* 38.1.16.1.

difficulties, the freedman was required to support 'his needy patron'.[36] The 'concessive' nature of what Paul was actually saying has not always been correctly perceived, for the 'freedom' sought was from social stigma, not from the legal and financial obligations subsequent to manumission. So Paul was encouraging what Roman law permitted when he wrote that slaves should secure their freedom if they could (v. 21b).[37] However, this is not the import of the whole passage, although it has been a centre of interest in the debate about Paul's attitude to slavery. The passage actually belongs in a context explaining why Christians who are slaves should not be anxious about their secular status (v. 22) and is not unconnected to the preceding and subsequent discussion on God's calling and to their revolutionary status in Christ (1:26ff.).

III. Voluntary Slavery by Free Men[38]

In a recent treatment, D.B. Martin has suggested that the argument in 1 Corinthians 7:23 is as follows: 'Because they are now slaves of Christ, they should not willingly become slaves of any human being. To do so would be to pass from high status in a highly placed household to a position in a lesser household'. He adds, 'Verse 23 indicates that, ideally, Paul considers slavery to Christ and slavery to a human owner as mutually exclusive'.[39]

However, from the secular point of view, the move from freedom to slavery was for the very purpose of moving from a lesser household to a position in a highly placed one and was undertaken for financial and social reasons. J. Crook notes that self-enslavement was undertaken 'in order to secure the post of *servus actor*, the chief accountant of a big household (and in due course to become later their freedman

---

[36]Watson, *Roman Slave Law*, 40.

[37]On the application of Roman law and the Roman character of the colony see D.W.J. Gill, 'Corinth: A Roman Colony of Achaea', *Biblische Zeitschrift* 37 (1993) 259-64 esp. 264. 'Classicists are in no doubt as to the Roman nature of the colony'.

[38]Paul does not appear to be discussing the re-enslavement of a freedman for ingratitude towards his patron. For the provision against *libertus ingratus*, see W.W. Buckland, *The Roman Law of Slavery: The Condition of the Slave in Private Law from Augustus to Justinian* (Cambridge: CUP, 1908) 422ff. The reference is clearly to free men (v. 23).

[39]*Slavery as Salvation: The Metaphor of Slavery in Pauline Christianity* (New Haven: Yale University Press, 1990) 66, 70 n. 21. See Scott Bartchy, *First-Century Slavery and 1 Corinthians 7:21*, 47-8 for the evidence.

procurator in the same post and eventually a rich citizen with free–
born children)'.[40] *The Digest* recognises that 'free men too, if in particular being over twenty they allow themselves to be sold. . .are not
barred from proclaiming freedom'.[41]

In *Satyricon* 57 Petronius, who wrote this work possibly in Nero's
Principate,[42] records both the procedures and the advantages of such
a move.[43] The scene is a dinner given by the enormously wealthy
Trimalchio, himself a freedman. In Hermeros's quarrel with Ascylton,
the latter's status is solicited ('are you a Roman knight?') to which he
replies that concerning his status, he is a king's son. The retort 'why
have you been a slave?' ('*Quare ergo servivisti*') demands an explanation
which reveals the motivation of Hermeros who describes his present
status as a freedman (58) but also his history as a free man who sold
himself into slavery.

> I went into service to please myself, and preferred being a Roman cit-
> izen to going on paying taxes as a provincial. And now I hope I live
> such a life that no one can jeer at me. I am a man among men; I walk
> about bare-headed; I owe nobody a brass farthing; I have never been
> in the Courts; no one has ever said to me in public, 'Pay me what you
> owe me!'; I have bought a few acres and collected a little capital; I have
> to feed twenty bellies and a dog; I ransomed my fellow slave to pre-
> serve her from indignities; I paid a thousand silver pennies for my
> own freedom; I was made a priest of Augustus and excused the fees;
> I hope to die so that I need not blush in my grave.

---

[40]*Law and Life of Rome* 60, although it must be remembered that only those who
were formally manumitted were eligible for Roman citizenship. See Weaver,
Familia Caesaris: A Social Study of the Emperor's Freedmen and Slaves, 1.
[41]Ulpian, *Edict* 54, XL.12.7 cf. XL.13.1.
[42]See H.C. Schnur, 'The Economic Background of the Satyricon', *Latomus* 18 (1959)
790–9 for its date; J.P. Sullivan, *The Satyricon of Petronius* (London: Faber and Faber,
1968) 24–5; and K.F.C. Rose, *The Date and the Author of the Satyricon* (Leiden: E.J.
Brill, 1971). Scott Bartchy, *First–Century Slavery and 1 Corinthians 7:21*, 47–8 briefly
discusses this passage, citing Crook, *Law and Life of Rome* 60 and stating without
further explanation that it was done in order 'to obtain a place in Roman society'.
[43]While the *Satyricon* is a novel, its witness to the conventions and attitudes of its
day should not be dismissed. As in the case of Apuleius' *The Golden Ass*, a novel
written in A.D. *c.* 180 which has proved a source of information on Corinth and
which reflects aspects of its life and times (see F. Millar, 'The World of *The Golden
Ass*,' *JRS* 71 (1981) 63–75), so too Petronius' work reflects attitudes as well as social
and legal conventions of Nero's era which make it an invaluable source especially
on the subject in question.

A number of important points emerge from this autobiographical statement. His decision to become enslaved was not made because of debt nor for any misdemeanour, but purely for his own advantage: 'I went into service to please myself'. This is explained in the following statement which outlines the status and financial advantages of Roman citizenship, to which he was entitled after his manumission, and the avoidance of the provincial tax to which he had previously been subject.

He was obviously conscious of his status, for he tells his opponent that, even though he was a slave, nobody knew whether he was slave or free (57). To his mind his tasks and lifestyle were such that they could not discern his legal status. His many achievements had secured for him a status and make him feel 'a man among men', *i.e.* as good as the next man (*cf.* 39.4; 74.13).

He does not need 'to cover his head in shame'. He is not in debt, which means that he is under no financial obligations. He has never been 'humiliated by a court action', something dreaded by Roman citizens,[44] nor has he suffered the indignity of being challenged in public for the failure to pay a debt on time—'pay me what you owe me'.[45] He is a landowner and presides over a household of twenty. He has also secured the manumission of an exploited female slave. On the matter of his own manumission, he has paid for it himself,[46] for he holds a position in the extremely wealthy household of Trimalchio.[47]

He has achieved the important status of a priest of Augustus and more significantly has done so without the fees. The office of *serviratus Augustalis* had been established in Italy as a means of attracting the loyalty of the wealthy by appealing to their ambition. It comprised a board of six and usually consisted of freedmen—such membership signalling a pinnacle of success among freedmen. The waiving of payment was an exceptional honour.[48] It is possible that his influential

---

[44]Epstein, *Personal Enmity in Roman Politics*, 90ff., especially the personal humiliation and possible destruction of the social standing felt by Romans.

[45]See M.S. Smith, *Petronii Arbitri Cena Trimalchionis* (Oxford: Clarendon Press, 1975) 156, for a discussion of the use of the term *constitutum*, 'an agreement to repay a debt on a fixed date'.

[46]He had obviously gainfully invested his 'working capital' (*peculium*) borrowed from his master; see Hopkins, *Conquerors and Slaves*, 125.

[47]For a discussion of his wealth and that of others during this period, see Schnur, 'The Economic Background of the Satyricon', 92ff.

[48]See Smith, *Petronii Arbitri Cena Trimalchionis*, 62, 157 for a discussion of the office and the waiving of the fee. He cites as an example *CIL* X.3959: '*sevir Aug(ustalis) decr(eto) decur(ionum) gratis factus*'.

patron procured this for his freedman as an honour in return for benefactions.[49] The freedman thanks God for his education: 'it made me
what I am, as you see'. It suggests that his formal education could have
been to the third level of παιδεία, viz. in the school of the sophists.[50] To
it he attributes the entrepreneurial skills which have secured his
standing.[51]

Hermeros engages in invective against his opponent, Ascylton
—'You can see the lice on others, but not the bugs on yourself'. It
reveals his awareness of the status into which he has sold himself.
Ascylton alone finds Hermeros amusing, but by contrast the school-
master of Ascylton, who is older and wiser than his student, likes him.
Ascylton may be richer and 'able to have two breakfasts a day as well
as two dinners', born with a silver spoon in his mouth, but Hermeros
includes the cutting remark, 'I prefer my reputation to any riches'. He
refers to his own tomb, which will reflect either his wealth or that he
has maintained his honour.

Even making allowance for exaggerated boasts by Hermeros, *The
Satyricon* reflects the economic and legal realities of Paul's period and
provides important evidence of the quest for status and money which
motivated a free man to enslave himself for ultimate gain.

There is also a brief second century A.D. letter which parallels
the situation of Hermeros. Its main objective was to convey the information 'Know, then, that Herminos went off to Rome and became a
freedman of Caesar in order to take appointments'.[52] It is not only the
lure of *officia*—the term ὁπίκια is used in *l.* 13 to denote public offices—
that is of interest, but the fact that Herminos became 'a freedman of
Caesar'. While it has been said that his reason for relinquishing his free
status 'is hard to imagine',[53] the above discussion explains why this
was done. There has been conjecture that Herminos was an Imperial
slave without status in the Egyptian administration or that he was
transferred as a slave of an non–imperial owner to the emperor's own-
ership and then manumitted.[54] The letter may reflect the something of

---

[49]See R. Gordon, 'The Veil of Power: Emperors, Sacrifices and Benefactors', 219ff.
esp. 225 for the unusual exemption from the *summum* bearing in mind the link
between the priesthood and benefactions.
[50]H.I. Marrou, *History of Education in Antiquity* (ET; London: Sheed and Ward,
1956) ch. 10.
[51]On the recruiting of 'the highly cultured' from the East to work in Roman Italy
as slaves, see Hopkins, *Conquerors and Slaves*, 123–4.
[52]*P.Oxy.* 3312 *ll.* 10–13.
[53]G.H.R. Horsley, 'Joining the Household of Caesar' *New Docs.* 3 (1983) 8.

the situation of Hermeros who said he sold himself into slavery to escape the provincial tax, although his reasons were for increased financial and social status and not really tax relief, as the discussion has shown. Here the free man's explanation given in Egypt to the family and passed on in the letter was not that he was selling himself into slavery, but that he was securing a career path in the imperial household. It might well be that he became an imperial servant in Caesar's household and that the report of the matter seeks to glide over the realities of selling himself into slavery. There is uncertainty concerning this man's legal status as such a situation has not been encountered before by ancient historians. The letter is helpful in that it shows that this person is seeking advancement in the imperial service with all the attendant advantages of the full manumission and Roman citizenship that entry and into the imperial household would provide.

Lucian wrote two essays, the former, 'On Salaried Posts in Great Houses' denouncing those who sought such posts, and the latter, an 'Apology for the "Salaried Posts in Great Houses"', retracting some of the things he had written in the former since he himself had then taken up a salaried post in the imperial administration. The first work is highly informative because it describes something of the motivation and humiliation which could be experienced by those who undertook salaried posts in the houses of the rich. It is a revealing insight into the way 'class' not only affected the world of *politeia*, but reached to the centre of much activity in the ancient world, *viz.* the household. This move into 'great houses' is seen by Lucian as slavery—'of his own free will rush headlong into slavery so manifest and conspicuous' (*Apology* 1).

In Lucian's first essay he explains that those who enter these posts may seek to defend their actions by claiming poverty, but that they really expect to enjoy the benefits of living out their lives in the context of the great luxury of leading households. He adds, 'They plunge themselves into these households for the sake of pleasure and that is what seduces them and makes them slaves instead of free men' (7). He also argues that status is a motivating factor for they think that their new position 'exalts them above the masses' (9). Lucian warns that life in a famous house could be a demeaning experience even for a salaried free man. While the situation is not exactly the same, it can be concluded that if free men who undertook salaried posts could be

---

[54]P.R.C. Weaver *per litt.* to G.H.R. Horsley, 'Joining the Household of Caesar' 8.

humiliated and put to shame, how much more would those who sold themselves into slavery be subjected to even greater humiliation.

While Paul does not specify why he is so concerned, noting simply that Christ secured the free man's real manumission, other background evidence may provide an additional clue. Those who voluntarily sold themselves into slavery would have been expected to swear by the *genius* of their master. It was a veiled form of worship, as is evident in the case of those who swore by the *genius* of the emperor. The latter imitated the cult that developed from that which 'the genius of the family head (*paterfamilias*) received from his household'.[55] Free men had no such obligation, and it is interesting to note that it was not until the reign of Nero that developments in the imperial cult sought to draw in this class.[56] Paul would have had substantial reservations about a free man voluntarily putting himself in this position.

Unlike the Augustan era, in the Principate of Claudius there was considerable 'enthusiasm of provincials' for the Roman citizenship which was acquired as a direct result of imperial encouragement.[57] This may well account for the desire to provide a Christian 'tradition' on this matter for all the Pauline churches.

IV. Calling and Social Status in 1 Corinthians 7:17–24

The evidence discussed in sections I, II and III points to the common factor of social status. The background evidence also reveals the accompanying financial benefits which accrued as the motive for some Christians in the Pauline churches wanting to undergo epispasm, voluntary slavery and manumission.[58] Does the nexus between possible

---

[55]J. Rives, 'The *iuno feminae* in Roman Society', *Echos du Monde Classique/ Classical Views* 36.1 n.s. (1992) 39–42. I am grateful to Dr. T. Hillard for drawing my attention to this important consideration.

[56]S. Weinstock, *Divus Julius* (Oxford: Clarendon Press, 1971) 214–6.

[57]F. Millar, *The Emperor in the Roman World* (31 B.C.–A.D. 337) (London: Duckworth, 1977) 481 on Augustus. See E.M. Smallwood, 'The Claudian Problem and *Viritane* Grants', *The Jews under the Roman Rule*, ch. 9 citation 249 on the change of policy with Claudius and see also A. Lintott, *Imperium Romanum: Politics and Administrations* (London: Routledge, 1993) 167.

[58]This does not explain why some Christian Gentiles sought to undergo circumcision (1 Cor. 7:18b). It must be remembered that Paul is simply repeating a summary of his tradition. Galatians provides clues as to why some Christians sought this Jewish rite, see chapter 7.

'career' paths and the search for status fit into the immediate context of vv. 17–24?

The meaning of Paul's term 'calling' (κλῆσις) and its cognates in vv. 17–24 suggests that it does. These were tied up with social status in the Graeco–Roman world and were clearly related to class. Dionysius of Halicarnassus, in his Greek work on *Roman Antiquities*, offers a discussion of the origins of the Latin word *classis*. 'There were six divisions which the Romans called *classes*, by a slight change of the Greek word κλήσεις for the verb which we Greeks pronounce in the imperative mood κάλει, the Romans called *cala*, and the classes they anciently called *caleses*.'[59] When Dionysius describes the Roman class system, he likewise uses the term κλῆσις and its cognates. 'Those who were eminent for their birth, approved for their virtue (ἀρετή) and wealth, were distinguished from the class of the obscure, the lowly and the poor' (II.8).[60] Others might call clients 'hirelings' as in the case of Athenians, or 'serfs' (πενέσται) in the case of the Thessalonians, with the choice of term epitomized by their status (εὐθύς ἐν τῇ κλήσει τὴν τύχην, II.9).[61] The Latin term signals in the first-century 'class'.

> A *classis* was a 'summoning' or 'calling out' of the Roman people for military action. When the Romans assembled in this way, they arranged themselves in groups (*classes*) which were distinguished according to the financial resources and pride of lineage of their members. The adjective *classicus* thus came to mean 'of or pertaining to class' in a general way, but most often it referred to things associated with the upper classes. From this it acquired the general sense of 'first class' or 'of the highest rank'.[62]

---

[59]Dionysius of Halicarnassus, *Roman Antiquities* IV.18.

[60]It is his belief that the patronage system was copied from the Athenians (the Greek origins of Rome are an essential part of the thesis of his history) who divided their population into εὐπατρίδαι or well-born 'as they called those who were of noble families and powerful by reason of their wealth, to whom the government of the city was committed', and the ἀγροίκοι who constituted the remainder of the population (II.8).

[61]Rome however used a handsome designation, calling the protection of the poor and lowly class 'patronage' (πατρώνια), the 'bond of kindness befitting fellow citizens' (II.9). He also notes that the patronage was not restricted to Rome 'but each of Rome's colonies. . .had Romans of their own choosing as their protectors and patrons' (II.1). See Saller, *Personal Patronage under the Early Empire* 168ff. on 'provincials and their mediators'.

[62]J.J. Pollitt, 'On the meaning of "classical"', *Art and Experience in Classical Greece* (Cambridge: CUP, 1972) 1. I am grateful to Dr. T. Hillard for this reference.

Paul states that each Christian is to 'remain in the calling', *i.e.* class, to which he has been called (ἕκαστος ἐν τῇ κλήσει ᾖ ἐκλήθη ἐν ταύτῃ μενέτω, v. 20). He likewise uses κλῆσις to refer to the racial and social groupings to which his congregation belonged.[63] The social dichotomy between Jews and Gentiles is discussed in 1 Corinthians 7:18–19. In both instances they are to remain in the ethnic κλῆσις in which they were born. They must not remove their distinguishing racial marks.[64]

It is in this context that Paul's statement in v. 19 is to be interpreted. 'Circumcision is nothing' although some mistakenly underwent this Jewish rite for particular reasons,[65] 'and uncircumcision is nothing' although some believed that it was the key to their social ascent, 'but the keeping of the commandments of God' (v. 18c) is everything.[66] What are these commands? P.J. Tomson has suggested that 'the message [*viz.* keeping the commandments of God] is that one should fear God and be intent on what is fundamentally commanded'.[67] It may be possible to be more specific than that. Paul's previous discussion provides a theological framework within which a later issue can be understood by means of a careful cumulative approach in 1 Corinthians.[68] He has already warned the Corinthians against keeping company with a fellow Christian who is a covetous person (5:11) and against covetousness as the grounds for exclusion from the kingdom of God (6:10). Would not the first-century Christians in Corinth and elsewhere have been only too aware of the reasons why the Christian Jews underwent the operation? There were obvious

---

[63]*Cf.* 1:26ff. where the term also refers to social distinctions.

[64]Martin, *Slavery as Salvation*, 65–6. He rightly observes, 'Paul's language. . .clearly reflects the Greco–Roman preoccupation with status and the place of persons. . .within society', although there is no discussion of the meaning of the term.

[65]See chapter 7.

[66]Far too much has been made of this statement, almost to the stage of making it into a proof text. E.P. Sanders, *Paul, the Law and the Jewish People* (Philadelphia: Fortress Press, 1983) calls this 'one of the most amazing sentences he ever wrote'. This passage does not reflect aspects of a new 'covenantal nomism'. For a brief critique of aspects of Sanders on this point see P.J. Tomson, *Paul and the Jewish Law: Halakha in the Letters of the Apostle to the Gentiles* (Assen, Netherlands and Minneapolis: Van Gorcum and Fortress Press, 1990) 17.

[67]Tomson, *Paul and the Jewish Law*, 271–2, draws a dichotomy between Jews and Gentiles and argues that the latter's obligations are not to the Torah but to the Noachian code.

[68]See B. Rosner, 'Temple and Holiness in 1 Corinthians 5', *Tyn.B.* 42 (1991) 142, where he cites K. Snodgrass, 'Spheres of Influence: A Possible Solution to the Problem of Paul and the Law', *JSNT* 32 (1988) 104.

advantages to renouncing one's ethnic identity during one's education, especially as one's spiritual status even as a Jew in the new
covenant was no longer necessarily connected with circumcision.

A similar theological significance was later attached to epispasm
by Rabbi Eleazar who died during the revolt of Bar Kochba. He
declared that a man who underwent epispasm 'broke the covenant of
Abraham', *i.e.* obliterated his circumcision by epispasm and thereby
forfeited his inheritance in the life to come.[69] Paul may also have
observed, as did Romans and Jews, that a Jew undergoing epispasm
became an apostate. Although Paul does not elucidate the reasons for
this proscription in any other letters, it was obviously an important
part of his 'apostolic teaching' (παράδοσις) that the Jewish Christian
was not to seek to obscure his racial identity. God's calling provided
sufficient theological reason, even as it forbade Christian Gentiles from
undergoing circumcision (v. 18b).[70]

The above discussion suggests that Paul's concern was with the
Christian Jew who sought to escape from the social disadvantages of
his ethnic status during the Claudian period by undergoing epispasm
(v. 18a).[71] It does not support the view that 'the rule has to do with
"circumcised" and "uncircumcised" and their respective status in the
church'.[72] Both groups are exhorted to remain in their ethnic status.

Paul did not allow non–Roman Christian free men to sell
themselves into slavery as a route to Roman citizenship. He has
already discussed the irrelevance of social status in relation to
salvation in 1:26ff., and the status of Christians who are 'in Christ Jesus'
(ἐν Χριστῷ Ἰησοῦ) in 1:30. Aspiring to the status of Roman citizenship,
with its attendant financial and social benefits via the route of
voluntary slavery was therefore forbidden. In a subsequent discussion
Paul calls upon Christians to adopt a new attitude towards their
existence. In 7:30 'those who buy [are to live] as if they possessed
nothing' (οἱ ἀγοράζοντες ὡς μὴ κατέχοντες).[73] This exhortation would
not have been lost on those who contemplated selling themselves into

---

[69]Mishnah *Aboth* 3.12; BT *Sanh*, 99a; *Strack Billerbeck*, 4.1.31–57.
[70]He states elsewhere that this was being done in order to escape persecution for
the cross of Christ (Gal. 6:12). For a discussion see chapter 7.
[71]*Cf.* Tomson, *Paul and the Jewish Law*, 270, who feels that the passage is fragmen-
tary and yet that there is sufficient to conclude that the essence differs from the
polemics of Galatians and 'the balanced dialectics' of Romans.
[72]Tomson, *Paul and the Jewish Law*, 270.
[73]On the use of κατέχοντες see 2 Cor. 6:10: 'As having nothing, yet possessing all
things' (ὡς μηδὲν ἔχοντες καὶ πάντα κατέχοντες). See also *P.Tebt*. 5.47 on the possession of property.

slavery in order to undertake commercial activity and thus secure a financial and social future for themselves and their children. Wimbush has argued that ὡς μὴ κατέχοντες does not prohibit involvement in commercial affairs but only 'the attitude that leads to grasping and covetousness'.[74]

While the rehearsal of Paul's standard teaching or 'tradition' in vv. 17–24 is succinct in that there is none of the extensive argumentation which often accompanied his ethical discussion, the apostle clearly has been concerned to provide, for all his churches, authoritative teaching on this first-century preoccupation with social status in *politeia*.[75]

V. Calling and Christians in *politeia*

There may have been some who argued that because Paul taught Christians to be civic benefactors, the pursuit of higher social status was thus inherently justified. Christians moving to secure high-status positions in the public place could not do so. If ever that was an argument, and again it must be born in mind that verses 17–24 are a summary without arguments or responses, it would not have persuaded Paul for the summary in vv. 17–24 is part of a much larger argument in 1 Corinthians 7. It concerns one's relational status, *i.e.* married, widowed or betrothed, and one's ethnic origins and social status, *i.e.* Jew or Gentile, slave, or free, and the complexity as to what should be done about any changes in these because of the present 'dislocation' in Corinth (7:26).[76]

Paul has very clear teaching on the matter of 'gift' (χάρισμα) and 'calling' (κλῆσις), both of which he sees as having been providentially ordered for each Christian. This is his over–arching theological framework. He rules in v. 17, 'as the Lord has distributed to each, as the Lord has called each. . .thus he must walk'.

---

[74]V.L. Wimbush, *Paul the Worldly Ascetic: Response to the World and Self–understanding according to 1 Corinthians 7* (Macon: Mercer University Press, 1987). 30. *Cf.* W. Schrage, 'Die Stellung zur Welt bei Paulus, Epiket und in der Apokalyptik. Ein Beitrag zur 1 Kor. 7:29–31', *ZThK* 61 (1964) 151, who suggests that the reference is to the grasping of these things as inappropriate.

[75]On the importance of the social status of clients and Paul's response, see the discussion in ch. 3.

[76]For a discussion of that background see p. 53ff. and also 'Secular and Christian Responses to Corinthian Famines', *Tyn.B.* 40 (1989) 88-106.

It was the Corinthians' inability to grasp the significance of being 'in Christ' which caused Paul in his introductory prayer of thanksgiving to reflect on their feelings of inferiority that they 'came behind' others socially or intellectually, and the remedy for that was to be found 'in Christ' (1:4–7). There was no deficiency in Christ for the Christian either in 'gift' (χάρισμα) or 'calling' (κλῆσις) (1:7, 26ff.). Those Christians who yearned to join the 'class' of the 'wise, mighty and well–born' whose significance was most visible in the public place were forbidden to do so. Their aspirations represent a failure thankfully to acknowledge what they were by virtue of their calling in Christ (1:26–31). Their conduct and that of other Christians in the Pauline churches reflects a perception of themselves determined by the concerns of those who sought social mobility in *politeia*.

CHAPTER NINE

CIVIC RIGHTS

1 Corinthians 8-11:1

If Christians were precluded from 'social climbing' (see chapter 8), then what could be done about those who already possessed high social status? The Christian faith might interfere with existing privileges or rights conferred by such status. In 1 Corinthians 8:9 Paul refers to 'this "right" of yours' (ἡ. . .αὕτη) as a cause of difficulty for some Christians. It will be argued that 'this right' was a civic privilege which entitled Corinthian citizens to dine on 'civic' occasions in a temple.

One way to enhance the life of the city was to endow an annual feast as a benefactor. The other was to give one while holding an annual public office. The entitlement to attend these endowed feasts could be restricted to citizens who had been honoured, or to those who had held public office.[1] They might also include those who were 'active' citizens, for participation in the life of *politeia* was dependent upon the payment of a sum of money which enabled them to exercise their civic rights.[2]

There are a number of reasons for believing that this passage deals with a civic privilege which conferred the right to attend civic dinners in a temple. In order to demonstrate this, it will be argued that (I) in spite of its inconsistent rendering by translators and commentators, the term ἐξουσία in 1 Corinthians 8:9 refers to a 'right' possessed by some Corinthian Christians to dine in the temple, (II) there is extant evidence of the right of Corinthian citizens, as distinct from other inhabitants of this Roman colony, to participate in certain public feasts, (III) these feasts most likely refer to those given at the famous Isthmian games, (IV) while participation could be justified on the grounds that 'it is lawful' (ἔξεστιν) and to one's own 'advantage' (σύμφορον), Paul rejects this by invoking the paradigm of his ministry which was based on Christ's as that which sought both the physical and spiritual welfare of others (11:1).

I. The 'right' (ἐξουσία) of 1 Corinthians 8:9

The word ἐξουσία has been translated in this verse as 'liberty' by the RV, NASB and REB, with the RV suggesting in a footnote, 'power'. The NIV curiously renders the term 'exercise of your freedom', thus omitting the word 'this', for the phrase reads ἡ ἐξουσία ὑμῶν αὕτη. The

---

[1]See p. 168ff. for examples and further the collection of documents in Hands, *Charities and Social Aid in Greece and Rome*, 175ff.

[2]Jones, *The Roman World of Dio Chrysostom*, 80–1.

assumption made by such translations is that the 'liberty' or 'freedom' (ἐξουσία) of some Corinthians to eat in the temple springs from know ledge that an idol was nothing (8:4).

What is the justification for the translation of this term as 'liberty' or 'freedom' in 8:9? Paul uses the same term repeatedly in the following chapter. In none of these cases does his argument allow us to render the word 'liberty' or 'freedom'. Furthermore he uses the term 'free' (ἐλεύθερος) some five verses later (9:1), so that one would have expected the term ἐλευθερία in 8:9 had he meant 'liberty' (*cf.* 9:19). On the contrary, he himself argues cogently that his 'right' (ἐξουσία) is his entitlement by reason of his apostleship, at least as far as the Corinthian church is concerned (9:1-2). As such, he is entitled to take a spouse on his travels and to be supported financially by his converts (9:4–6). His entitlement to such a 'right' is reiterated by means of a number of questions in which he lists the equivalent rights of soldiers, vine-dressers, shepherds, oxen according to the OT, ploughmen and reapers, and OT priests (9:7-13). The implication is clear. Paul and others are entitled to such support from the Corinthians (9:11–12a).

However, Paul himself has never claimed his right (9:12b). He has not availed himself of it, nor was he claiming it when he wrote (9:12c, 15). The word 'wage' is used of his just entitlement or 'right' (9:17). Rather he speaks of his satisfaction in preaching the gospel without charge to anyone, not having made use of his 'right' in the gospel, *viz.* a wage as an evangelist and apostle (9:18). It is clear from the context that Paul uses this term to refer to his inalienable right as an apostle to receive financial support, a right clearly ordained by the Lord for his apostles (9:14).

Paul, then, has gone to great lengths to argue his case concerning the correctness of not exercising his right. This is important, not only for his defence (9:3), but also for the contrast which he is making between his apostolic right and an established 'right' which was held and exercised by some Corinthian Christians. This becomes clear when, at the end of the whole discussion, he commands the Corinthians to imitate him in his Christ-like conduct, following his example of seeking not one's own advantage but that of others, both outside and inside the church (10:33). The contrast, therefore, is between two comparable matters—his right and theirs. These determine the conduct of both and have a bearing on their spiritual health (10:14ff.). It is a specific 'right' rather than 'rights' in general to which Paul refers in 8:9. Why then is another rendering required for the phrase, 'this right of yours', considering that Paul contrasts it with his own right?

The discussion of 'this right' does not end in chapter 9. In the discussion about reclining in a temple at an idol's feasts, it is possible to overlook the linguistic connection between 'right' (ἐξουσία) and 'it is lawful' (ἔξεστιν) used in 1 Corinthians 8–10. A legal right can be introduced by the verbal form 'it is lawful', 'it is allowed'.[3] A right established by a law (νόμος) or custom (ἔθος) can be referred to as what is lawful. This semantic connection further supports the view that in 8:9 ἐξουσία relates to a specific 'right'.

Paul's treatment of idolatry and the jealousy of God is based on the outcome of Israel's experience in a comparable situation (10:1–22). It is followed by an ethical challenge to the decision of some Corinthians to participate in the public feasts (10:23). '"All things may be lawful", but not all things build up others' (10:23b). Here Paul is returning to his discussion of the possible destructive effects on some 'weaker' Christians if others were to exercise their right (8:7ff.). He has already dealt with the deleterious effect that participating in public feasts had on the persons themselves (10:6ff.). Ethical decisions are not to be made on the grounds of personal rights. Paul has shown that this was the case in his own apostolic ministry (ch. 9). He again affirms this in his concluding comments, 'even as I also please all men in all things, not seeking my own benefit or advantage but the advantage of the many' (10:33).

Christian concern would also express itself in great sensitivity to the highly developed social interaction that existed at private dinner parties in the first century. There presumably the host, or perhaps a guest, might warn the Christian that the food they were eating had been offered to idols. Respect for the other person's comment comes into consideration. By this Paul means that what the non-Christian believes to be right or wrong for the Christian, will determine the latter's response (10:28-29a). He is thus not to exercise his right to eat.

II. Citizenship Rights and Civic Feasts

'Candidates for election promised to perform important benefactions for their fellow [Roman] citizens upon election, such as fund. . .banquets'.[4] These banquets could be connected with temples, as shown by the following inscription, which records the restoration of a temple

---

[3] ἔξεστιν ('it is allowed', 'it is possible'), ἐξόν (participle), ἐξεῖναι (infinitive), and ἐξουσία (noun), all of which are cited under ἔξεστι in Liddell and Scott.

and the building of additional dining rooms by Euphrosynus and his wife, Epigone.

> They rebuilt the temples which had been in utter ruins and they added dining–rooms to those existing and they provided the [religious] societies with treasuries. . .worshipping the gods reverently at sacrificial expense, in providing all men alike with a festive banquet.[5]

Some inscriptions state who could attend a particular benefactor's feast. In the first century A.D. in Epidaurus, south of Corinth, Soteles set up a statue and 'sacrificed to all the gods and gave a dinner to all the citizens and residents (πάροικοι) and to all the Romans residing with us and to the slaves of all these and their sons and the slaves' children'.[6] Other evidence indicates that separate feasts were held, one given by the magistrates at which the 'townspeople' present received 8 *sesterces* each, and another involving elite members of the city such as the priests of the *Lares* of Augustus and the officers of the city–wards, *i.e.* administrative divisions.[7]

Kritolaos, the son of Alkimedon, gave a large sum of money for the holding of an annual public feast in the gymnasium and an athletic contest in Aigiale, Amorgos in the second century B.C. because his son had been declared a hero. He gave specific details concerning the investment of his endowment, the minimum age of the two commissioners appointed to run the feast, the guests, the table decorations and the carrying away of food after the feast.

> Let them provide the dinner for all the citizens who are resident at Aigiale and the alien residents and the foreigners and those of the Romans and their wives who are present. . .And let the feast be a compulsory feast in the gymnasium, and let the commissioners set aside those in the dining–room a dinner, regardless of expense, and flowers. . .and all that is set before them may be carried away from the dining room.[8]

---

[4]D. Engels, *Roman Corinth: An Alternative Model for the Classical City* (Chicago: University of Chicago Press, 1990) 68.

[5]*IG* V², 268 (end of first century A.D.) Mantinea, Antogonea, Greece.

[6]*IG* IV², 65 first century A.D. (Epidaurus).

[7]*CIL* X, 4815 after A.D. 100. (Spoletium, central Italy), translated by N. Lewis and M. Reinhold, *Roman Civilization Source Book II: The Empire* (New York: Harper and Row, 1955) 356.

[8]*IG* XII, 7515

In the penultimate paragraph an inscription recorded that
money could be distributed to those eligible to attend the feast. In
Petelia in southern Italy an inscription was erected in *c.* A.D. 138–61 to
Manius Megonius Leo noting the amounts to be given. 'There may be
a distribution to the *decuriones* (magistrates) at a feast, of 300
denarii. . .the rest to be divided among those who shall be present. Also
to the *Augustales* (priests of Augustus) on the same condition I wish 150
denarii to be given.' It seems that not all were eligible because of their
status, although the benefactor prescribed that all the inhabitants were
to be given one *denarius* on the anniversary of his birthday.[9] Again in
Corfinium in central Italy *c.* A.D. 180 Priscinus 'gave to the town-
counsellors attending the feasts and to their children 30 *sesterces*, to the
board of six at the meal 20 *sesterces*, and to the whole people, to each
attending the feast, 8 *sesterces*'.[10]

Turning to Corinth there is also evidence of feasts. It has been
suggested that the idol temple referred to in 1 Corinthians 8:10 could
have been the sanctuary of Demeter, where dining occurred in small
rooms in the Greek period.[11] The archaeological evidence, however,
suggests that there was a break between activities in the sanctuary
during both the Greek period, when there were ritual dinners of small,
segregated groups of worshippers, and the Roman period. As Stroud
notes, 'Conceivably, there was still some kind of communal dining in
the open air, but it seems clear from the excavated remains that in the
Roman period small groups of segregated worshippers no longer
assembled indoors for ritual dining as they had in Greek times'.[12]
Given that the text in 1 Corinthians 8:10 specifies 'sitting at meat in an
idol's temple', the possibility that the incident relates to activities at the
Demeter sanctuary is unlikely, especially as the restoration occurred
later than the writing of 1 Corinthians. Furthermore, feasting there
would not be connected with any 'right' and this makes the possibility

---

[9]Dessau, *ILS* 6468.

[10]*Ibid.*, 6530.

[11]'The numerous dining–rooms of the Sanctuary of Demeter and Kore. . .are an eloquent testimony to the wider popularity of the symposium, at least in a religious
context.' J.B. Salmon, *Wealthy Corinth: a History of the City to 338 B.C.* (Oxford:
Clarendon Press, 1984) 403. See most recently P.D. Gooch, *Dangerous Food: 1 Corinthians 8–10 in Its Context;* Studies in Christianity and Judaism 5 (Waterloo,
Ontario: Wilfrid Laurier University Press, 1993) ch. 1 and 2 for the use of this in
relation to Roman Corinth.

[12]R.S. Stroud, 'The Sanctuary of Demeter on Acrocorinth in the Roman Period', in
T.E. Gregory (ed.), *The Corinthia in the Roman Period*, Journal of Roman Archaeology Mono. Supp. 8 (Ann Arbor: Cushing–Malloy, 1994) 69.

that this was the temple to which Paul refers in 1 Corinthians 8:10 still less likely.

It has been suggested that the *Asklepion* was the building in which the incident involving Christians occurred. However, while eating did occur, the activity was related to individual healing connected with dietary restrictions and the like.[13] There is no healing context mentioned in 1 Corinthians 8:1–11:1 and it is unlikely that Christians would have resorted to that temple for healing, since later in the letter gifts of healing are listed as operating inside the Christian community (12:29). Moreover, healing activities were not connected with any 'right' in the Temple of Asklepius, but were open to all.

We know that well before Paul's time the games were of such fame that the task of financing and running them was enormous. These duties had been transferred from the *aedile* to the president of the games who was ranked in status above the president of the city magistrates.[14] The games were moved from Sicyon to Corinth soon after the latter was declared a Roman colony.[15] Recent work has shown that it is unlikely that the games were taken back to the ancient site at Isthmia until a much later period.[16] The first recorded games appear to have been held there in the A.D. 50s, some ninety years after they were moved to Corinth. It is assumed that the site where they were held after they were returned to the colony was somewhere in the environs of Corinth.

> Lucius Castricus Regulus. . .who was [the first] to preside over the Isthmian games at the Isthmus under the sponsorship of *Colonia Laus Julia Corinthiensis*. . .and after the buildings of Caesarea were renovated. . .gave a banquet for all the colonists' (*epulumo omnibus colonis*).[17]

---

[13]See *IG* IV.1(2) 126 *ll.* 5ff. which recounts these activities connected with the cult. Communal dining is not certain if this inscription from Epidaurus is any guide. See Gooch, *Dangerous Food: 1 Corinthians 8–10 in its Context,* ch. 1 & 2 for a discussion of 1 Cor. 8–10 in relation to this particular temple complex in Corinth.

[14]See Kent, *Corinth,* 8.3.30 for the list of *agonothetai* and the more recent discussion of those who held both liturgies of magistrate and president of the Games in M. Amandry, *Le monnayage des duovirs corinthiens,* Bulletin de Correspondance Hellénique Supp. 15 (1988).

[15]E.R. Gebhard, 'The Isthmian Games and the Sanctuary of Poseidon in the Early Empire', in T.E. Gregory (ed.), *The Corinthia in the Roman Period,* Journal of Roman Archaeology Mono. Supp. 8 (Ann Arbor: Cushing–Malloy, 1994) 79–82 where she estimates the date to bec. 40 B.C. based on coins struck at the time.

[16] Gebhard, 'The Isthmian Games and the Sanctuary of Poseidon in the Early Empire', 78–94.

Gebhard rightly notes, 'As a final celebration, he hosted a banquet for the citizens of Corinth', *i.e.* Roman citizens.[18] This particular banquet at Isthmia would have occurred in the early years following the form ation of the church, and would have been subsequent to Regulus acting as a magistrate *(duovir)* in A.D. 50/51.

The president of the games was expected to entertain the citizens at a feast. Given the prestige of the games, an invitation to the banquet was considered a special privilege. Because the non–Roman inhabitants of Corinth were known as *incolae* ('inhabitants', 'residents'), the above reference to the guests at this banquet was only to citizens. There was a distinction between those who were citizens of the Roman colony of Corinth and those who were provincials. Roman citizens possessed privileges that others did not.[19]

> The non–Romans residing in Corinth were legally classified as *incolae*. They were not citizens of the colony, and they could not vote, hold magistracies, or be members of the *curia* unless they were given a special grant of citizenship. [20]

The citizens of Corinth were entertained on a number of occasions by the president of the games while they were in progress. Plutarch records this custom as he recounts his own experience of a more select dinner party which he attended with the president.[21]

> During the Isthmian games, the second time Sospis was president, I avoided the other banquets, at which he entertained a great many foreign visitors at one, and several times entertained all the citizens... *(Quaes. Conviv.* 723A).

---

[17]Kent, *Corinth,* 8.3.153. For the redating of the inscription and the discussion of the president of the games held in the Isthmia, see E.R. Gebhard, 'The Isthmian Games and the Sanctuary of Poseidon in the Early Empire', 87.

[18]Gebhard, 'The Isthmian Games and the Sanctuary of Poseidon in the Early Empire', 88. 'Citizens' is the correct translation for *colonus*. *Cf.* Kent, *Corinth,* 8.3.151, where he correctly renders the term there despite failing inexplicably to do so in no. 153.

[19]Sherwin–White, *The Roman Citizenship,* 245.

[20]Engels, *Roman Corinth,* 68, 70.

[21]C.P. Jones, *Plutarch and Rome,* (Oxford: Clarendon Press, 1971) 72 and Murphy-O'Connor, *St. Paul's Corinth* 101, who comments, 'It appears that Plutarch was a frequent visitor to Corinth, presumably on the occasion of the great panhellenic festival, the Isthmian games'.

It has been estimated that the population of Corinth at this time was approximately one hundred thousand.[22] This further substantiates the view that those who attended this banquet did so on the basis of their citizenship. It was their 'right' to do so.

III. 1 Corinthians 8–10 and the Isthmian Feasts

The problem about which the Corinthians wrote had not arisen when Paul was in Corinth.[23] He cites no 'tradition' that he had delivered to them on the matter in his discussion in 8:1–11:1, although he does so in the following verse and commends the Corinthians for their adherence to the traditions which he had delivered to them (11:2). The reason this matter may not have arisen before is that no games occurred during Paul's ministry in Corinth to which Christians who were Roman citizens were invited.

The text itself indicates that the person who is 'reclining' at a meal [at a dinner] (κατακείμενον) in the idol temple is seen by another Christian. The latter is described as being 'built up' (οἰκοδομηθήσεται), *i.e.* gaining confidence that eating idol food in a temple is not a wrong practice for a Christian, following the example of the Christian person reclining at a feast in an idol temple (8:10). It is the imitation of the other person's conduct to which Paul refers. That the president of the games gave several dinners to the citizens of Corinth could well mean that the weaker Christian exercised his civic right to join in another presidential dinner having declined an earlier feast. It was the eating of food specifically in the idol temple that caused the difficulty, as later in the discussion Christians so disposed are permitted to eat food which has been offered to idols at a private dinner (10:27).

The athletic imagery used later in the discussion perhaps provides further evidence that the Games constitute the *Sitz im Leben* in which the problem arises. Paul notes that 'all who strive in the Games. . .do so to receive a corruptible crown' (1 Cor. 9:24–25).

Later he refers to the experience of Israel in its eating and drinking and rising up to play (10:8). Both pagan and Christian writers

---

[22]J. Wiseman, *The Land of Ancient Corinth, Studies in Mediterranean Archaeology* (Göteberg, P. Artiöms Förlag, 1978) 11–12, rightly notes that no contemporary sources exist that provide such information. For a recent discussion of estimates see Engels, *Roman Corinth*, 79–84.

[23]On the use of περὶ δέ when replying to matters raised in correspondence, see *BGU* 1141.

discussed the nexus between feasts and immorality. Booth, after sum-
marising the evidence, states that 'eating and drinking and sexual
indulgence constitute. . .an unholy trinity'.[24] There were peripatetic
brothel keepers who supplied prostitutes for grand occasions and it
may have been that they provided services at dinners on such great festive gatherings as the Games.[25] The concern, then, about immorality at
feasts on the part of Paul was not unfounded (1 Cor. 10:8a cf. also 6:15).

In addition, as Engels notes, 'The Isthmian Games were linked to
the imperial cult through the Caesarean Games and the Imperial Con-
tests'.[26] The connection with the imperial cult and 'the gods on the
earth' (8:5) has already been explored.[27] This provides further cumulative evidence to support the view that the issue in Paul's mind is the
dining 'right' of Christian Roman citizens to attend the 'several' feasts
given by the President of the Games.

There were certainly rights attached to Roman citizenship,[28] but
can the established custom of entertaining the Corinthian citizens, one
of the privileges of Roman citizenship in the colony, be described as
such? It was Dio Chrysostom in his oration on 'custom' who defined
it as 'an unwritten law of a tribe [an administrative division in a city]
or city' and notes that 'it is impossible to destroy' (Or. 76.1, 3).[29] The
answer is that such a convention was attached to the office of President
of the Games. He extended dinner invitations to those who possessed
citizenship of the Roman colony. Paul and those who possessed this
status could legitimately be described as owning a 'right'.

IV. Christians and the Welfare of Others

In the concluding section of his lengthy discussion (10:23–11:1) Paul
deals specifically with the theme of the 'welfare' of others in contrast

---

[24]A. Booth, 'The Art of Reclining and Its Attendant Perils', in W.J. Slater (ed.),
Dining in a Classical Context (Ann Arbor: University of Michigan Press, 1991) 105,
where he cites pagan and Christian writers alike. See also Dio Chrysostom 77/
78.28, 30.

[25]Dio Chrysostom, *Or.* 77/78.4 refers to brothel-keepers who were 'dragging their
stock about to the congress. . .of other great festive gatherings'.

[26]Engels, *Roman Corinth*, 102.

[27]See p. 126ff.

[28]Sherwin–White, *The Roman Citizenship*, 245.

[29]On the definition of a law and a custom, see Dio Chrysostom's discourses, 'On
law' and 'On custom' (*Or.* 75 and 76).

to one's rights. He begins this discussion with the use of the term 'welfare' (σύμφερον, 10:23), the neuter substantive of the verb συμφέρω.[30]

It is significant that the argument concerning the personal civic right of the Corinthians that 'all things are lawful' is countered by Paul's argument concerning the welfare of others *i.e.* 'not all things are beneficial (οὐ πάντα συμφέρει)'. Paul refutes the Corinthian argument using the synonymous term for welfare, *viz.* 'edification'—'all things do not build up' (10:23b). The concept of 'building up' (οἰκοδομεῖ) is not found in pagan religious language. 'Edification' was a unique term which Paul coined for the Christian faith which reflects the responsibility individuals should assume for the welfare of others as a matter of 'religious' obligation.

Paul uses 'welfare' and 'building up'as synonyms and expands them in the following verse with language belonging to the semantic field of benefactions: He commands, 'No man must seek his own [good], but each must seek [the good] of his neighbour' (μηδεὶς τὸ ἑαυτοῦ ζητείτω ἀλλὰ τὸ τοῦ ἑτέρου, 10:24 cf. 8:10). Later in the discussion Paul repeats this Christian orientation towards the welfare of others when he affirms, 'I also please all men in all things (κἀγὼ πάντα πᾶσιν ἀρέσκω). I do not seek my own welfare, but the welfare of the many' (μὴ ζητῶν τὸ ἐμαυτοῦ σύμφορον ἀλλὰ τὸ τῶν πολλῶν, 10:33).

These important statements bring us to the heart of the definition of 'welfare' which is the main subject of this book. The important parallels elucidate the meaning of the term 'welfare' (10:23, 33). The pursuit of one's rights on the grounds that it is lawful (πάντα ἔξεστιν) cannot be undertaken at the same time as the pursuit of the 'welfare of all' (πάντα συμφέρει) or the 'building up of all'. This is confirmed twice by the use of the strong adversative (10:23). Paul illustrates this from his own example, and claims that his concept of 'welfare' is the same as that of Christ on whose his ministry he has modelled his own (11:1).

From this discussion it may be concluded that those Christians who possessed a civic right should not necessarily exercise it. The consideration of their fellow Christian's conscience certainly had to be taken into account (8:10–11). In the 'private' sphere of a dinner party in another's home, the conscience of the non–Christian may determine how the Christian should act. In that case a host might possibly expect that Christians should not eat idol meat (10:28–29a). To inform the Christian of the origin of the meat would be a courtesy on the part of the host. It would be in keeping with the etiquette associated with

---

[30]Liddell and Scott.

inviting a guest to a meal and seeking to avoid giving any offence. Having shown consideration for the scruples of one's guest, the Christian was required to take into account his host's perceptions.

Civic rights must now be evaluated as to the effect they have on one's relationship with Christian and non-Christian alike. Do they contribute to the welfare of others as well as one's own spiritual edification. Paul has expanded this to encompass the welfare of the inhabitants of the city (10:32). When Paul gave the command not to be a stumbling block either to the church, or to Jew or Greek, he intended that Christians not exercise their civic rights of reclining at dinner in the idol temple (8:9). This was a practice which the early church proscribed for its members,[31] and one which would create problems for those who were Jews.[32] But in what way would the exercise of this civic right cause the Greek to stumble? To recline at a civic banquet would surely give the impression that the Christian faith was simply about another god and lord on earth and in the heavens viz. Jesus (8:5–6).

Paul also added, 'whatever you do, do all to the glory of God' (10:31). What would this general command include? He sees the seeking of the welfare of others in terms of trying to 'please all men in all things' (10:33). It would certainly concern the welfare of the city, including the good works of Christian civic benefactors (Rom. 13:3–4) and private benefactions for a neighbour (10:24).[33] However it was not restricted to material welfare, as he makes clear in 10:33, for he seeks the welfare of many 'that they may be saved'. This also comes within the purview of the welfare of the city.

One can readily appreciate the strength of the argument of the Christian citizens of Corinth. In their mind there was no reason to surrender their civic right of dining at the president's invitation on 'several' occasions with dignitaries in an idol temple. They knew that 'an idol was nothing' (8:4). If the Christian faith had simply been a matter of theological knowledge or personal 'religion' whereby one sought one's own advantage, then their encouragement to other Christians who possessed that right not to have any scruples over

---

[31]See B. Witherington III, 'Not so idle thoughts about *eidolothuton*', *Tyn.B.* 44 (1993) 237–54, who argues that the term refers to eating food in the precincts of a pagan temple and it is this that the Jerusalem Council proscribes in Acts 15:29.

[32]For evidence of Jewish reactions to idol temples and prohibitions on actually entering them, see the evidence gathered in my 'Theological and Ethical Responses to Religious Pluralism in 1 Corinthians 8–10', 215–219.

[33]See chapters 2 and 3.

dining in the temple on these civic occasions would have been explicable. The lengthy argument to which Paul resorted in 8:1–11:1 shows not only the need to demolish the substantial case which they had mounted, but to reaffirm that the Christian's task was to seek the physical and spiritual welfare of others, as Paul himself had done in imitation of Christ (11:1).

CHAPTER TEN

AN EARLY CHRISTIAN BENEFACTOR AND PROMINENT CITIZEN

Romans 16:23

It is in a Roman colony with its heightened sense of loyalty to Rome and its deep pride in its civic privileges, that we may find the name of an early civic benefactor and leading citizen who is a Christian. This concluding chapter provides an opportunity to examine the possible rôle played by him and the implications for this study as a whole. It will be argued that activities in both the temporal and spiritual spheres were accommodated by him in what the epistle to Diognetus calls 'a wonderful and confessedly strange characteristic of the order of their own citizenship'.[1]

There were two ways in which benefactors could seek the welfare of the city. One was to donate, for example, buildings, aqueducts, or pavements, or provide corn subsidies in times of food shortages. These were duly honoured by the Council and the People. The other was to provide a benefaction in fulfilment of an election promise, having won an honorary public office in a city. The name of one early Christian who may have been a civic benefactor in either capacity has been preserved. It is that of Erastus of Corinth who was a benefactor elected to public office.[2] Could this *aedile* be the 'city treasurer' or 'business manager' (οἰκονόμος τῆς πόλεως), as Kent calls him, who sent his greetings via Paul from Corinth to the Christians in Rome?[3] Discussion on the probable link has been divided.[4] Those in favour include the editor of volume III of the Corinthian inscriptions in which that of Erastus was discussed, and also an ancient historian specialising in Greek terms used in the Roman empire for posts with Latin titles.[5] If their identification is correct, then we have evidence of an early Christian who sought the welfare of the city in this capacity.

According to an inscription dated to the Neronean era, 'Erastus laid the pavement at his own expense in return for his aedileship'. The actual area was nineteen metres by nineteen metres and consisted of large slabs of Acrocorinthian limestone. The lettering of this

---

[1]*The Epistle to Diognetus* V.4.
[2]See D.W.J. Gill, 'Erastus the Aedile' *Tyn.B.* 40 (1989) 294–301, for a full description of the inscription, and A.D. Clarke, 'Another Corinthian Erastus Inscription' *Tyn.B.* 42 (1991) 146–151, esp. 151, who lays down helpful parameters for identification. See also his *Secular and Christian Leadership in Corinth* (Leiden: E.J. Brill, 1993) ch. 4 esp. 46–56, which offer a full discussion of Erastus and presents a judicious assessment of the views of others.
[3]Kent, *Corinth*, 8.3, No. 27 and Rom. 16:23.
[4]For the secondary literature see Clarke, *Secular and Christian Leadership in Corinth*, 46ff.
[5]Kent, *Corinth*, 8.3 99–100 and H.J. Mason, *Greek Terms for Roman Institutions - A Lexicon and Analysis*, ASP 13 (1974) 71.

inscription would have stood out because it was in bronze. In fact, it is the largest metal lettering extant in the Corinthian inscriptions. The pavement was located in a conspicuous place next to the theatre and bordering the road which led to the closest city, Sikyon.[6] Here was a benefactor of considerable wealth who had secured election to the annual office of *aedile*.[7]

In order to assess whether this Erastus of Corinth was indeed a Christian public benefactor, it is necessary to discuss (I) procedures for electing an *aedile* to the city, (II) the role of this honorary public office, (III) the use of Latin and Greek terms to describe this office, (IV) the oath of Erastus, the city official and Romans 16:23, and (V) whether the assumption of public office was an outworking of the social ethics of a civic benefactor referred to in Romans 13:3–4 and 1 Peter 2:14–15.

I. The Election of an *aedile* in the City

According to the constitution of a Spanish Roman colony,

> The aediles. . .are chosen from among those who are of free birth. . .A candidate for the aedileship. . .must be at least twenty-five years old and free from any impediment which would debar him from becoming a *decurio* [magistrate] or *senator* if he were a Roman citizen. . .on election. . .he should take the oath and give security for public money . . .[8]

The 'constitution' of Roman Corinth has not survived. The status of some of the holders of the aedileship suggests that it could be held by a freedman or a free man. M.A. Achaicus was an Argive with Corinthian citizenship and hence a free man.[9] L. Antonius Priscus, son of Lucius of the tribe of Meninia would have been a free-born holder of this office.[10] Some, such as Cn. Babbius Philinus who held this office, had names which betray freedman status or origins.[11] Corinth was

---

[6]Kent, *Corinth*, 8.3, No. 232. For details, see D.W.J. Gill, 'Erastus the Aedile', 293–4 and, for the plan in relation to the theatre, 301.

[7]A.D. Clarke, *Secular and Christian Leadership in Corinth*, 47.

[8]*Lex Malacitana* (c. A.D. 84) ch. 54, 57, cited by Staveley, *Greek and Roman Voting and Elections*, 234-5.

[9]For discussion see A. Spawforth, 'Roman Corinth: The Formation of a Colonial Elite'. I am grateful to him for permitting me to see this article which is forthcoming in a volume of *Meletemata* (Athens).

[10]Kent, *Corinth* 8.3 No. 177.

'freedman-friendly', to quote Spawforth, and 'continued to attract freedmen in the years after its foundation'.[12] Certainly, some of the magistrates were of freedman status. Others were Roman free men with freedman origins.[13] There were holders of public office who were Corinthian citizens of Greek origins from other cities who are known from the principate of Claudius onwards.

To date the final section of the Erastus inscription has not been found, and therefore his *praenomen* and *nomen* are not known. Kent observes that the number of letters for his *nomen* provide no place for his patronymic or tribal abbreviation and so concludes that he was a freedman.[14] However, there is no certainty that this was the case and unless the remainder of the slab is found, his civic status is not absolutely certain. It is certain, however, that he was a Roman Corinthian citizen; otherwise he could not have held this office.

The election of Erastus to this office was done under a well-known convention called *pollicitatio* whereby the contending candidates made pledges, *i.e.* election promises. They fulfilled these at their own expense rather than the city's, if elected to office. Such a liturgy would have been an expensive undertaking. Although it is not possible to estimate the cost to Erastus, in North Africa there was a custom of levying a cost on various offices and the honour of the office of the aedileship varied from 4,000 to 20,000 H.S. according to the importance and number of the cities in question.[15] Garnsey notes 'a Carthaginian who was *aedile*. . .and *pontifex* spent 90,000 H.S. and more besides to celebrate these offices'. He also provides evidence that such payments were known in the East.[16] How the illustrious Roman colony of Corinth organised its financial guarantees for this prestigious office is not known. The pavement which was given to honour an election promise was only part of an expensive financial undertaking for Erastus in holding the office of *aedile*.

Inscriptions to the Corinthians who undertook this particular office were erected by the Council and the People. They usually record

---

[11]Kent, *Corinth* 8.3 No. 155.

[12] Spawforth 'Roman Corinth: The Formation of a Colonial Elite'.

[13]In Caesar's colonies exception was made to this rule, although normally only free men held these posts: see Treggiari, *Roman Freedmen during the Late Republic* 63–4.

[14]Kent, *Corinth* 8.3, 100.

[15]R.P. Duncan-Jones, 'Costs, Outlays and *Summae Honorariae* from Roman Africa', *Papers of the British School at Rome* 17 (1962) 103 Nos. 349-53a.

[16]P. Garnsey, '*Honorarium decurionatus*', *Historia* 20 (1971) 325. He also cites from the East *CIG* 2683 (Iasos), 2981 (Miletus), 2987 (Ephesus); *IGR* III.800 (Syllii), IV.1637 (Philadelphia) 325, n. 97.

the performance of other liturgies as well,[17] among which the *aedile* appears to have been third in status.[18] If his public service followed the normal course of events, this may have been but one of the Corinthian liturgies undertaken by Erastus.

There are extant 'posters' which indicate that sponsors were needed by a candidate for the aedileship. For example, 'M. Cerrinus Vatia is proposed for the aedilate by Nymphodotus and Caprasia'. The robust nature of elections is reflected in some of the posters. One opposition poster obviously aimed at thoroughly discrediting the candidate for this office, which involved the handling of public funds, *e.g.* 'Vatia is supported for the aedilate by all the petty thieves'.[19] Another explains why he should be supported, even if the implications of the statement are lost on us: 'I ask you to elect Marcus Cerrinius Vatia to the aedileship. All the late drinkers support him.'[20] For Erastus to have been elected to office, he must have enjoyed the confidence of important citizens to sponsor his nomination. He would also have had to possess sufficient means to provide the substantial financial guarantees required for an office where considerable revenues were collected.[21] It is certain that the Erastus who laid the pavement must have been a leading citizen who commanded the respect of the Roman citizens. Sufficient people voted for his election to this initial office in the hierarchy of liturgies, most likely in the face of other candidates.

---

[17]See West, *Corinth*, 8.2 No. 70, 80-1, 93, 104b, 132. Kent, *Corinth*, 8.3, No. 152-156, 157, 164, 166, 168, *et. al.* Many of the inscriptions were destroyed during the sacking of the city by the Herulians and the Goths in A.D. 267 and 395. It is possible that an inscription recording the liturgies of Erastus may have been erected as in the case of Tiberius Claudius Dinippus and it could yet come to light in the excavations at Corinth.

[18]The President of the Games was first in status, followed by the chief magistrates and then the aedileships. See Kent, *Corinth*, 8.3 Nos. 70, 80-1, 93, 104b, 132, 152-156, 157, 164, 166, 168, *et. al.* Cf. the evidence of Epictetus on p. 186.

[19]Cited Staveley, *Greek and Roman Voting*, 224-5.

[20]*CIL* IV.3702.

[21]See C.K. Williams II, 'Roman Corinth as a Commercial Center', in T.E. Gregory (ed.), *The Corinthia in the Roman Period*, Journal of Roman Archaeology Supp. 8 (Ann Arbor: Cushing–Malloy, 1994) 31–46 on the rapid expansion of Corinth's commerce in the Claudian principate.

II. The Rôle of the *aedile* in the City

The honorary office of *aedile* was held in Corinth for one year.[22] Kent sees the *aedile* primarily as a business manager who was

> responsible for the upkeep and welfare of city property such as streets, public buildings, and especially the market places [hence their Greek title ἀγορανόμοι], as well as the public revenue therefrom. They also served as judges, and it is probable that most of a colony's commercial and financial litigation was decided by them rather than the magistrates (*duoviri*). The third responsibility of colonial aediles was for public games.[23]

The paving of a street was not an unknown benefaction for the aedile to promise, according to an inscription in Venusia.[24] Given the responsibility for the maintenance of streets and walkways, it was appropriate that Erastus should have laid the pavement to honour his election promise. In the same way other Corinthian citizens undertook this office in exchange for the honour of providing benefactions for the city. We know that in the second half of the first century A.D., 'Hicesius the aedile built this [?] at his own expense with the official permission of the Council', and that a statue was erected for Stationus, 'who was honoured by decree of the Council with the prerequisites of aedile'. In the second century A.D., P. Licinius Priscus Iuventianus undertook his aedileship in exchange for erecting buildings connected with the Isthmian Games which were held in the environs of Corinth.[25]

Plutarch provides an insight into some of the demands of the aedileship. It was expected that the holder of this public office would stand and watch tiles being measured and stores delivered.

> A man would be paltry and sordid who managed them for himself and attended to them for his own sake, but if he does it for the public and for the State's sake, he is not ignoble; on the contrary his attention to duty and his zeal are all the greater when applied to little things.[26]

---

[22]For an extant list of aediles see Kent, *Corinth* 8.3, 27-8.
[23]Kent, *Corinth* 8.3, 27. See also J. Wiseman, 'Corinth and Rome I', *ANRW* II.7.1 (1979) 499 and G. Theissen, *The Social Setting of Pauline Christianity*, 77-8.
[24]*CIL* IX 442, cited by A.G. Roos, 'De titulo quodam latino corintho nuper reperto', *Mnemosyne* 58 (1930) 163.
[25]*CIG* 1104 cited H.J. Cadbury, 'Erastus of Corinth', *JBL* 50 (1930) 54, and Kent, *Corinth* 8.3 Nos. 231, 237.
[26]Plutarch, *Politics* 811C–D.

III. Greek and Latin Terms for the Aedileship

Because Corinth was a Roman colony, one of the ways in which it demonstrated its status was the use of Latin in its inscriptions. This practice continued throughout the first century in the East until the influence of the emperor Hadrian, when offices were officially rendered in Greek out of deference to his love of all things Greek. This identification creates some difficulty in the case of Erastus, whose official rôle in Corinth is described in Greek in the New Testament while the description of his office in the Corinthian inscription is in Latin. This difficulty, however, is no greater than comparable situations in Greek cities and it is not impossible for the ancient historian to identify the particular office.

It should be noted that, over a period of time, there was a wide variation in terminology from city to city, and even within individual cities in the East. It is clear from the primary material gathered by H.J. Mason, *Greek Terms for Roman Institutions - A Lexicon and Analysis*, that there was no standardised provincial or empire-wide designation in Greek of official positions in cities by either Roman or Greek authorities. His work shows that it was not unusual for an office described in Latin to be rendered by a large number of Greek terms.[27] Any insistence on uniformity of terminology across the empire, or even in individual cities over the centuries, is therefore unreasonable.

The aedile and the three Corinthian Greek terms

Mason identifies three Greek words as having been used for the local *aedile* in the East. They are ἀστυνόμος, ἀγορανόμος and οἰκονόμος.[28] It is significant that all three are used of a civic office in Corinth in the first and second centuries—one in an official inscription, the second in a literary work describing its various public liturgies, and the third as the designation of a person who sends his greeting from Corinth to the church in Rome.

The evidence of Epictetus, a noted Stoic philosopher in Nicopolis in the adjacent province to Achaea (A.D. 55 – c. 135), has not been noted in discussions of the Greek terminology for this Corinthian liturgy (III.1.34).[29] His discourses were dedicated to the well-known aristocrat

---

[27]See Mason, 'Latin-to-Greek Reverse Index', *Greek Terms for Roman Institutions - A Lexicon and Analysis*, 175–204.

[28]Mason, *Greek Terms for Roman Institutions - A Lexicon and Analysis*, 91.

of Corinth, L. Gellius Menander. This philosopher not only knew the city, but was also well acquainted with the liturgies of this Roman colony.[30] A student of rhetoric from Corinth paid him a visit and was told of the future opportunities for his advancement in public offices in Corinth, given his status and training.

In enumerating these annual offices, Epictetus reveals his knowledge of the official liturgies of Corinth and the subsequent permanent appointment to its ruling body, the Council, which could be attained by a young man who had secured the former appointments. He mentions a title which indicates that one who had held the annual liturgies would be considered a benefactor, since he had held public offices in exchange for the requisite benefactions; he would be designated a 'generous citizen' (καλὸς πολίτης).[31] There was also a strong possibility of his election as a member of the Council (βουλευτής), a life appointment. Finally, he would be described as an 'orator' (ῥήτωρ), a title which appears on a number of second-century inscriptions of citizens who had participated in civic life in all its facets during the Second Sophistic in the second century.[32] This accolade was a much-coveted title in the heyday of Corinth. Epictetus' accurate knowledge of Corinth's civil structures is demonstrated when he places 'the President of the Games' at the head of the annual liturgies and demonstrates the honour attached to the term 'orator'. He was aware of the separation of the office of 'president' from the aedileship. The four official Greek terms of the office in Corinth used by Epictetus are ἀστυνόμος, ἐφήβαρχος, στρατηγός and ἀγωνοθέτης, the last three of which can be translated as 'superintendent of the *ephebi*', 'magistrate'[33] and 'President of the

---

[29]For the evidence cited in support of a publication date of A.D. 115, see F.H. Sandbach, *The Stoics* (London: Chatto & Windus, 1975) 164. His discourses, based on the shorthand notes made by his pupil, Flavius Arrianus, in c. A.D. 108, are considered a reliable record of his teaching.

[30]G.B. Bowersock, 'A New Inscription of Arrian', *GRBS* 8 (1967) 279-80. Epictetus is regarded as a reliable witness of his day alongside Plutarch and Dio Chrysostom and provides important evidence of the imperial world. See F. Millar, 'Epictetus and the Imperial Court', *JRS* 55 (1965) 141-60, esp. 142.

[31]See p. 32.

[32]Kent, *Corinth* 8.3 Nos. 226 (where the orator undertook the costly liturgy of *agonthete* on three occasions), 264 (where he was a member of the Panhellenion) and 307 (where he was a Helladarch and priest); see also *SEG* XVIII.137 for a third-century A.D. Corinthian orator who was 'first among orators, pre-eminent as *agonethetes*, having acquired glory in every public office'.

[33]ἄρχων, τοῦτ' ἔστιν ὁ στρατηγός (*Digest* xxvii.1.15.9). See Cornelius Pulcher from Corinth who is described as στρατηγός τῆς πόλεως Κορινθίων (Kent, *Corinth* 8.3 No. 80).

Games', respectively. According to Mason, ἀστυνόμος used in a municipal setting refers to the office of *aedile*.[34]

The term ἀγορανόμος described, among others,[35] the Corinthian aedile P. Licinius Priscus Iuventianus in the late second century when official inscriptions were in Greek. It has been held by New Testament scholars to be the term normally used in the first century to translate the office of *aedile*. Although he is not cited as the basis for this, it might be thought that this conclusion can be supported by the early twelfth-century A.D. writer, Zonaras, who wrote on the history of the office of *aedile*.

> Originally, therefore, they were chosen for this purpose [*viz.* assisting the tribunes] and the trying of cases; afterwards they were granted the supervision of the public market, when they came to be called *agoranomoi* [clerks of the market] by those who put their names into Greek.[36]

Mason has shown that this was not the only Greek term that was used of the aedile. Recent constitutional evidence of the first century has shown that the duties connected with the Roman office and a provincial one bearing the same title were not the same.[37]

In Romans 16:23 Erastus is described as an οἰκονόμος. There are three inscriptions cited by Mason containing the term *aedile*.[38] In two of the three instances it is followed by the phrase 'of the city' (τῆς πόλεως) and in the third the context suggests that the same phrase is meant. Of the various positions held by a sophist of Philadelphia there is mentioned 'the administration of the city' (ὁ τῆς πόλεως οἰκονόμος).

Changes in designations and duties

Precisely what the official terms might mean in a given situation may be complicated, for the same title could be used in the same city in a different era even when the duties originally attached to it had

---

[34]He cites Epictetus III.1.34 and *IGBulg.* 1023.

[35]*IGRom.* 1.769.

[36]Zonaras, *Ann.* VII.15.i.f.

[37]See J. González, 'The Lex Irnitana: a New Flavian Municipal Law', *JRS* 76 (1986) 201, on the duties and jurisdiction of the municipal *aedile* and that of Rome.

[38]Mason, *Greek Terms for Roman Institutions - A Lexicon and Analysis,* 71 who cites *IGRom.* 4.813 (Hierapolis) *IGRom.* 4.1630 (Philadelphia) and *IGRom.* 4.1435 (Smyrna).

changed partially or even radically. This was the case in Corinth. The task of rendering official Greek terms in Latin and *vice versa* can be complex for the ancient historian. Nowhere is this better illustrated than in the liturgy undertaken by the sophist Lollianus, who operated in Athens during the Principate of Hadrian. Philostratus records,

> He held the office of hoplite general in that city (στρατηγήσας ἐπὶ τῶν ὅπλων). The functions of this office were formerly to levy troops and lead them to war, but now the holder was in charge of food-supplies and the provision market (νυνὶ δὲ τροφῶν ἐπιμελεῖται καὶ σίτου ἀγορᾶς).[39]

The term used of such an office had previously been στρατοπεδάρχης or στρατηγὸς ἐπὶ τῶν ὅπλων. If the inscription erected to Lollianus by his 'star' pupils had been in Latin rather than Greek and had recorded not his great ability in forensic oratory but his public office,[40] precisely how would the Greek term be rendered in Latin? Had those who erected the statue and inscribed the pedestal not understood the actual duties he was expected to perform, then they would have rendered it prescriptively as 'hoplite general' (στρατηγὸς ἐπὶ τῶν ὅπλων) while those in the city who knew what they were might have rendered it descriptively as superintendent of the market.[41] The editor of Philostratus renders the liturgy held by him as *curator annonae* and notes that 'food-controller' was the nearest equivalent for στρατοπεδάρχης.[42] The duties he normally undertook were those of superintendent of the grain and the market. The text of Philostratus indicates that he was also held responsible for the supply of grain in times of dearth in Athens. The liturgy that covered that emergency was not an annual one but an appointment made only when there was a grain shortage. The wealthy citizen appointed to that temporary liturgy agreed to subsidise the price of grain himself or to take up a collection by means of subscriptions. In this particular case Lollianus asked the students in his own school to subscribe to it, and a large sum of money was collected which provided the necessary money to pay for the cargo of grain. He remitted the substantial fees of those of his students who subscribed.[43] How then would his office be rendered descriptively in

---

[39]*Lives of the Sophists* 526.

[40]See G. Kaibel, *Epigrammata Graeca* (Berlin, 1878) 362.

[41]See 'The Life of Prohaeresius', *Lives of Eunapius* 492, where the term clearly does not describe the temporary office of *curator annonae*.

[42]*Lives of the Sophists*, xiii, xv. See however *IG* IV 795 where the Greek for the office of *curator annonae* was ἐπιμελητὴς εὐθηνίας and also Meritt, *Corinth* 8.1 No. 76.

either Latin or Greek? On face value the use of the term 'hoplite general' of Athens of Lollianus on an inscription might be assumed to be a military one, but that would be entirely misleading.

These examples show that there is a need to exercise care when pronouncing on the titles of offices where changes occur in the way a city is administered from one period to another. The term ἀγορανόμος usually involved the organisation of the games in cities in the East as well as administrative and financial duties. However, the job description of the *aedile* was determined by a situation peculiar to Corinth. The holder of that office would be responsible for sponsoring the games, which returned to Corinth *c.* 40 B.C., soon after it was founded as a colony.[44] Precisely when the duties of running the Games were separated from the aedileship is not unclear but the office of 'President of the Games' (ἀγωνοθέτης) in Corinth was created as a separate liturgy no later than the beginning of the first century A.D.[45] Such was their fame and the burden of private sponsorship borne by the president that the office was given precedence over any other liturgy in Corinth, including that of magistrates who normally held the most senior position.[46] This change in the duties of the *aedile* in Roman Corinth meant that his function was that of chief administrative officer and city treasurer. Such duties could best be rendered descriptively by the term οἰκονόμος, a natural and entirely appropriate term. It was used in the first century of the steward who was the custodian of the resources and financial matters of a large household or estate.[47] Paul uses the term in 1 Corinthians 4:1 by way of analogy for his ministry and that of Apollos, describing him as a custodian of the revelation of God. The same term would be an apposite one for a civic office, since it described the function of a manager as the custodian of the city's resources, including legal matters of a fiscal nature.

---

[43]*Lives of the Sophists*, 526–7.

[44]See Gebhard, 'The Isthmian Games and the Sanctuary of Poseidon in the Early Empire' 82.

[45]See Kent, *Corinth*, 8.3, 30-31 for the extant list of those who held the office.

[46]This provides a good example of the distinction drawn between rank and status by E.A. Judge, *Rank and Status in the World of the Caesars and St. Paul*, University of Canterbury Publications 29 (Christchurch: University of Canterbury, 1982). The presidency of the games which was normally a liturgy included in the aedileship had so grown in prestige that the status of the former responsibility outstripped the rank of the most senior appointment of magistrate.

[47]I am grateful to Dr Andrew Clarke who drew my attention to the connection.

Official v. unofficial terms

It should also be remembered that there was no 'official' Greek term used by the Council in the annual election for this office. Those who voted for the candidates for this or any other elected position were Roman citizens, and only Latin terms would be appropriate on that and other official occasions. This is borne out by the insistence on the use of Latin terminology in the colony in all official inscriptions and reflected its particular pride in its special status with regard to Rome.

The term οἰκονόμος may well have been used unofficially by the inhabitants of Corinth to describe in Greek the peculiar duties attached to the office in the colony. It is not until the second century that official Greek terms appear in inscriptions. In the case of P. Licinius Priscus Iuventianus (*c.* A.D. 170), the word chosen was ἀγορανόμος, the first extant appearance of this word in Corinth.[48] It must be stressed that there was no Greek term used in first-century official sources for the office of *aedile* in this Roman colony.

Because the designation of the office in Romans 16:23 is found in the context of a personal greeting from Erastus himself, the Greek term is very likely to be self-descriptive. It is improbable that the author recorded the actual title wrongly, as Erastus had asked that his personal salutations to the Roman Christians be sent. If the Acts 19:22 evidence is accepted, his close relationship with Paul was clearly such as to guarantee even further the accuracy of the term used. The designation in the pavement inscription is that inserted by the person who laid it, and declared that he bestowed it upon the city in exchange for the office of *aedile*. The Latin term could not be incorrect. So the terminology in both the Latin inscription and Romans 16:23, therefore, is certainly correct.

How the recipients of the letter to the Romans would have understood the term is not certain.[49] There must have been some confidence on the part of Paul that the word would be understood by those in Rome to mean that this person was a custodian of the resources of the city and therefore its chief administrator.[50] That they would have

---

[48]On the dating of the inscription see Kent, *Corinth* 8.3, 121. There is no record of terms used in pre-Roman Corinth for this office or of precisely how individual offices functioned in Greek Corinth: see J.B. Salmon, *Wealthy Corinth: a History of the City to 338 B.C.* (Oxford: Clarendon Press, 184) 201ff., 385.

[49]Rom. 16 is here regarded as part of the letter to the Romans. For a discussion of its integrity, see H. Gamble, *The Textual History of the Letter to the Romans*, Studies and Documents 42 (Grand Rapids: Eerdmans, 1977).

been unaware that another office of President of the Games existed which had been carved out of the original liturgy is not important. The most likely understanding would be of a 'civic administrator' or 'manager'. The terms *dispensator* ('manager' or 'treasurer') and *vilicus* ('steward') are synonyms for a household steward and an association of a 'city-wide' steward with *aedile* could easily be made.[51]

The *aedile* and the οἰκονόμος of the city belong to the same area of *politeia, viz.* positions connected with the administration of Corinth. Attempts to argue that the οἰκονόμος occupied a lesser office, and that the Latin equivalent for it was *quaestor* cannot be sustained; the Greek term supplied by Mason for the latter term is καμίας and not οἰκονόμος.[52]

In concluding this section a good case can be put forward that the Latin term used of the office occupied by Erastus for one year was a prescriptive one. The Greek word for the office of Erastus in Romans 16:23 was descriptive. The term may well have been used by some Greek-speaking Corinthians to refer to the civic administrator. Those who were Roman citizens could have retained the Latin term even when speaking Greek, or may have used synonymous terms (*viz.* ἀγορανόμος and ἀστυνόμος) such as were used in the following century in the official inscription or the literary source. All would have been aware of the duties attaching to the 'occasional' or *ad hoc* office of the President of the Games in Corinth, and that the remainder of the duties of the *aedile* related to financial and administrative matters connected with the running of the largest city in the province.

On the question of identification, Kent concludes that the Erastus of the inscription was the same person who sent his greetings to the church in Rome. He gives three reasons: the laying of the pavement can be dated to the middle of the first century; the name of Erastus was

---

[50]The much later discussion of Zonaras, *Ann.* VII.15.i.f. on the office of *aedile* in Rome and its Greek equivalent does not permit the conclusion that there was an official set of Latin/Greek equivalents which were generally understood, any more than this was so in the East.

[51]Mason, *Greek Terms for Roman Institutions - A Lexicon and Analysis*, 71. In Aphrodisias the 'treasurer' (ἀρκάριος) was the Greek transliteration of the Latin *arcarius*. It has been suggested that in the third century A.D., 'Aphrodisias the city and most private households would surely have used a Greek word, οἰκονόμος.' J. Reynolds and R. Tannenbaum, *Jews and Godfearers at Aphrodisias*, 119.

[52]*E.g.* Theissen, *The Social Setting of Pauline Christianity*, 79–82, who suggests that the term οἰκόνομος is equivalent to *quaestor, contra* Gill, 'Erastus the Aedile', 299. The latter term was the equivalent of καμίας, according to Mason, *Greek Terms for Roman Institutions - A Lexicon and Analysis*, 91.

rare in Corinth; and the term οἰκονόμος 'describes with reasonable accuracy the function of a Corinthian aedile'.[53] No epigraphist has subsequently questioned the dating of the pavement inscription. While a second Erastus has been located in Corinth, the date is much later and he was not the same person.[54] Because of the subsequent wholesale sacking of Corinth by the Herulians (A.D. 267) and the Goths (A.D. 395) there is limited extant epigraphic evidence and therefore the argument on the rare occurrence is not a strong one. The view that the term in Romans 16:23 is an appropriate description is fully endorsed, as are other terms used of this office in the following century, viz. ἀγορανόμος and ἀστυνόμος. They confirm the use of synonymous Greek terms to render a particular official Latin name. This is not peculiar, for in Mason's list there are very few Latin words which do not have at least two Greek equivalents, and in a large number of cases there are more than three—in some instances there are up to ten Greek terms.[55]

The first-century historian can feel confident in the light of the evidence of three Greek terms being used in Corinth—two of which come from the second century A.D.—that *aedile* was equivalent to οἰκονόμος in the Julio-Claudian period, as indeed ἀγορανόμος and ἀστυνόμος would be in the next century. The self-descriptive term οἰκονόμος has been rendered 'the treasurer of the city' by NT scholars. 'Business manager' is Kent's translation,[56] although 'city administrator' might more accurately encompass the job description of this civic office in Corinth for the twentieth-century reader. On the basis of the present literary and non-literary evidence we possess, the identification of the Erastus in the inscription with the Erastus in Romans 16:23 can be made with confidence.

IV. Romans 16:23 and the Oath of Office

One of the early arguments felt to carry weight against the occupation by the Erastus of Romans 16:23 of an official position in Corinth is that he would not be able to swear the required oath at the time of his inauguration or soon after. In more recent times this point has been rightly

---

[53]Kent, *Corinth* 8.3, 99–100.
[54]Clarke, 'Another Erastus Inscription'.
[55]Mason, *Greek Terms for Roman Institutions - A Lexicon and Analysis*, 175ff.
[56]Kent, *Corinth* 8.3, 27.

raised again.[57] In the *lex Malacitana* (*c.* A.D. 84) cited above, one of the requirements of the *aedile* was that he swore an oath. The *lex Salpens* of the Domitian Principate stipulated that within five days of assuming public office an oath had to be sworn. The oath which the magistrates were to undertake at the end of the century required the newly-elected person to swear by Jupiter, Augustus, Claudius, Vespasian, Titus and the *genius* of Domitian.[58] On these grounds it has been argued that Erastus as a Christian would have been unable to do so and therefore that Christians could never have undertaken public office.

If this was the case, did Jews, who would have been faced with the same problem, undertake public office? We know that there were Alexandrian Jews who held office in the Roman administration during the Claudian period. Philo is critical of them because they used education (παιδεία) not in the pursuit of 'virtue', its theoretical purpose, but to parade their superiority or 'for office or magistracy for our rulers' (ἀρχῆς τῆς πρὸς τοὺς ἡγεμόνας, *LA* III.167). Philo does not mention the danger of apostasy which he most likely would have done had they sworn an oath in the name of Jupiter, and the pagan deities. Rather the intention of education as perceived by philosophers had been devalued by his young countrymen to the securing of 'office' or 'magistracy' (the term ἀρχή can carry either meaning). We know that education was the prerequisite for public offices such as magistracies, as Epictetus reminded the young student from Corinth.[59] Abramos, a Jew from Leontopolis is recorded in his epitaph as having been 'crowned with a magistracy over all the people' and that he held 'a magistracy in two places, fulfilling the double expense with gracious liberality'. This inscription is dated between the mid-second century B.C. and early second century A.D. and, while these magistracies have been attributed to jurisdiction over Jews, the term 'all the people' (πανδήμῳ) and 'city magistracy' (πολιταρχῶν) would suggest a civic context that was not exclusively Jewish. The customary costly liturgy would support this.[60] The Jewish Aurelius Frugianus Menocritus held a number of

---

[57]*E.g.* Roos, 'De titulo quodam latino corintho nuper reperto', 160–5; Cadbury, 'Erastus of Corinth'; and Clarke, *Secular and Christian Leadership in Corinth*, 53.

[58]*Lex Salpens* 26 cited by Clarke, *Secular and Christian Leadership in Corinth*, 53 n. 80. The same applied in the *Lex Irnitana* ch. 25, 26 and 73.

[59]Epictetus, III.1.34.

[60]*CPJ* no. 1530a. For discussion see W. Horbury and D. Noy, *Jewish Inscriptions of Graeco–Roman Egypt* (Cambridge: CUP, 1992) 95ff. and more recently W. Horbury, 'Jewish Inscriptions and Jewish Literature in Egypt' in edd. J.W. van Henten and P.W. van der Horst, *Studies in Early Jewish Epigraphy* (Leiden: E.J. Brill, 1994) 22–6.

posts, including the office of *aedile*, in the third century A.D.[61] 'Greek and Latin inscriptions show that Jews actively participated in the economic, military and political institutions of the Graeco-Roman world.'[62]

How did the Jews cope with the problem of the required oath of office? If there was a way around that for them, then at least in the province of Achaea there must surely have been a similar concession for Christians in Paul's day, given the identification of Christianity with Judaism in Gallio's ruling (Acts 18:12–15).[63] There is second-century evidence which shows that in the Principates of Marcus Aurelius and Commodus, Jews were definitely participating in public office. The source is Modestinus, *Excuses* book 6, where it was stated that 'Jews are to be tutors to non-Jews just as they undertake all other public duties; for *constitutiones* provide only that they are not to be troubled with matters which appear to be defiling their religion'.[64] We also learn, 'The deified Severus and Caracalla [c. A.D. 198–211] allowed those who profess the Jewish *superstitio* to hold city office (*honores*), but also imposed on them only the obligations which would not damage their superstition'.[65] Two points need to be made. The first is that in discussing the rôle of Jews as tutors, the law was formulated on the basis of an existing principle, *viz.* that Jews were already undertaking 'all other public offices'. The second observation is that both laws recognised the scruples of the Jews and only applied those 'obligations' (*necessitates*), which may not mean anything more than the payment of the customary *summae honorariae* for the office.[66] It has been suggested that 'we should not expect to find practising Jews in civic office before the edict of the emperors Severus and Caracalla', and, it is added, 'we should not expect to find many anywhere' after it.[67] The evidence of Modestinus shows the opposite to be the case.

---

[61]*CIJ* II 770 cited by Reynolds and Tannenbaum, *Jews and Godfearers at Aphrodisias*, 66.

[62]See L.H. Kant, 'Jewish Inscriptions in Greek and Latin', *ANRW* II.20.2 (1987) 692.

[63]See pp. 142-3 and my further discussion of it in 'Acts and Roman Religion', in D. Gill and C. Gempf (edd.), *The Book of Acts in its Graeco-Roman Setting*, The Book of Acts in its First Century Setting (Grand Rapids and Carlisle: Eerdmans and Paternoster, 1994) vol. 2, 98–103.

[64]*Digest* xxvii.1.15.6. For discussion see P.R. Trebilco, *Jewish Communities in Asia Minor*, SNTS 69 (Cambridge: CUP, 1991) 209 n. 36.

[65]*Digest* l.2.3.3. See Trebilco, *Jewish Communities in Asia Minor*, 47.

[66]See p. 182 on the *summae honorariae* and Reynolds and Tannenbaum, *Jews and Godfearers at Aphrodisias*, 66.

[67]Reynolds and Tannenbaum, *Jews and Godfearers at Aphrodisias*, 66.

Both in the time of Philo and in the second century, public office was open to Jews. The concession referred to in the legal codes mentioned earlier exempted them from swearing the customary oath in a name other than that of their God. In Achaea what applied to Jews in the Julio-Claudian period was applicable to Christians because of Gallio's ruling.[68] Would this peculiar situation not have allowed Erastus to have taken up this liturgy without swearing a pagan oath?

V. Erastus, Romans 13:3–4 and 1 Peter 2:14–15

In the light of the above discussion the present writer concurs with Theissen concerning the identification of Erastus the *aedile* and the person in Romans 16:23 when he wrote that there is 'no compelling argument against this identification of the Christian Erastus. . .We can assume Erastus belonged to the οὐ πολοί δυνατοί. To have been chosen *aedile* he must have been a full citizen.'[69]

Paul did not normally mention the present, secular occupations of the other Christians who are mentioned in his letters. In doing so in the case of Erastus, he was able to provide an example for his readers of the rôle that the well-to-do Christian could undertake in seeking the welfare of the city. The filling of this public office by Erastus was an outworking of the rôle of the Christian as a civic benefactor referred to in Romans 13:3–4 and 1 Peter 2:14–15. He was engaging in the time-consuming office of *aedile* during the year in which the letter to the Romans was written.[70] The difference between the unelected benefactor and the one who undertook public office may have been largely one of resources and, for the high-minded person, a commitment to the well-being of the city. The former was given immediate honours appropriate to the size of the benefaction by 'the Council and the People' (see p. 30). The latter served the city at his own expense in an annually-elected public office. He provided, in addition, a benefaction which was judged to be appropriate to the importance of that office by

---

[68]See *lex Irnitana* ch. 73, where a city scribe swears the same oath as the *praefectus* (ch. 25) and the *aedile* (ch. 26).

[69]G. Theissen, 'Social Stratification in the Corinthian Community: A Contribution to the Sociology of Early Hellenistic Christianity', *The Social Setting of Pauline Christianity*, 83.

[70]If Erastus had been a former *aedile*, the greeting would have indicated this. Distinctions were drawn between those who had held office and those who were presently doing so: see *e.g. P.Fouad.* 26 (A.D. 157–9) *l.* 38.

the majority of the electors, *viz.* a year of service in the actual running of an important aspect of the city of Corinth.[71] From a Christian perspective, both forms of benefaction would have constituted 'good works' performed in *politeia*, and would have been high-profile (1 Pet. 2:12). The latter benefaction would have been a greater commitment to the welfare of the community because of the actual service it rendered to the city.

If the evidence of Acts 19:22 is accepted,[72] Erastus was a Christian of substantial financial means, active in two spheres. After he 'ministered to Paul' in Ephesus as part of the apostolic team, he was sent into Macedonia to the churches. He subsequently engaged in civic duties in Corinth. The ordering of these events is important. Had the civic liturgy preceded the period of missionary activity with Paul, then it could be argued that his conversion occurred during his period as *aedile*.[73] That his activities happened the other way around, as extant evidence suggests,[74] supports the view that it was as a Christian that he undertook this public duty. The office undertaken then by Erastus in Corinth for the year demanded commitment and accountability for it was no sinecure as the duties show.[75]

If this is correct, then there was no dichotomy in the thinking of the early church between the gospel/church ministry and the seeking the welfare of the city of Corinth as benefactors. This conclusion based on the discussion of 1 Corinthians 10:23–33 in the previous chapter appears to find confirmation in the person of Erastus. There it was

---

[71]On the price set by some cities for the office rather than a promise of a benefaction, see p. 182. In that case election was on the grounds of the popular vote. In the case of Erastus it was his election promise that secured the votes.

[72]Some would see the Erastus of Rom. 16:23 as different from that of Acts 19:22. See Theissen, *The Social Setting of Pauline Christianity*, 76, who rejects the identification, although he concedes that there was a common connection with Corinth. The basis for this was his conjecture that he was a slave and that it is therefore unlikely that he would have been travelling.

[73]Cf. J. Murphy-O'Connor, 'The Corinth that Paul saw', *Biblical Archaeology* 47 (1984) 155, who suggests, 'Since the pavement antedates the middle of the first century A.D., this person is identified with the Erastus who became one of Paul's converts. . .It is not impossible that Paul met Erastus in the latter's official capacity, that is when paying rent or taxes for his workspace, which would explain why he calls Erastus, "treasurer of the city"'.

[74]On the dating of the third missionary journey and Paul's writing of Romans, see for example the chart of R. Jewett, *A Chronology of Paul's Life* (Philadelphia: Fortress, 1979) 161, and C.E.B. Cranfield, *The Epistle to the Romans*, I, 12.

[75]See p. 184. On the large body of law governing commercial and other activities under the *aedile*'s jurisdiction, see 'The Edict of the Aedile', *Digest* 21.

argued that Paul wrote in such a way as to imply that the secular and spiritual welfare of the city were two sides of a single coin and not separate spheres. The combination of these activities in this prominent Christian citizen may never have been perceived by him as incompatible or autonomous entities for Christians. Both rôles were concerned with the welfare of those who lived in the city. They were what Paul saw as an imitation of the ministry of Christ who, in Acts 10:38, was recorded as 'having gone about [undertaking] benefactions or 'doing good works' (ὃς διῆλθεν εὐεργετῶν) as part of the gospel.[76]

---

[76]1 Cor. 11:1. See F.W. Danker, *Luke* (ed 2; Philadelphia: Fortress Press, 1987) v.

CHAPTER 11

CONCLUSIONS

I. An Ambivalence or a Paradox?

It has been recently suggested by Wayne Meeks that the attitude of the majority of early Christians towards 'the city' is best described as 'the ambivalent middle way' between the extreme positions of the demonic nature of Rome and the cities, and of the desert as the temporary place to flee before entering the heavenly Jerusalem. He sees the ambivalent nature of the *via media* most eloquently expressed in the epistle to Diognetus and notes that '. . .the Christians keep all the local customs. . .while somehow at the same time demonstrating "the amazing and admittedly strange establishment of their own republic"'. The term πολιτεία is here translated by Meeks as 'republic' in his summary of this second-century Christian self–description.[1] He also suggests that the problem of their ambivalent attitude to the *politeia* to which they subscribed was not resolved by the early Christians and is still something which confronts Christians and their neighbours today.[2]

The anonymous writer of the epistle to Diognetus may not have written about the rôle of Christians in *politeia* in the way Meeks suggests. There was a paradox in their existence that was acknowledged in their self–definition but is it rightly described as an 'ambivalence'?

> They reside in their respective countries, but only as aliens (πάροικοι) they take part in everything as citizens (πολῖται) and put up with everything as foreigners (ὑπομένουσιν ὡς ξένοι). . .Every foreign land is their home and every home a foreign land. They find themselves in the flesh, but do not live according to the flesh.[3]

This statement was preceded by the declaration that 'they show forth the amazing and admittedly strange nature of their *politeia*, which best renders θαυμαστὴν καὶ ὁμολογουμένως παράδοξον ἐνδείκνυνται τὴν κατάστασιν τῆς ἑαυτῶν πολιτείας. It was not only 'amazing' but it was 'strange' in that the 'nature' (κατάστασις) of their *politeia* was admittedly 'contrary to expectation' (παράδοξος). The context suggests that one reason why it was contrary was that they continued to participate in everything as citizens, even though the society in which they lived at times treated them in a shabby way as if they were 'foreigners'. The ancient writer saw that the nature of the Christian's

---

[1]*The Epistle to Diognetus*, V.4.
[2]Meeks, *The Origins of Christian Morality*, 50.
[3]*The Epistle to Diognetus* V.5, 8.

politeia was not related simply to their dual citizenship in this *apologia* but that they participated in civic life in spite of the attitude of other citizens towards them (V.17).

The ten chapters of this book have sought to chart something of the paradoxical situation of Christians in *politeia* as both benefactors and citizens. The case studies have shown not so much an 'ambivalence' on the part of Christians, but rather, like the chameleon which can focus its eyes separately in different directions at the same time, Christian instruction aimed to develop a heavenly and an earthly focus. The former encouraged them as the diaspora or exiled people of God to fix their hope fully on the grace that was coming to them at the revelation of Jesus Christ, having already been given assurance of their reaching their heavenly inheritance. This helped them to cope with the uncertainties of the present created by the suspicions of the fellow citizens who were mistreating them as if 'foreigners' (1 Pet. 1:3ff.). The nature of the earthly focus was described as an alternative to living 'after the flesh' while 'in the flesh'.[4] The Christian mandate committed them to secure the welfare of others in *politeia* as well as in the private sphere (1 Pet. 2:11ff.).

The welfare of the city was seen to be two-fold. It was 'physical' and 'spiritual', and in the former case it was revolutionary in certain respects. It linked wealthy Christian members of the city into the civic benefaction convention . At the same time it expanded the definition of 'benefactor' to encompass all those in the Christian community who had the capacity to meet the needs of others from self-generated resources. It required all to be the doers of good. This involved the renunciation of the client's full-time rôle in *politeia* forcing Christians to withdraw from an unproductive existence where they were part of the paid retinue of a patron. Unlike the secular trends of the first century with the development of a welfare syndrome favouring those with status and/or wealth,[5] the Christian community was to be discriminating in the distribution of 'benefactions' to its members, 'honouring' only those who were genuinely needy *e.g.* the godly Christian widows without relatives.

Paul was concerned that as an 'association' they lived in a way that was worthy of the gospel. This involved securing concord in their midst to be a gospel witness in *politeia* where discord could be the rule rather than the exception. To live in a manner worthy of the gospel

---

[4]Citing *The Epistle to Diognetus*, V.8.
[5]See p. 209.

proscribed its members struggling for 'primacy' in their Christian community (Phil. 1:27ff.). It also required them to abandon the use of vexatious litigation in civil actions which was one of the secular means of securing power in any group (1 Cor. 6:1-8).

Unlike the Essenes, the Therapeutai and the Qumran communities, Christians were not to be a 'withdrawn' community. They were taught to participate in public life in the first and subsequent centuries. This was not a pragmatic decision but was seen positively as 'the will of God' (1 Pet. 2:15). Tertullian was to insist that Christians did take an active part in the observances and institutions of public life. They engaged in its ordinary callings with the exception of religious observances and feasts.[6] However, some Christians in the first century had sought to deal with the problem of their obligation to the imperial cult by demanding in effect Jewish ethnicity for all Christians (Gal. 6:11ff.). Others had insisted that they could exercise their civic right to participate in feasts in idol temples because of the theological fact 'that an idol is nothing' (1 Cor. 8:4).

There was a preoccupation with social status even among many Jewish and Gentile Christians, including household servants. To counter this there was standard teaching on these issues for slaves and free men alike in all the Pauline churches. The unholy scramble for secular status was proscribed for Christians who were to recognise the divine ordering of the 'status' both ethnically and socially (1 Cor. 7:17-24), for God conferred a wonderful calling and status in Christ (1 Cor. 1:26ff.).

It was not social 'status' (κλῆσις) but the call to seek the welfare of the city both physically and spiritually that was to be the focus of the Christian community. Christians were required to seek the advantage or well-being of the inhabitant of their earthly cities in imitation of Paul's life-style, who in turn had imitated Christ's (1 Cor. 8-11:1). It has been suggested in the previous chapter that we find in the person of Erastus someone who fulfilled both the rôle of a civic and spiritual benefactor. He provides for Paul an example of the Christian teaching on benefactors in Romans 13:3-4.

For Meeks, 'ambivalence' means that the majority of early Christian communities in Gentile areas had mixed feelings towards the city which were not and still cannot be resolved. This study has shown that the apostolic traditions created a positive attitude to the city and indicated how Christians could contribution to the welfare of others there.

---

[6]*Apology* 42.

II. The Social Register of Early Christians

This study has raised indirectly the question of the social register of
early Christians. The view that they were drawn predominantly from
the lower echelons of society is challenged by the evidence of the Gentile churches. Clients of patrons were not drawn from the bottom of
the social scale. They were recruited by a patron from the ranks of
those who were of a slightly lower status. The fact that they longed for
a substantial gift of money which enabled some, for example, to
become knights confirms this contention.[7] With respect to the Thessalonian Christians, the social register of those who were clients prevents
us concluding that they were largely artisans and non-slave labourers.
The injunction that Christians operate as civic benefactors in Rome and
Anatolia also supports the view that, while there were 'not many powerful', they were by no means absent from Christian communities.[8]

This raises questions about the description of early Christians as
largely low-profile and low-status members of the city. The concept of
'rich' and 'poor' is an imprecise and misleading description of the
social dichotomy of any Roman colony or any Greek city in the first
century. It is better not to use such categories but rather to resort to a
term current in the ancient world which Paul also chose *viz.* 'the have
nots' (τοὺς μὴ ἔχοντας) (1 Cor. 11:22) and its antonym 'the haves'. The
'have nots' did not belong to a household. They were not close or
extended members of the family, clients, servants or freedmen, i.e. they
did not 'have' households. They could have been artisans and may
even have held property. They were society's insecure members. They
lacked the safety net which a master or a patron afforded in times of
uncertainty or adversity such as famines or strife caused by political
machinations. On the other hand, 'the secure' or 'the haves' may not
have been materially wealthy. They may have possessed very little,
but they did have a household which guaranteed them protection.

The classifications 'haves' and 'have nots', if correctly understood, help to avoid the misreading of that situation. Terminology
such as 'rich' and 'poor' and even 'middle class' is unhelpful when discussing the social register of first-century Christians, and there should
perhaps be a moratorium on their use when describing Christianity in
Gentile regions.[9]

---

[7]See Juvenal, *Satires* V, *ll.* 132-5, and discussion p. 45.
[8]See recent secondary literature cited on the élite p. 38 n. 44.

III. The Distinctiveness of Christian *politeia*

By ancient standards, the 'nature of *politeia*' (κατάστασις τῆς πολιτείας) for Christians was commended as something unique.[10] It was not that they were postulating heaven as a 'republic'.[11] Rather, Christian conduct in the *politeia* of their present cities was seen as a 'selling point' for the Christian message in the *apologia* to Diognetus. It was sufficiently different from that of others to draw attention to its distinguishing and startling characteristics. What made it different? In answering this question it is not intended to undertake a full scale comparison with first-century discussions of *politeia*. It is sufficient for our purposes to make some comparison with other views of three first-century authors who wrote on important aspects of *politeia*, not as detached philosophers, but as active participants.

The nature of *politeia* in Plutarch, examined for a young man considering entry into active political life, has already been discussed. It dealt largely with negotiating some of the realities and pitfalls of first-century politics.[12] Dio Chrysostom, like Plutarch, also grappled with the complexities of *politeia* both as a civic benefactor and politician.[13] He concluded that 'no one knows of a good city made wholly of good elements as having existed in the past, that is, a city of mortal men', (37.22) and that 'the only *politeia* or city that may be called genuinely happy' is 'the partnership (κοινωνία) of god with god' (36.23). In his orations he reflects aspects of the Stoics' 'cosmic city'.[14] There are two such strands running through Dio's discussion of the city. The first sees the *cosmos* as a city in the sense that it is a habitation for the community of gods and men. The second is a mix of Platonic and Aristotelian views of kingship and uses the city as an analogy for the

---

[9]For a further discussion of this point see my 'Civil Litigation in Secular Corinth and the Church: The Forensic Background to 1 Corinthians 6:1–8', in B. Rosner (ed.), *Understanding Paul's Ethics: Twentieth Century Approaches* (Grand Rapids: Eerdmans, 1995) 101–3.

[10]*The Epistle to Diognetus*, V.4.

[11]Meeks, *The Origins of Christian Morality*, 50 translates the term πολιτεία in Diognetus thus.

[12]For a discussion of this see pp. 86-9.

[13]Jones, 'Local Politics' *The Roman World of Dio Chrysostom*, ch. 11.

[14]For a helpful discussion of how Dio presents and interacts with Stoic philosophy especially in *Or.* 36 see M. Schofield, *The Stoic Idea of the City* (Cambridge: CUP, 1991) 57–63, Jones, 'Ideal Communities' and 'Benefactions', in *The Roman World of Dio Chrysostom*, ch. 7 and the conclusions he draws on p. 64 and ch. 12. respectively. See also the discussion of discord and concord on p. 88ff.

structure and order of the cosmos itself.[15] This helps account for Dio's ambivalent attitude towards the city and also his writings on utopian communities and *politeia* in 'utopian terms'.[16]

Dio's ideal *politeia* was seen as divine in origin. It encapsulated that which 'the wisest and eldest ruler and law–giver ordains for all' and saw 'the leader of all heaven and lord of all being, himself thus expounding the term and offering his own administration as a pattern of the happy and blessed condition' (36.31–2). When he mentioned a 'divine form of government' in a particular oration, it appealed greatly to the whole of his audience who wanted to know about that ' divine city—where it is and what it is like' (36.26, 27). He explained that 'the doctrine, in brief, aims to harmonise the human race with the divine, and to embrace. . .everything endowed with reason [as] the only sure and indissoluble foundation for fellowship and justice' (36.31).[17] He justified the idea of a cosmic city by an analogy, for Zeus rules over the entire universe and governs the affairs of men who are in effect his citizens. Dio believed that the divine *politeia* was a more righteous code than the proverbial one possessed by Sparta (36.38).[18] Therefore it was not inappropriate to use the term *politeia* (πολιτεία) of such activity or 'city' or 'something like it' to describe that which Zeus administers (36.37).[19]

Philo, the Hellenized Jew from Alexandria, was a contemporary of Paul who discussed the city from the OT perspective. Given the common scriptures used by him and the NT writers one would expect would him to come closest to the latter's perception of *politeia*.[20] In a recent paper on 'The Idea and the Reality of the City in the Thought of Philo of Alexander' D.T. Runia has shown that Philo endorsed the classical Greek concept of the city as the ideal and natural structure for humanity.[21] He suggests that this Greek ideal of the 'well-organized and well-governed city. . .informs Philo's presentation of the Mosaic

---

[15]Schofield, 'The Cosmic City' *The Stoic Idea of the City*, ch. 3.

[16]Jones, 'Ideal Communities' *The Roman World of Dio Chrysostom*, ch. 7.

[17]Elsewhere, he spoke of 'the theory of the philosophers. . .which sets up a noble fellowship of gods and men which gives a share in law and citizenship. . .to such as have a share in intellect and reason' (36.38).

[18]On the myth of the Spartans' constitution that 'alone in the whole world they have now lived for more than seven hundred years with the same customs and laws', see Cicero's comment in *Pro Flacco* 63.

[19]Here Dio is indebted to Cicero's thesis on the 'cosmic city'. See Schofield, *The Stoic Idea of the City*, 78.

[20]R.G. Barraclough, 'Philo's Politics. Roman Rule and Hellenistic Judaism', *ANRW*, II. 21, (1984) 538.

politeia'. Philo's constitutional views are clear. Moses is the lawgiver for the cities of the world, but he has been rejected. In his place the law-givers of the Greeks have emerged (*Mos.* I.43-44).[22] Philo judges that it was only envy and anti-Semitism that has precluded the Gentile world from adopting the divine Law or Logos mediated through Moses as the basis for *politeia* (*Mos.* II. 49-51).

Runia uses the term 'ambivalent' to describe Philo's personal attitude to the city and therefore to *politeia*. He describes Philo as *homo urbanus* because of his participation in the social life of the city. As a member of the élite of society he was 'accustomed to living in the hubbub of the large city'.[23] However, Philo is critical of the way it provides the opportunity for its inhabitants to live 'after the flesh' because it is there that sexual licence and slander flourish (*Det.* 99, *Spec.* III.37). The law of Moses was given in the desert because cities are full of evil and promote pride (*Decal.* 2-17). For Philo the desert is the place of purification, yet he gives personal testimony that in the desert he has found himself bitten by passion as he was in the city. He wrote that 'God. . .has taught me that it is not differences of place that effect good and bad dispositions (*Mos.* II.41, *Leg.* II.85).

Philo treats Jerusalem as the city above all others. It is the holy city because of the temple. In an exposition of Psalm 45:5 he calls it the city of God (*Som.* II.245–54). However, it would be incorrect to con-clude that as such it could be paralleled with heaven in 1 Peter. Runia notes that for Philo 'The city of God is not only the cosmos, but also the soul of the wise man' (*Som.* II.249).[24]

Substantial use is made by Philo of the term 'benefaction' (εὐεργεσία) and its cognates. It is highly probable, given the status of his family and his possession of Alexandrian citizenship, that he would have participated in civic benefactions.[25] Yet he never suggests, let

---

[21]This paper was read at the SNTS conferene held in Edinburgh in August, 1994 and I am grateful to Professor D.T. Runia for his kindness in making this essay available to me.

[22]Runia, 'The Idea and the Reality of the City in Philo'.

[23]Runia, 'The Idea and the Reality of the City in Philo'.

[24]While elements of Augustine's city of God may be found in Philo he is not regarded as the sole progenitor of subsequent discussion of Augustine's city of God. For discussion of this point see J.P. Martín, 'Philo and Augustine, *De civitate Dei* XIV 28 and XV: Some Preliminary Observations' in edd. D.T. Runia, D.M. Hay and D. Winston *Heirs of the Septuagint: Philo, Hellenistic Judaism and Early Christian-ity, Festscrift for Earle Hilgert*, The Studia Philonica Annual 3 (1991) 286ff. and J. van Oort, *Jerusalem and Babylon: A Study of Augustine's City of God and the Sources of his Doctrine of the Two Cities* (Leiden: E.J. Brill, 1991) 250–2.

alone commands the Alexandrian Jews to undertake public benefactions for either pragmatic or theological reasons such as 'the will of God'.[26] Yet, according to the prophets they were technically Jews of 'the exile', or to use a contemporary term, 'diaspora'. As such one would expect Philo to teach them that they were obligated by Jeremiah's instructions to seek the welfare of the city of Alexandria. However, Philo operated from a Mosaic perspective of 'the land of Israel' and not 'the exile' in his discussion of *politeia* with Alexandrian Jews.

Having briefly laid out important views on *politeia* in the first century, what comparisons can be made with those of the early Christians? Plutarch, Dio, Philo and Paul were all only too well aware of the perennial problem of discord in *politeia* and its debilitating effects on the city's welfare. All were concerned that citizens were law-abiding. After the experience of bloody civil strife with Alexandrian Greeks, Philo's particular emphasis was for Alexandrian Jew to live as tranquil lives as citizens.[27]

What is to be made of the benefaction tradition of Christians and others in the first century? It would perhaps be unrealistic to expect Plutarch or Dio Chrysostom to engage in the discussion of any practical transformation of the great benefaction convention in *politeia* such as is found in the New Testament. Even had they believed in such a revolutionary idea, to require their audiences to be 'benefactors' would have been seen as a ruse by the rich to avoid costly civic obligations for 'the People'. It would have provoked a constitutional crisis in the city and a riot, which was the form of protest used in the first century against the ruling class.[28] Philo nowhere seeks the transformation of the benefaction convention or even its commendation.

Like Dio Chrysostom, Philo had seen and experienced hostility in *politeia*. The perpetrators of *stasis* were condemned by them both. In

---

[25]In conversation Professor Runia pointed out that Philo discloses little about himself in his corpus so that one does not expect him to provide of evidence of this.

[26]Philo uses εὐεργεσία and its cognates 127 times in his *corpus*, primarily with reference to God as the Benefactor bestowing blessings on the creation. It can be said that he uses the terms and conventions of praise and obligations to describe God whose works demand the right response by men. He does not draw the conclusions of Rom. 13:3-4 and 1 Pet. 2:14. G. Bertram, *TWNT*, II, 655 comments on Philo's strong Hellenistic usage.

[27]Barraclough, 'Philo's Politics: Roman Rule and Hellenistic Judaism', 533-5 on the ideal citizen.

[28]For a discussion of some of public hostility which arose when it was felt that civic responsibilities were being avoided, see Jones, *The Roman World of Dio Chrysostom*, 100.

the case of Dio he threatens to withdraw from civic benefactions.[29] By comparison, in 1 Peter 2:15 civic benefactions were commanded even in the face of hostility. They were declared to be 'the will of God' and also the means of silencing unwarranted accusations against Christians as evil-doers. There was to be no withdrawal of civic benefactions because of the attitude of others in *politeia*.

All writers accepted the structures of *politeia* as the reality in which they lived. What made the Christians different was the eschatological perspective from which they perceived those structures. They had a paradigm derived from the Jewish Exile or Diaspora in the sixth century B.C. (1 Pet. 1:1ff.). It was the author of 1 Peter's hermeneutical judgement that there was an identical dispensation in the economy of salvation for the people of God in the OT and in his day. It was this that created the unique characteristic of the Christian *politeia*. Like the other first-century writers who have been examined, Philo shared no such eschatological framework and therefore did not have this hermeneutical key of 'exile' or 'disapora'. His 'working canon' was restricted primarily to the Books of Moses where Israel was dwelling in their promised land.[30] It was in the Christian view of *politeia* that eschatology, with its emphasis of heaven as the promised land, and social ethics came together.

It is felt that this study as a whole and this brief comparative discussion, have been sufficient to show that the writer of the *apologia* to Diognetus would have been justified in making claims of unique attitudes to *politeia* for the Christians in both his and the first century. Christian teaching certainly did not share the ambivalence of Dio and Philo towards *politeia* in spite of the peculiar difficulties they experienced as citizens. What then made Christian perception different? Meeks believes that

> it was in certain of their social practices that the Christian groups most effectively distinguished themselves from other cult associations, clubs, or philosophical schools—their special rituals of initiation and communion, their practice of communal admonition and discipline, the organization of aid for widows, orphans, prisoners, and other weaker members of the movement.[31]

---

[29]Barraclough, 'Philo's Politics: Roman Rule and Hellenistic Judaism', 429ff.

[30]*Contra* Meeks,*The Origins of Christian Morality*, ch. 3 who argues for the contemporary model of the Jewish Diaspora as a paradigm for the early Christians. The Jews however were not taught to seek the welfare of the cities such as Alexandria in which they dwelt in the first century A.D.

[31]Meeks, *The Origins of Christian Morality*, 213.

However, none of these characteristics was singled out by the writer of
the epistle to Diognetus in his *apologia*. He suggested that what distinguished them from others was not their country, language or customs,
(V.1) but how they acted in that area which the ancient world defined
as *politeia*.[32] They did everything as citizens in spite of the attitude of
hostility displayed towards them in *politeia* (V.11–7). It was declared to
Diognetus that 'they show forth the amazing and admittedly strange
nature of their *politeia*' (5.4). They did this by continuing to seek the
welfare of the city. While there must be some modification of the claim
of participation in 'everything' as citizens, because they abstained from
pagan religious observances, it is clear that they 'belonged' to their
earthly city and sought its welfare.

If the command to seek the welfare of the city was a remarkable
one for Jews of the Exile in Babylon when judged against their
traditions,[33] it was no less amazing for Christians of 'the Diaspora'
when seen in the light of *politeia* of the first century. Their century saw
the introduction of child benefits for those with status from civic
endowments,[34] the continuing tradition of the rich endowing feasts
normally provided only for those with social status,[35] rich Roman
citizens, including their infants, fully using the corn dole, and the rich
being driven to give subsidies for grain in times of shortages because
of their fear that social unrest would see the plundering of their own
goods.[36] The Christian social ethic, by contrast, can only be described
as an unprecedented social revolution of the ancient benefaction
tradition. All able-bodied members of the Christian community were
to seek the welfare of others in their city, even though they might be
treated as 'foreigners'. Eschatologically, for them 'every home was a
foreign land', but in terms of their social ethics 'every foreign land was
their home'. They themselves perceived this to be 'the remarkable and
admittedly unexpected nature of their *politeia*'.[37]

---

[32]For its reference to activities outside the 'private sphere' see p. 2.
[33]J. Bright, *Jeremiah*, 211.
[34]Hands, *Charities and Social Aid in Greece and Rome*, 108ff. It went back to the Prici-
pate of Nero, although it blossomed in Trajan's reign. See also Garnsey, Trajan's
Alimenta: Some Problems' 367–81.
[35]Hands, *Charities and Social Aid in Greece and Rome*, 107ff.
[36]See pp. 53–4.
[37]For the justification of the literal translation of *The Epistle to Diognetus*, V.4 see p.
200.

SELECTED BIBLIOGRAPHY

Amandry, M., *Le monnayage des duovirs corinthiens*, BCH Supp. 15 (1988).

Bahr, G., 'The Subscriptions in the Pauline Letters' *JBL* 89 (1969) 27-41.

Balch, D.L., 'Hellenization Acculturation in 1 Peter', *Perspectives on First Peter*, NABPR Special Studies Series, 9 (1986).

Balch, D.L., *Let Wives Be Submissive: The Domestic Code of 1 Peter*, S.B.L: Monograph 26 (Chico: Scholars Press, 1981).

Balsdon, J.P.V.D., *Roman Women: Their History and Habits* (London: Bodley Head, 1974²).

Balsdon, J.P.V.D., *Romans and Aliens* (London: Duckworth, 1979).

Bammel, E., 'Romans 13' edd. E. Bammel and C.F.D. Moule, *Jesus and the Politics of His Day* (Cambridge: Cambridge University Press, 1984) 365-83.

Barclay, J., *Obeying the Truth: A Study of Paul's Ethics in Galatians* (Edinburgh: T.&T. Clark, 1988).

Barraclough, R.G. 'Philo's Politics: Roman Rule and Hellenistic Judaism', *ANRW*, II. 21.1, (1984) 417-533.

Bartchy, Scott S., *ΜΑΛΛΟΝ ΧΡΗΣΑΙ: First-Century Slavery and 1 Corinthians 7:21*, SBL Dissertation Series 11 (Missoula: Scholars Press, 1973).

Barton, S. and Horsley, G.H.R. 'A Hellenistic Cult Group and the New Testament Churches' *JbAC* 24 (1981) 7–41.

Bartsch, H.W., *Die Anfänge: Evangelischer Rechtsbildungen: Studien zu den Pastoralbriefen* (Hamburg: Herbert Reich, 1965).

Bassler, J.M., 'The Widows' Tale: A Fresh Look at 1 Tim. 5:3-16' *JBL* 103 (1984) 23-41.

Booth, A., 'The Art of Reclining and Its Attendant Perils' in ed. W.J. Slater *Dining in a Classical Context* (Ann Arbor: University of Michigan Press, 1991) 106-20.

Bordes, J., *Politeia dans la pensée grecque jusqu'à Aristote,* (Paris: 'Les Belles Lettres' 1982).

Borg, M., 'A New Context for Romans XIII', *NTS* 19 (1973) 205-18.

Bosch, J. S., *'Gloriarse' Segun San Pablo: Sentido y teologia de* καυχάομαι, Analecta Biblica (Rome and Barcelona: Biblical Institute Press, 1970).

Bradley, K.R., *Slaves and Masters in the Roman Empire: A Study in Social Control* (Oxford: OUP, 1987).

Bremmer, J.N., 'The Old Women of Ancient Greece' in edd. J. Blok and P. Mason *A Sexual Asymmetry: Studies in Ancient Society* (Amsterdam: J.C. Gießen, 1987) 191-205.

Brewer, R.R., 'The Meaning of *politeuesthe* in Philippians 1:27' *JBL* lxxii (1954) 76-83.

Brunt, P.A., 'The Romanization of the Local Ruling Classes in the Roman Empire', in ed. D.M. Pippidi, *Assimilation et résistance `a la culture gréco-romaine dans le monde ancien: Travaux du VI e Congrès International d'Etudes Classiques,* (Bucharest and Paris: 'Les Belles Lettres', 1976) 161-73.

Cadbury, H.J., 'Erastus of Corinth' *JBL,* 50 (1930) 42-58.

Chin, M., 'A Heavenly Home for the Homeless: Aliens and Strangers in 1 Peter' *Tyn.B.* 42.1 (1991) 96-112.

Cipriani, S., 'Saint Paul et la "Politique"' in ed. L. De Lorenzi *Paul de Tarse: apôtre du notre temps* (Rome: Abbaye de S. Paul, 1979) 596-618.

Clarke, A.D., 'The Good and the Just in Romans 5:7', *Tyn.B.* 41 (1990) 129-142.

Clarke, A.D., *Secular and Christian Leadership in Corinth: A Socio-Historical and Exegetical Study of 1 Corinthians 1-6* (Leiden: E.J. Brill, 1993).

Clarke, M.L., *Higher Education in the Ancient World* (London: Routledge & Kegan Paul, 1971)

Cranfield, C.E.B., 'Some Observations on Romans XIII.1-7' *NTS* 6 (1959-60) 241-49.

Cranfield, C.E.B., *A Commentary on Romans 12-13,* SJT Occasional Papers 12 (Edinburgh and London: 1965)

Cranfield, C.E.B., *A Critical and Exegetical Commentary on the Epistle to the Romans* (Edinburgh: T. & T. Clark, 1975 and 1979) I and II.

Cranfield, C.E.B., *Romans: a Shorter Commentary* (Edinburgh: T. & T. Clark, 1985)

Crook, J.A., *Law and Life in Rome* (London: Thames and Hudson, 1967).

Danker, F.W., *Benefactor: Epigraphic Study of a Graeco-Roman and New Testament Semantic Field* (St Louis, Missouri: Clayton Publishing House, 1982).

Dawes, G.W., "'But if you can gain your freedom' (1 Cor. 7:17-24)", *CBQ* 52 (1990) 681-697.

De Ste Croix, G.E.M., 'Additional Note on KALOS KAGATHOS, KALOKAGATHIA', *The Origins of the Peloponnesian War* (London: Duckworth, 1972) 371–6.

Delcor, M., 'The Courts of the Church of Corinth and the Courts of Qumran' in ed. J. Murphy-O'Connor *Paul and Qumran: Studies in New Testament Exegesis*, (London: Geoffrey Chapman, 1968) ch. 4.

Den Boer, W., *Private Morality in Greece and Rome* (Leiden: Brill, 1979).

Derrett, J.D.M., 'Judgement and I Corinthians 6' *NTS* 37 (1991) 22-36.

Dinkler, E., 'Zum Problem der Ethik bei Paulus: Rechtsnahme und Rechtsversicht, I Kor. 6,1-11', *ZThK* (1952) 167-200, reprinted in *Signum Crucis: Aufsätze zum Neuen Testament und zur christlichen Archäologie* (Tübingen: J.C.B. Mohr [Paul Siebeck], 1967) 204-240.

Dixon, S., *The Roman Mother* (London and Sydney: Croom Helm, 1988).

Duff, A.M., *Freedmen in the Early Roman Empire* (Cambridge: Heffer, 1958).

Dunbabin, K.M.D. and Dickie, M.W., 'Invidia rumpantur pactora: Iconography of Phthonos/Invidia in Graeco-Roman Art', *JbAC* (1983) 7–37.

Duncker, P.G., '"...quae vere viduae sunt"(1 Tim. 5.3)', *Angelicum* 35 (1958) 121-38.

Elliott, J.H., 'Peter, Its situation and strategy: A Discussion with D. Balch', in ed. C.H. Talbert, *Perspectives on 1 Peter*, NABPR Special Studies Series 9 (Macon, Georgia: Mercer University Press 1986) ch 4.

Elliott, J.H., *A Home for the Homeless: A Sociological Exegesis of 1 Peter, Its Situation and Strategy* (Philadelphia: Fortress, 1981).

Elliott, J.H., *The Elect and the Holy. An Exegetical Examination of 1 Peter . 2.4-10 and the Phrase basileion hierateuma*, Nov.T. Sup. 12 (Leiden: E.J. Brill, 1966).

Engels, D., *Roman Corinth: An Alternative Model for the Classical City* (Chicago: University of Chicago Press, 1990).

Eph'al, E., 'The Western Minorities in Babylon in the 6th-5th Centuries B.C. : Maintenance and Cohesion, *Orientalia* 47 (1978) 74-90.

Epstein, D.F., *Personal Enmity in Roman Politics* 218-43 BC, (London and New York: Routledge, 1987).

Erskine, A., 'The Romans as Common Benefactors' *Historia* 43 (1994) 70–87.

Finley, M.I., *The Ancient Economy* (London: Hogarth, 19852)

Fiori, B., ' "Covert Allusion" in 1 Corinthians 1-4' *CBQ* 47 (1985) 85-102.

Fishwick, D., *The Imperial Cult in the Latin West* (Leiden: E.J. Brill, 1987-1992) I.1 and II.

Friesen, S.J., *Twice Neokoros: Ephesus, Asia and the Cult of the Flavian Imperial Family* (Leiden: E.J. Brill, 1993).

Fuller, R.H., 'First Corinthians 6:1-11—An Exegetical Paper' *Ex Auditu* 2 (1986) 96-104.

Furnish, V.P., 'Elect Sojourners in Christ: An Approach to the Theology of 1 Peter' *Perkins School of Theology Journal*, 28 (1975) 1-11.

Gamble, H., *The Textual History of the Letter to the Romans*, Studies and Documents 42 (Grand Rapids: Eerdmans, 1977).

Gardner, J.F., *Women in Roman Law and Society* (London and Sydney: Croom Helm, 1986).

Garland, D.E. 'Composition and Unity of Philippians: Some Neglected Literary Factors' *NovT* 27 (1985) 141-173.

Garnsey, P. and Saller, R., *The Roman Empire: Economy: Society and Culture*, (London: Duckworth, 1987) 33.

Garnsey, P., *Famine and Food Supply in the Graeco-Roman World: Responses to Risk and Crisis* (Cambridge: Cambridge University Press, 1988).

Garnsey, P., 'Taxatio and pollicitatio in Roman Africa' *JRS* 61 (1971) 116-29.

Garnsey, P., 'The Civil Suit', *Social Status and Legal Privilege in the Roman Empire* (Oxford: Clarendon Press, 1970) Part III.

Garnsey, P., *Social Status and Legal Privilege in the Roman Empire* (Oxford: Clarendon Press, 1970).

Gauthier, P., Les Cités grecques et leurs bienfaiteurs, *BCH Supp.* XII (1985).

Gebhard, E.R., 'The Isthmian Games and the Sanctuary of Poseidon in the Early Empire' in ed. T.E. Gregory *The Corinthia in the Roman Period*, Journal of Roman Archaeology Supp. 8 (Ann Arbor: publisher, 1994) 78-94.

Gill, D.W.J., 'Acts and Urban Élites' in edd. D.W.J. Gill and C. Gempf *The Book of Acts in its Graeco-Roman Setting*, The Book of Acts in its First Century Setting(Grand Rapids and Carlisle: Eerdmans and Paternoster, 1994) ch. 5.

Gill, D.W.J., 'Corinth: A Roman Colony of Achaea' *Biblische Zeitschrift* (1993) 259-64.

Gill, D.W.J., 'Erastus the Aedile' *Tyn.B.* 40 (1989) 294-301.

Goldstein, J., 'Jewish Acceptance and Rejection of Hellenism', in edd. E.P. Sanders, A.I. Baumgarten and A. Mendelson *Aspects of Judaism in the Greco-Roman Period: Jewish and Christian Self-definition* (London: SCM, 1981) II. ch. 4.

Gomme, A.W., 'The Interpretation of KALOI KAGAQOI in Thucydides 4.40.2', *CQ* (1953) 65–8.

González, J., 'The Lex Irnitana: a New Flavian Municipal Law' *JRS* lxxvi (1986) 147-243.

Gooch, P. D., *Dangerous Food: 1 Corinthians 8-10 in Its Context*, Studies in Christianity and Judaism 5 (Waterloo, Ontario: Wilfrid Laurier University Press, 1993).

Goodman, M., *The Ruling Class of Judaea: The Origins of the Jewish Revolt against Rome A.D. 66-70* (Cambridge, Cambridge University Press, 1987).

Gordon, R., 'The Veil of Power: Emperors, Sacrificers and Benefactors' in edd. M. Beard and J. North *Pagan Priests: Religion and Power in the Ancient World* (London: Duckworth, 1990) ch. 8.

Green, G.L., 'The Use of the Old Testament for Christian Ethics in 1 Peter' *Tyn.B.* 41.2 (1990) 276-89.

Hamel, G., *Poverty and Charity in Roman Palestine: First Three Centuries C.E.*, Near Eastern Studies 23 (Berkeley and Oxford: University of California Press, 1990).

Hands, A.R., *Charities and Social Aid in Greece and Rome* (London: Thames and Hudson, 1968).

Hansen, G.W., *Abraham in Galatians: Epistolary and Rhetorical Contexts*, JSNT Supp. Series 29 (Sheffield: Sheffield Academic Press, 1989).

Harris, H.A., *Greek Athletics and the Jews* (Cardiff: University of Wales Press, 1976).

Harrison, A.R.W., *The Law of Athens: Family and Property* I and II (Oxford: Clarendon Press, 1968 and 1971).

Hemer, C.J., *The Book of Acts in the Setting of Hellenistic History* (Tübingen: J.C.B. Mohr [Paul Siebeck], 1989)

Hengel, M., *The Hellenization of Judaea in the First Century after Christ* (London: SCM,1989).

Henry, A.S., *Honours and Privileges in Athenian Decrees: The Principal Formulae of Athenian Honorary Decrees* (Hildesheim and New York: G. Olms, 1983).

Hewitt, J.W., 'The Development of Political Gratitude' *TAPA* 55 (1924) 35-51

Hiebert, D.E., 'Designation of the Readers of 1 Peter 1:1-2', *Bibliotheca Sacra* 137 (1980) 64-75.

Hock, R.F., *The Social Context of Paul's Ministry: Tentmaking and Apostleship* (Philadelphia: Fortress Press, 1980).

Holland, G.S., *The Tradition that You Received from Us: 2 Thessalonians in the Pauline Tradition* (Tübingen: J.C.B. Mohr [Paul Siebeck], 1988).

Hopkins, K., *Conquerors and Slaves, Sociological Studies in Roman History* I (Cambridge: CUP, 1978).

Horsley, G.H.R., ''Joining the Household of Caesar' *New Documents Illustrating Early Christianity*, 3, 7-9.

Horbury, W. , 'Jewish Inscriptions and Jewish Literature in Egypt' in edd. J.W. van Henten and P.W. van der Horst *Studies in Early Jewish Epigraphy* (Leiden: E.J. Brill, 1994) 9-43.

Humphries, S.C., *The Family, Women and Death: Comparative Studies* (London: Routledge and Kegan Paul, 1983).

Hunter, V.J., *Policing Athens: Social Control in the Attic Lawsuits, 420-320 B.C.* (Princeton, Princeton University Press, 1994).

Hurd, J.C., *The Origins of 1 Corinthians* (London: SPCK, 1965) 125.

Jewett, R., 'The Agitators and the Galatian Congregation' *NTS* 17 (1971) 198-212.

Jewett, R., *A Chronology of Paul's Life* (Philadelphia: Fortress, 1979).

Jewett, R., *The Thessalonian Correspondence: Pauline Rhetoric and Millenarian Piety* (Philadelphia: Fortress Press, 1986)

Jones, A.H.M., *The Criminal Courts of the Roman Republic and Principate* (Oxford: Blackwells, 1972).

Jones, B.W., *The Emperor Domitian* (London and New York: Routledge, 1992).

Jones, C.P., *Plutarch and Rome* (Oxford: Clarendon Press, 1971).

Jones, C.P., *The Roman World of Dio Chrysostom*, Loeb Classical Monographs (Cambridge, Mass. and London, Harvard University Press 1978)

Jones, J.W., *The Law and Legal Theory of the Greeks* (Oxford: OUP, 1956)

Judge, E.A., *The Social Pattern of Early Christian Groups in the First Century* (London: Tyndale, 1960).

Judge, E.A., 'The Early Christians as a Scholastic Community' *Journal of Religious History* I (1960-61) 125-137.

Judge, E.A., 'The Social Identity of the First Christians: A Question of Method in Religious History' *Journal of Religious History* 11 (1980) 201-7.

Judge, E.A., *Rank and Status in the World of the Caesars and St. Paul* (Christchurch: University of Canterbury Publications, 1982) No. 29.

Judge, E.A., 'Judaism and the Rise of Christianity: A Roman Perspective' *Tyn.B.* 45.2 (1993) 355-68.

Kampen, N., *Image and Status: Roman Working Women in Ostia* (Berlin: Gerb. Mann Verlag, 1981).

Käsemann, E., *Commentary on Romans* (E.T. London: SCM Press, 1980).

Kasher, A., *Jews in Hellenistic and Roman Egypt* (Tübingen: J.C.B. Mohr, [Paul Siebeck], 1985)

Kelly, J.M., *Roman Litigation* (Oxford: Clarendon Press, 1966).

Kelly, J.M., *Studies in the Civil Judicature of the Roman Republic* (Oxford: Clarendon Press, 1976).

Kokkinos, N., *Antonia Augusta: Portrait of a Great Lady* (London: Routledge, 1992).

Kunkel, W., *An Introduction to Roman Legal and Constitutional History* (Oxford: Clarendon Press, 19732).

Lacey, W.K., *The Family in Classical Greece* (London: Thames and Hudson, 1968).

Levick, B., *Tiberius the Politican* (London: Thames and Hudson, 1976).

Levick, B., *Claudius* (London: Batsford, 1990).

Lightman, M., and W. Zeisel, 'Univira: An Example of Continuity and Change in Roman Society', *Church History* 46 (1977) 19-32.

Lintott, A., *Violence, Civil Strife and Revolution in the Classical City* (London & Canberra: Croom Helm, 1982)

Lintott, A., *Imperium Romanum: Politics and Administrations* (London: Routledge, 1993).

Lull, D.J., 'The Servant-Benefactor as a Model of Greatness (Luke 22:24-30)' *Nov.T.* 28 (1986) 296.

MacMullen, R., 'Women in Public in the Roman Empire' *Historia* 29 (1980) 208-20.

Malherbe, A.J, *Paul and the Thessalonians* (Philadelphia: Fortress Press, 1987)

Malherbe, A.J., 'The Beasts at Ephesus' *JBL* 87 (1968) 71-80.

Malherbe, A.J., *Social Aspects of Early Christianity* (Philadelphia: Fortress, 1983).

Malina, B.J., *The New Testament World: Insights from Cultural Anthropology* (Atlanta: John Knox Press, 1981)

Marrou, H.I., *History of Education in Antiquity* (ET London: Sheed and Ward, 1956).

Marshall, A.J., 'Roman Women and the Provinces' *Ancient Society* 6 (1975) 108-27.

Marshall, P., *Enmity in Corinth: Social Conventions in Paul's Relations with the Corinthians* (Tübingen: J.C.B. Mohr [Paul Siebeck], 1987).

Martin, D.B., *Slavery as Salvation: The Metaphor of Slavery in Pauline Christianity* (New Haven and London: Yale University Press, 1990).

Mason, H.J., *Greek Terms for Roman Institutions—A Lexicon and Analysis*, ASP 13 (1974).

Meeks, W.A., *The First Urban Christians: The Social World of the Apostle Paul* (New Haven: Yale University Press, 1983).

Meeks, W.A., *The Origins of Christian Morality: The First Two Centuries* (New Haven: Yale University Press, 1994)

Meier, C., *The Greek Discovery of Politics* (ET Harvard: University Press, 1990)

Mellor, R., *ΘΕΑ ΡΩΜΗ: The Worship of the Goddess Roma in the Greek World*, Hypomnemata 42 (Göttingen: Vandenhoeck & Ruprecht, 1975).

Mengel, B., *Studien zum Philipperbrief: Untersuchungen zum situativen Kontext unter besonderer Berücksichtigung der Frage nach der Ganzheitlichkeit oder Einheitlichkeit eines paulinischen Briefes* (Tübingen: J.C.B. Mohr [Paul Siebeck], 1982).

Menken, J.J., 'Paradise Regained or Lost? Eschatology and Disorderly Behaviour in 2 Thessalonians' *NTS* 38 (1992) 271-89.

Meurer, S., *Das Recht im Dienst der Versöhnung und des Friedens: Studien zur Frage der Rechts nach dem Neuen Testament* (Zürich: Theologischer Verlag, 1972).

Michaels, J. R., 'Eschatology in 1 Peter II.17' *NTS* 13 (1967) 394–401.

Miller, E.C., 'Πολιτεύεσθε in Philippians 1.27: Some Philological and Thematic Observations' *JSNT* 15, 1982, 86-96.

Millar, F., 'Epictetus and the Imperial Court', *JRS* lv (1965) 141-60

Millar, F., 'The Imperial Cult and the Persecutions' in ed. M. den Boer *Le Culte des Souverains dans l'Empire romain* (Geneva: Vandoeuvres, 1972) 145-65.

Millar, F., 'The World of The Golden Ass' *JRS* 71 (1981) 63-75).

Millar, F., *The Emperor in the Roman World (31 B.C.-A.D. 337)* (London: Duckworth, 1977).

Millett, P., 'Patronage and its avoidance in Classical Athens,' in A. Wallace-Hadrill (ed.), *Patronage in Ancient Society* (London and New York: Routledge, 1989) ch. 1.

Mitchell, A.J., 'Rich and Poor in the Courts of Corinth: Litigiousness and Status in 1 Corinthians 6.1-11' *NTS* 39 (1993) 562-586.

Mitchell, M.M., *Paul and the Rhetoric of Reconciliation* (Tübingen: J.C.B. Mohr [Paul Siebeck], 1991).

Mitchell, S., *Anatolia: Land, Men, and Gods in Asia Minor* (Clarendon: Oxford, 1993) I and II.

Mott, S.C., 'The Power of Giving and Receiving: Reciprocity in Hellenistic Benevolence', in ed. G.F. Hawthorne *Current Issues in Biblical and Patristic Interpretation: Studies in Honor of Merril C. Tenney* (Grand Rapids: Eerdmans, 1975) 60-72.

Murphy-O'Connor, J., 'Archaeology', *St. Paul's Corinth: Texts and Archaeology* (Wilmington: Michael Glazier, 1983) Part 3.

Murphy-O'Connor, J., 'The Corinth that Saint Paul Saw' *The Biblical Archaeologist* 47 (1984) 147-159

Nédoncelle, M., 'Prosopon et persona dans l'antiquité classique' *Revue des Sciences Religieuses* 22 (1948) 277-99.

Nelson, C.A., 'Epikrisis: The Identity and Function of the Officials', in edd. E. Kiessling and H.A. Rupprecht *Akten XIII Internationalen Papyrologenkongresses* (München, 1974) 309-14.

Nickle, K.F., *The Collection: A Study in Paul's Strategy*, SBT 48 (London: SCM, 1966).

Nobbs, A., 'Cyprus' in edd. D.W.J. Gill and C. Gempf *The Book of Acts in its Graeco-Roman Setting*, The Book of Acts in its First Century Setting (Grand Rapids and Carlisle, Eerdmans and Paternoster, 1994) ch. 8.

Osborne, M.J., *Naturalization in Athens: The Law and Practice of Naturalization in Athens from the Origins to the Roman Period* (Brussels: AWL^{S}K, 1983).

Padgett, A., 'Wealthy Women at Ephesus: I Timothy 2:8-15 in Social Context' *Interpretation* 41 (1987) 19-31

Pallas, D.I., 'Inscriptions Lyciennes trouvées à Solomos près de Corinthe' *BCH* 58 (1959) 498-500.

Pollitt, J.J., 'On the meaning of "classical"' *Art and Experience in Classical Greece* (Cambridge: Cambridge University Press, 1972) Introduction.

Pomeroy, S.B., 'Charities for Greek Women', *Mnemosyne* XXXV (1982) 115-135.

Price, S.R.F., *Rituals and Power: The Imperial Cult and Asia Minor* (Cambridge: Cambridge University Press 1984²).

Pryor, J.W., 'First Peter and the New Covenant' *Reformed Theological Review* XLV.2, (1986) 44-51

Rajak, T and Noy, D., '*Archisynogogoi*: Office, Social Status in the Graeco–Roman World' *JRS* 83 (1993) 75–93.

Rapske, B., 'The Importance of Helpers to the Imprisoned Paul in the Book of Acts' *Tyn.B.* 42.1 (1991) 1-30.

Raubitschek, A.E., 'Octavia's Deification at Athens' *TAPA* 77 (1946) 146-50.

Rawson, B., *The Politics of Friendship, Pompey and Cicero* (Sydney: Sydney University Press, 1978).

Rawson, B., 'The Roman Family' in ed. B. Rawson *The Family in Ancient Rome: New Perspectives* (London and Sydney: Croom Helm, 1986) ch. 1.

Reynolds, J.M., 'The Origins and Beginnings of the Imperial Cult in Aphrodisias' *Proceedings of the Philological Society* 206 (1980) 70-82.

Reynolds, J.M., 'New Evidence for the Imperial Cult in Julio-Claudian Aphrodisias' *ZPE* 43 (1981) 317-27.

Reynolds, J.M., 'Further Information on Imperial Cult at Aphrodisias' *St. Cl.* xxiv (1986) 109-117.

Reynolds J. and Tannenbaum, R., *Jews and Godfearers at Aphrodisias*, Proceedings of the Cambridge Philological Society Association, Supp 12, Cambridge: Philological Society (1987).

Rhodes, P.J., 'Political Activity in Classical Athens' *JHS* cvi (1986) 137

Rives, J., 'The *iuno feminae* in Roman Society' *Echos du Monde Classique/ Classical Views* 36.1 n.s. (1992) 39-42.

Roberts, R., 'Old Texts in Modern Translation: Philippians 1.27' *ET* 49 (1937-38) 325-6.

Robinson, D.W.B., 'To Submit to the Judgement of the Saints' *Tyn.B.* 10 (April 1962) 1-8.

Robinson, D.W.B., 'The Deliverance Jesus Refused' *ET* 80 (May, 1969) 253-4.

Rosner, B., '"No Other Gods": The Jealousy of God and Religious Pluralism' in edd. A.D. Clarke and B.W. Winter, *One God and One Lord: Christianity in a World of Religious Pluralism* (Grand Rapids and Carlisle: Baker and Paternoster, 1992²) ch. 7.

Rosner, B., 'Temple and Holiness in 1 Corinthians 5' *Tyn.B.* 42.1 (1991) 137-145.

Roueché, C., 'Gladiators and Wild-beast Fighters' *Performers and Partisans at Aphrodisias in the Roman and late Roman Periods,* JRS monograph ser. 6 (1993) ch. 5.

Rousell, A., *Porneia* (Oxford: Blackwells, 1988).

Rowland, R.J., 'The "Very Poor" and the Grain Dole at Rome and Oxyrhynchus' *ZPE* 21 (1976) 69-72.

Runia, D.T., 'The Idea and the Reality of the City in the Thought of Philo of Alexandria' *(forthcoming)*.

Russell, R., 'The Idle in 2 Thess 3:6-12: an Eschatological or a Social Problem?' *NTS* 34 (1988) 105-119.

Saller, R.P., *Personal Patronage under the Early Empire* (Cambridge: Cambridge University Press, 1982).

Salmon, J.B., *Wealthy Corinth: a History of the City to 338 B.C.* (Oxford: Clarendon Press, 1984).

Sanders, E.P., *Paul, the Law and the Jewish People* (Philadelphia: Fortress Press, 1983).

Schaps, D.M., *Economic Rights of Women in Ancient Greece* (Edinburgh: Edinburgh University Press, 1979).

Schofield, M., *The Stoic Idea of the City* (Cambridge: Cambridge University Press, 1991).

Schlossmann, S., *Persona und πρόσωπον im Recht und im christlichen Dogma* (Kiel, 1906).

Schnur, H.C., 'The Economic Background of the Satyricon' *Latomus* 18 (1959) 790-9.

Schröger, F., *Gemeinde im 1 Petrusbrief* (Passau: Passavia Universitäts-verlag, 1981)

Schürer, E., *The History of the Jewish People in the Age of Jesus Christ* (175 BC-AD 135) (Edinburgh: T. & T. Clark, 1973² and 1979²) I and II.

Selwyn, E.G., 'The Persecutions in 1 Peter', *BNTS* 1 (1950) 39-50.

Sherwin-White, A.N., *Roman Society and Roman Law in the New Testament* (Oxford: Clarendon Press, 1963).

Sherwin-White, A.N., *The Roman Citizenship* (Oxford: Clarendon Press, 1973[2]).

Skard, E., 'Zwei religios—politische Begriffe: Euergetes Concordia', *Norske Videskaps Akademi i Oslo*, Avhandlinger 13 (1932) 1-66.

Smallwood, E.M., *The Jews under Roman Rule from Pompey to Diocletian: A Study in Political Relations* (Leiden: Brill, 19812)

Spawforth, A., 'Corinth, Argos, and the Imperial Cult: A Reconsideration of Psuedo-Julian Letters 198 Bidez' *Hesperia* 63.2 (1994) 211–32.

Spawforth, A., 'Roman Corinth: The Formation of a Colonial Elite' *Meletemata* (Athens) forthcoming.

Staveley, E.S., *Greek and Roman Voting and Elections* (London: Thames and Hudson, 1972)

Stein, A., 'Wo trugen die korinthischen Christen ihre Rechtshandel aus?' *ZNW* 59 (1968) 86-90.

Stowers, S.K., 'Friends and Enemies in the Politics of Heaven: Reading Theology in Philippians' in ed. J.M. Bassler, *Pauline Theology* (Minneapolis, Fortress Press 1991) I, ch. 9.

Strobel, A.,'Zum Verständnis von Rm 13', *ZNW* 47 (1956) 67-93.

Stroud, R.S., 'The Sanctuary of Demeter on Acrocorinth in the Roman Period' in ed. T.E. Gregory*The Corinthia in the Roman Period*, Journal of Roman Archaeology Supp. 8 (Ann Arbor, 1994) 65-77.

Sullivan, J.P., *The Satyricon of Petronius* (London: Faber and Faber, 1968).

Synge, F.C., 'Studies in texts: 1 Timothy 5.3-16' *Theology* 108 (1968) 200-1.

Taubenschlag, R., *The Law of Greco-Roman Egypt in the Light of the Papyri 332 B.C - 640 A.D.* (Warsaw: Panstwowe Wydawnictwo Naukowe, 1955)

Taylor, J., 'Why were the Disciples first called "Christians" at Antioch? (Acts 11:26)' *Revue Biblique* 101.1 (1994) 75-94.

Theissen, G., *The Social Setting of Pauline Christianity* (Philadelphia: Fortress Press, 1982).

Thurston, B.B., *The Widows: A Women's Ministry in the Early Church* (Minneapolis: Fortress Press, 1989).

Tomson, P.J., *Paul and the Jewish Law: Halakha in the Letters of the Apostle to the Gentiles* (Assen, Netherlands and Minneapolis: Van Gorcum and Fortress Press, 1990).

Trebilco, P.R., *Jewish Communities in Asia Minor*; SNTSSM 69 (Cambridge: Cambridge University Press, 1991).

Treggiari, S., *Roman Freedmen during the Late Republic* (Oxford: Clarendon Press, 1969)

Treggiari, S., 'Jobs for Women', *AJAH* 1 (1976) 76-104.

Trilling, W., 'Untersuchungen zum 2. Thessalonicherbrief' *Erfurter theologische Studien* 27 (Leipzig: St. Benno-Verlag, 1972).

van Unnik, W.C., 'The Teaching of Good Works in 1 Peter' *NTS* 1 (1954) 92-110

van Unnik, W.C., 'Lob und Strafe durch die Obrigkeit Hellenistisches zu Röm. 13,3-4', in edd. E. Earle Ellis and Erich Gräßer (edd.), *Jesus und Paulus, Festschrift für Georg Kümmel zum 70. Geburtstag* (Göttingen: Vandenhoeck & Ruprecht, 1975) 334-343.

Verner, D.C., *The Household of God: The Social World of the Pastoral Epistles* (SBL Dissertation Series 71; Chico: Scholars Press, 1983).

Vischer, L., *Die Auslegungsgeschichte von 1 Kor. 6.1-11* (Tübingen: J.C.B. Mohr [Paul Siebeck], 1955).

Wallace-Hadrill, A., 'Family and Inheritance in the Augustan Marriage Laws', Proceedings of the Cambridge Philological Society 207 (1981) 58-80.

Wallbank, M., 'Pausanias, Octavia, Temple E' *Annual of the British School at Athens* 84 (1989) 361-94.

Watson, A., *Roman Slave Law* (Baltimore and London: Johns Hopkins University Press, 1987).

Watson, A., *The Law of Persons in the Later Roman Republic* (Oxford: Clarendon Press, 1967).

Watson, D.F., 'A Rhetorical Analysis of Philippians and Its Implications for the Unity Question' *Nov.T.* 30 (1988) 57-88.

Weaver, P.R.C., *Familia Caesaris: A Social Study fo the Emperor's Freedmen and Slaves* (Cambridge: Cambridge University Press, 1972).

Weinstock, S., *Divus Julius* (Oxford: Clarendon Press, 1971).

Welborn, L.L., 'On the Discord in Corinth: 1 Corinthians 1-4 and Ancient Politics', *JBL* 106.1 (1987) 85-111.

Welles, C.B., *Royal Correspondence in the Hellenistic Period* (New Haven: Yale University Press, 1934).

Williams II, C.K., 'Roman Corinth as a Commercial Center' in ed. T.E. Gregory *The Corinthia in the Roman Period*, Journal of Roman Archaeology Supp. 8 (Ann Arbor, 1994) 31-46.

Wimbush, V.L., *Paul the Worldly Ascetic: Response to the World and Self-understanding according to 1 Corinthians 7* (Macon: Mercer University Press, 1987).

Winter, B.W., 'Acts and Roman Religion' in edd. D. Gill and C. Gempf, *The Book of Acts in its Graeco-Roman Setting*, The Book of Acts in its First Century Setting, (Grand Rapids and Carlisle: Eerdmans and Paternoster, 1994) 2. 98-103.

Winter, B.W., 'Secular and Christian Responses to Corinthian Famines' *Tyn.B.* 40 (1989) 88-106.

Winter, B.W., 'Theological and Ethical Responses to Religious Pluralism in 1 Corinthians 8-10' *Tyn.B.* 41.2 (1990) 215-219.

Winter, B.W., 'The Importance of the *captatio benevolentiae* in the Speeches of Tertullus and Paul in Acts 24:1-21' *JTS* n.s. 42.2 (1991) 503-31.

Winter, B.W., 'In Public and in Private: Early Christianity and Religious Pluralism' in edd. A.D. Clarke and B.W. Winter, *One God and One Lord: Christianity in a World of Religious Pluralism* (Grand Rapids and Carlisle, Baker and Paternoster 1992[2]) ch. 6.

Winter, B.W., 'Official Proceedings and the Forensic Speeches in Acts 24-26', in edd. A.D. Clarke and B.W. Winter, *The Book of Acts in its Ancient Literary Setting*, The Book of Acts in its First Century Setting (Grand Rapids and Carlisle, Eerdmans and Paternoster, 1993) ch. 11.

Winter, B.W., 'Acts and Food Shortages', in edd. D.W.J. Gill and C. Gempf *The Book of Acts in its Graeco-Roman Setting*, The Book of Acts in its First Century Setting (Grand Rapids and Carlisle, Eerdmans and Paternoster, 1994) ch. 3.

Winter, B.W., 'The Problem with "church" for the Early Church' in edd. D. Peterson and J. Pryor *In the Fullness of Time: Biblical Studies in Honour of Archbishop Robinson* (Sydney: Lancer 1992) ch. 13.

Winter, B.W., *Philo and Paul among the Sophists: a Hellenistic Jewish and a Christ ian Response* (Macquarie University Ph. D. 1988) forthcoming SNTSMS.

Wiseman, J., 'Corinth and Rome I', *ANRW*, II.7.1 (1979) 438-548.

Wiseman, J., *The Land of Ancient Corinth, Studies in Mediterranean Archaeology* (Göteberg, P. Artiöms Förlag, 1978).

Witherington III, B., 'Not so idle thoughts about *eidolothuton*' *Tyn.B.* 44.2 (1993) 237-54.

Wright, N.T., *The Climax of the Covenant: Christ and the Law in Pauline Theology* (Edinburgh: T&T Clark, 1991).

Index of Biblical References

Index of Ancient Sources

Index of Authors

237

Index of Subjects

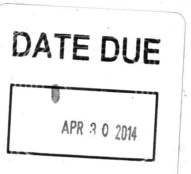